THE EROTIC MOTIVE
IN LITERATURE

ALBERT MORDELL

THE

IN

EROTIC MOTIVE LITERATURE

New, Revised Edition

COLLIER BOOKS
NEW YORK, N.Y.

This revised Collier Books edition is published by arrangement with the Liveright Publishing Corporation.

Collier Books is a division of The Crowell-Collier Publishing Company.

First Collier Books Edition 1962

Contents

Preface

THE PRESENT work is a revision of the volume originally published in 1919. New material has been added to bring a few matters up to date. Some pages have been here and there omitted and other data and conclusions have been substituted. There is, however, no substantial change in the present volume from the views I presented earlier.

First, how did the book come to be written and how did it get this title? Forty years ago Freud had only a few American followers. He was still looked upon as a kind of charlatan by some psychiatrists and literary critics, in spite of the fact that half a dozen of his books had been translated, and another half a dozen expounding and interpreting his views had been published in English. True, articles favorable to his theories had been printed, chiefly in psychiatrical journals and occasionally in literary periodicals and newspapers. *The Interpretation of Dreams* was not published in English until 1913.

My own interest in psychoanalysis derived from a concern with the subjective nature of literature. In my *The Shifting of Literary Values* (1912) I had devoted a chapter to showing that literary criticism itself was subjective. I had read a few articles in which the principles of psychoanalysis were applied to some isolated literary works. But it was Freud himself who influenced me by several essays and notably by two books *Delusion and Dream* and *Leonardo da Vinci: a Study in Psycho-sexuality* in which he took up the matter of the unconscious as a factor in the work of the novelist and the artist.

A few monographs in German had been written to show the unconscious factors in the work of a number of German poets little known here. Otto Rank had devoted a thick volume to the study of incest in connection with literature, *Das Inzest —Motiv*, but I was not interested in incest alone. In fact I had not read his book. I determined to apply psychoanalysis to the entire field of English literature, ancient and modern. However, I was able to occupy myself with only a part of this field, as I knew publishers would not want too large a volume on this new subject. Still I was able to deal with several great writers and books. Before submitting my manuscript to a publisher I decided to seek the opinion of two leading psychoanalysts practicing in America, Dr. Isidor H. Coriat, author of *The Hysteria of Lady Macbeth*, a pioneering brochure, and Dr. A. A. Brill who had already published a book on psychoanalysis. I was not a physician or a practicing psychoanalyst. I was, or at least I hoped I was, a literary critic. They both wrote me encouraging letters after reading my manuscript. Dr. Coriat made some suggestions which I adopted.

Thus fortified, I submitted the book to Horace B. Liveright who had already published one or two small books I had edited.

I had chosen the title, *Literature and the Unconscious*. Liveright gave the manuscript to Floyd Dell for his opinion. I was apprehensive that Dell might advise rejection as he was a follower of Jung rather than of Freud. But Dell recommended the book. Liveright then took up with me the matter of my title. He said it sounded rather dull and pompous; in his opinion it was not likely to attract many readers. He again turned to Floyd Dell who suggested the title *The Erotic Motive in Literature*. Many years later I asked him whether this title was his and he replied that it was. I was at first opposed to it, as I thought it might lead some people to think I was writing a pornographic book. Most people do not know Greek and are unaware that the word "*eros*" means normal love and does not imply necessarily an undue interest in the physical side of sex. As a matter of fact, some reviewers shied at the title, and one reader offered to lend me a number of pornographic books from his library. I soon realized however, that the title was really a true and good one, for the book showed the influence of a writer's love affairs upon his work, unconsciously and consciously. Today the word erotic has recovered its respectability and therefore I have retained the old title. In fact the phrase has become popular, but it is Floyd Dell who deserves the credit for it and not I.

In accordance with the new title, Liveright asked me to add a chapter on eroticism and to enlarge the one dealing with sexual symbolism. This latter chapter was somewhat original and startling and was the most attacked. Since then a number of critics have gone to a greater extent than I would warrant in finding sexual symbolism in literature. In fact I have often felt that like Frankenstein I was slain by the "monster" I had created. I spent a night at Liveright's home discussing the matter with him. We parted the next morning, and I believe he felt that he had a best seller in the book. He did not realize that numerous attacks which he expected upon the book might lessen the sales rather than stimulate them. Frankly, I was more concerned with the book's genuine contribution to literature than its sales.

The Erotic Motive in Literature attracted great attention and was reviewed in over a hundred newspapers and periodicals. In many, if not most, the tone was hostile. It met with disfavor from most of the New York newspapers.

Even critics who claimed to be Freudians or in sympathy with Freud were severe. Artillery was directed at it from the very start with the article by Laurence Gilman in the *North American Review* entitled "Literature Unveiled," although he gave it six pages under the caption "The Book of the Month." I had some of the leading critics in America against me: Francis Hackett in the *New Republic*, Mencken in the *Smart Set*, Conrad Aiken in the *Chicago News* and Simeon Strunsky in the *Atlantic Monthly*. Soon an English edition appeared and later Desmond McCarthy joined in the attack under his pseudonym "Affable Hawk" in the *New Statesman* and also Charles Whibley in his anonymous "Musings Without Method" in *Blackwood's Magazine*. Then a college professor, no less a person than Louis Cazamian in a book *Criticism in the Making* (1924), a translation and an abridgment from an article by him in the *Revue de Littérature Comparée*, handled me somewhat roughly.

Some reviews went beyond impersonal criticism in their attack. Here are a few specimens:

> The performance seems not a little like peeking through the keyhole of a lady's bedchamber.
> F. Parker Stockbridge in the New York *Sun*.

> The only divinity of the present volume is Venus libidinis Auctrix whose calumnies recall the scandalous tongue of Vivien when she let it "rage like a fire among the noblest names, defaming and defacing till she left not even Lancelot brave and Galahad clean."
> *The Nation.*

> Psychoanalysis describes a certain type of erotic named "voyeur," in plain English, the peeping Tom. A particularly odious type of "voyeur" is he who squints through keyholes and sees inside nasty things that are not there.
> *The Review.*

I did not reply to any of my critics. I had some very favorable notices, however, one by Idwal Jones in the *San Francisco Chronicle* and another in the *Seattle Post-Intelligencer*.

The real tributes came from leading psychoanalytic authors, Edwin B. Holt, Dr. William A. White, and Hanns Sachs. But what gave me courage was an unexpected article by Havelock Ellis in the *London Nation*, August 9, 1919. He did not wait for an English edition of my book. His title was "Unlocking the Heart of Genius" and he later included the article in his book *Views and Review*. I shall quote a sentence or two: "Mr. Mordell's scholarship, which is considerable, was not got up to prove a psycho-pathological thesis. He was a sympathetic, penetrating and original student of literature long before he ever heard of Freud. . . . It is in the sane and broad sense that, on the whole, Mr. Mordell understands psychoanalysis."

The other consolation I had was that without my knowledge the book in 1924 was translated into Japanese, probably because of the chapter on Hearn.

Some of the attacks on the book were confined to the chapter on symbolism and sex. Since then hundreds of writers have resorted to this theme and many of the other views in the book have been accepted. Indeed, a notable publisher of reprints ten years later did not want to issue it after it went out of print because, he said, it once may have been revolutionary, but now it represented the general attitude.

My real accolade was the following letter from Freud himself.

I read your book with great interest and I am glad you were able to do for the English-American literature something similar to what Rank did for the German in his book on Incest-Motive, I also would like to tell you that you should not take too seriously the attacks and unfavorable criticisms. At present we cannot expect anything else, and besides a good criticism by Havelock Ellis outweighs two dozen bad ones by the other side. I hope you will continue with your literary studies and often give us pleasure with their results. With hearty greetings and respect.[1]

---

[1] Ernest Jones printed this letter as the first among the letters from Freud to others in the third volume of his life of Freud, with a comment that it was "one of the many encouraging letters to young authors." Freud did not know that I was a young author. (As a matter of fact I was thirty-four years old and

Henry L. Mencken was writing the literary reviews for the *Smart Set*. The *American Mercury* was not dreamed of yet. He reviewed my book and concluded with the words "Let Freud pray to God to be delivered from ignorant disciples like Albert Mordell." I could not resist the impulse to send him a copy of Freud's letter which I received about the same time. He must have realized I had the laugh on him. In his review he also said that I applied Freud's notions in the manner of an owlish sophomore and that my criticisms were usually childish. What must have puzzled Mencken was that Havelock Ellis had praised my book for I informed him of this, and he had the highest regard for Ellis. Later on I found a copy of my book that Mencken had sold to a book store and there was pencilled in it the words "gossip" and the question: who cares how a book was written?

As for Francis Hackett I had an unexpected comeback later, though I never notified him of it. In the *New Republic* July 2, 1919 he quotes the following sentence from my book where I said that Swinburne's "Felise" may refer to a lost sweetheart. "Some new data may appear to tell us whether the facts of the poems had any basis in reality." "This last sentence," Hackett stated, "hints at Mr. Mordell's most serious limitation. Not only is he a half-baked Freudian but he takes literature without a primary interest in literature for its own sake. . . . Hence his lack of imagination and his failure to see the inapplicability of most of his formulas."

It happens that the new data did appear in a letter written by Swinburne and published subsequently in his *Life and Letters*, indicating that "Felise" was indeed a "personal" poem. When Ruskin had protested against the poem, Swinburne wrote to him:

> I recalcitrate vigorously against your opinion of "Felise" which is rather a favorite child of mine. As to the subject I thought it clear enough, and likely to recall to most people a similar passage of experience. A young fellow was left alone with a woman rather older, whom a year

had published two books.) If Freud encouraged young authors that was all right with me, but he was not encouraging me, e.g. because he said that he hoped I would continue writing. In fact I was then preparing another book. This hope was merely a formal conclusion to a letter. He was really telling me that he appreciated the fact that I was applying in America his ideas on literature, doing what Rank had done in Germany. I had written to him that the book was being attacked as a matter of information. I was not however seeking consolation. I had already some favorable notices, among them one by Havelock-Ellis of which I told Freud.

since he violently loved. Meantime he had been in town, she in the country; and in the year's lapse they have had time, he to become tired of her memory, she to fall in love with his. Surely I have expressed this plainly and 'cynically enough'; last year I loved you, and you were puzzled and didn't love me quite. This year (I perceive) you love me, and I feel puzzled, and I don't love you—quite.

I do not think that I was mistaken in saying the poem had a basis in reality. She was the same girl who inspired most of the love poems, particularly "The Triumph of Time," in *Poems and Ballads*.

Simon Strunsky's article in the *Atlantic Monthly* of September, 1919 "The Scandal of Euclid," a clever review of the fictitious book *Sex Elements in the First Five Books of Euclid* by a fictitious author Wilbur P. Birdwood was recognized as a satire on my book and was summarized in *Current Opinion*. Later it was expanded and published in book form but it no longer attracted attention, and was even slated.

A retraction came later from Strunsky who was conducting the "Topics of the Time" column on the editorial page of the *New York Times*. He wrote to me July 14, 1933:

It was my purpose in setting out to write the Topic on your *Quaker Militant: John Greenleaf Whittier to say* something about your book *The Erotic Motive*, fourteen years ago being a pioneer ... and then to go on to say that it was the work of a gentleman as well as a scholar by contrast with so much of the commercial muck that has since been discharged in the name of Freud and psychoanalysis. I didn't get around to making the point, but it was sincerely meant. As between me and you there is little disputing as to who foresaw the future in the year 1919.

I could not expect Conrad Aiken who had an article headed "Dam Up Your Libido! Be a Poet!" in the *Chicago News* to be favorable to my book, for he did not accept the conclusions of Freud or Jones or any of the Germans in their applications of psychoanalysis to literature, and yet he claimed to be a good Freudian. He challenged me to show how psychoanalysis could be applied to the work of Henry James. I hardly need say that since then there have been numerous applications of psychoanalysis to stories by Henry James. I did one myself of "Madame de Mauves." [2] Aiken's reviews were selected recently for book publication, and the writer of the introduction, Rufus A. Blanchard, said that the review of my book, which Aiken did not reprint, was the result of his feeling that there was a stultifying effect of Freud's theory in it. Aiken however called it a hasty and unassimilated hackwork. He became interested in Kostyleff's theory of poetry as a verbo-motor discharge, a theory that has not made much headway.

I shall mention a notice in the *Minneapolis Bellman*, an extinct periodical, because Hardin Craig who, as we all know, has become the great Shakespearean scholar, wrote it. His chief objection was that I went too far in applying psychoanalysis to Keats on the ground that some of his greatest poems were written before he met Fanny Brawne. I merely said that the affair with Fanny Brawne colored his later poetry. I never said that he could not write great poetry because he had not met her.

In England the application of Freud's theories to literature and art displeased some of the leading art critics like A. Clutton-Brock and Clive Bell, though two leading literary critics were interested—Robert Graves and Sir Herbert Read, and later, F. S. Lucas. I shall refer only to two who pounced on my book, first Charles Whibley who did me the honor of classifying me as a charlatan in literature to stand with Lloyd George, a charlatan in politics. I nead not summarize the abusive article he wrote for *Backwood's Magazine* except to quote one sentence, "The pupils of Herr Freud crawl like slugs, leaving a filthy trail behind them, over whatever is noble and comely in poetry and prose." He even quoted in disapproval of my book a passage from Freud's letter about my having done for literature in English what Rank had done in German with his *Das Inzest-Motif*, to prove that Freud and his disciples were obsessed with perversity. I was not disturbed by Whibley's article. I knew his prejudices and faults, and he had attacked me before.

But I was surprised by an attack coming from Desmond McCarthy under the pen name "Affable Hawk" in the *New Statesman*. He waited to make his attack two years later when he launched out at a new book of mine *The Literature of Ecstasy* which had just been published. He was a modern, a friend of the late Samuel Butler, and had a great reputation.

[2] *Literary Reviews and Essays* by Henry James. Edited by Albert Mordell.

He did not assail the *Erotic Motive* for its thesis. He merely selected a few passages of which he did not approve relating to my treatment of Gautier, Charlotte Bronte, and Kipling. He said that my book was typical of the poorest of such attempts to apply psychoanalysis to literature, that my analytical apparatus was more imposing than its results, and he concluded that I was not the man who ought to take up scientific ideas. He manifested his hostility to psychoanalysis many years later in an attack on Sir Herbert Read because he used psychoanalysis to defend Shelley from the attack by T. S. Eliot. He charged that Read lent "too uncritical an ear to the fuddled conjectures of second-rate intellects rejoicing in, and flourishing on, the present imprecision of psychoanalytic terminology." At least I was in good company with Sir Herbert Read.

Having related some of the attacks and having never before replied to them, I may be excused for giving some of the favorable notices. They take the form of stating that I was a pioneer, that I was correct in my applications, that I had ably performed my task, and that I was well equipped both as a literary critic and psychoanalyst.

As to being a pioneer I didn't give this a thought. I was following Freud and I knew there had already been several isolated instances in English where a book or an author came up for examination and I had originally cited them. The idea of being a pioneer was put into my head by Dr. Coriat when he read the manuscript: "It is," he said, "not only the first complete attempt to apply psychoanalytic conceptions to literature, but you have done it in a masterly and comprehensive manner."

Havelock Ellis had also said that there had been few attempts in English dealing with psychoanalytic studies of genius and therefore some interest attached to my book. The *Pittsburgh Gazette-Times* stated: "Mr. Mordell has given us perhaps the first comprehensive scientific estimate of literature and its ultimate relation to the life of its makers." The *Cincinnati Times-Star* said that the method in my book had been carried out on a broad scheme for the first time. The *American Journal of Psychology* stated that I had founded a new school of criticism: "The chief significance of the book however is the advent of a new school of criticism, which goes back of the conscious purpose of an author and shows conclusively that while he thinks he is saying or writing one thing, he is to the psychoanalyst of the unconscious, saying or writing something very different."

Of course I am not so deluded as to think that had my book not appeared there would not be any psychoanalytical biographies of writers and Freudian studies in literary criticism. Nor do I claim special influence. Though I learned that some critics and writers had read my book, I do not maintain that they would not have been doing what I had done. I do not claim to have wielded a direct influence. I was simply the first to be on the ground in America.

Since the chapter on sexual symbolism was so much attacked I may be justified in citing Dr. William A. White when he said, "There is a very interesting chapter on sexual symbolism in literature which is widely illustrated by literary references."

Isaac Goldberg writing under a pseudonym Irving Ormond in the *Stratford Journal*, called the book "a pioneer volume that must be owned by any man or woman who tries to look upon books and authors as living, rounded entities."

I give other citations without apologies:

The book gives more to the reader than the title seems to promise, at least in due respect: it does not content itself with following up the use made of erotic motives in literature, but points out their existence even where they do not seem to come to the surface—in short, the book has been written entirely from a psycho-analytic point of view . . . he arrives at a principle of the utmost importance. He maintains his points by referring to material which is rich, well chosen and thoroughly mastered. Hanns Sachs: *The International Journal of Psychoanalysis*, Vol. I, pt. 4 (1920). Edited by Ernest Jones.

In this volume we have Freudian principles applied to literature by a man whose knowledge and understanding of letters are more than those of an amateur. While Mr. Mordell's grasp of psychoanalytic principles is adequate, it is in his application of these to authors and their works that his judgment and skill are best evidenced and the result is, to be sure, itself literature, or literary criticism of a high order, rather than a contribution to psychoanalysis . . . Mr. Mordell's *Erotic Motive* is valuable as literary criticism, as a study in the psychology of literary composition and of "genius," and as one of the best applications of psychoanalysis to works of literature." Edwin B. Holt: *The American Journal of Abnormal Psychology*.

Erskine Caldwell in a letter to the author, June 21, 1936: "I have read and reread your *Erotic Motive* many times. It is one of the best pieces of creative writing I have ever had the opportunity of reading."

Andre Maurois in a letter to the author February 23, 1945: "I have just finished your book and I need hardly tell you how deeply it interested me. You deal with all the subjects I worked upon all my life, and also with some of the writers I prefer (Shelley, Kipling). You certainly were *the first* [italics supplied] to say many things that became themes for all the critics and biographers."

The late Edgar Lee Masters to the author in a letter (circa 1925): "A number of years ago I read your *Erotic Motive in Literature* and enjoyed it greatly."

The late Will Cuppy in a letter to the author (undated): *The Erotic Motive* really introduced me to what I think is the most interesting form of literary criticism, and I can never be too grateful."

I have said nothing of letters from people who were not famous authors. One reader sent me a very long index, saying that he had prepared it for his own reference to the many authors and works mentioned in *The Erotic Motive*. His name was Roger Lewis. The most interesting letters were very long ones from Katharine D. Osbourne, wife of Lloyd Osbourne who was a step-son of Robert Louis Stevenson, about whom she was writing a book and wanted some help in psychoanalytic matters. She found the tone of my book kindly and sympathetic.

The most flattering comment from an unknown correspondent was from a lawyer in Bay City, Texas, John Corbett:

"Pray do not consider me fulsome when I tell you that nothing I have ever read is so filled with novel and correct interpretations of scientific law as applied to literature as your *Erotic Motive in Literature*."

It is unsolicited praise like this that keeps an author going when the world is down on him.

The best answer to the view that psychoanalysis should not be applied to literature or biography was the fact that American writers were beginning to write books, particularly biographies and studies of authors, from a Freudian point of view. In some cases they were cautious and in others they did not shrink from following out the implications to courageous conclusions. Some of the authors were literary critics and others trained psychoanalysts. I shall mention only a few such works that appeared within a few years after my own work was published, but I do not maintain that they were influenced by it.

The first thorough application of the principles of psychoanalysis to a novelist's work was made by Lucille Dooley writing about Charlotte Bronte in 1920 in the *American Journal of Psychoanalysis*. She was especially qualified to apply the Freudian technique for she was familiar with the psychoanalytical studies made in German of various writers and had summarized them in an earlier issue of the same periodical.

The first nontechnical application of Freud's principles to the work of a popular writer appears to be Van Wyck Brooks's *Ordeal of Mark Twain*, issued in the summer of 1920. (I need not go into the extent to which Brooks later changed some of his views.)

Also in the same year Katherine S. Anthony in her *Margaret Fuller, a psychological biography* analyzed the hysteria of Margaret's childhood and the neurotic illness of her later life. In her subtitle she did not say that she was doing a psychoanalytical study, but this is what the book essentially was.

Also in the same year—October, 1920—there appeared in *The American Journal of Psychology* Lorine Pruette's psychoanalytical study of Poe, where frank acknowledgment is made to me.

In 1921 a real Freudian study was made of August Strindberg as the title *August Strindberg, a Psychoanalytical Study*, by Professor Axel Jonan Uppval of the University of Pennsylvania indicated. I was pleased to review this work in the old *New York Evening Post* (July 2, 1921).

In the following year Professor F. C. Prescott brought out *The Poetic Mind*, an expansion of his early brochure of 1912 *Dreams and Poetry*. Unfortunately Prescott avoided the subject of sex, giving about a page or two to it in his later volume, and his study tended to become an academic rather than a psychoanalytic analysis. Most of the Freudian phraseology was missing. Although I realized Professor Prescott had done pioneer work in his early brochure, I was compelled to draw attention to his failure to make sexual references in his later book in a review I regretfully wrote of it for *The Freeman*, August 16, 1922. Yet it is often stated that Professor Prescott was the first one to apply psychoanalysis to literature in America. This is hardly true for all the structures on which psychoanalysis are based are not touched in his work with the exception of the broad statement that poetry and dreams are related.

I shall mention only two more early psychoanalytical studies. There appeared in 1922 *Psychoanalysis and the Drama* by Louise Brink and Smith Eli Jeliffe.

In 1923 Eden and Cedar Paul translated *Psychoanalysis and Aesthetics* by Charles Baudouin, which was published the following year. It was an application of psychoanalysis to the theory of aesthetics as illustrated by a detailed study of the works of Verhaeren. Baudoin, however, made use of the techniques of other psychologists besides those of Freud.

From then on to the present day psychoanalytical biography and criticism have flourished. A bibliography would extend into hundreds of items. In American literature we have had psychoanalytical biographies of Hawthorne, Melville, Poe, Whitman, Holmes, Henry James, Whittier, etc. These biographies were different from former ones which often gave mere extracts from journals and letters without comment or psychological deductions. I must confess I have still a sneaking fondness for those old-fashioned biographies, many of which have become classics. I refer to the famous biographies of Cowper by William Hayley, Byron by Thomas Moore, Scott by Lockhart, Charlotte Bronte by Elizabeth Gaskell, Macaulay by Trevelyan, Dickens by Forster, Carlyle by Froude, and that of Tennyson by his son.

In the twenties there were several approaches to biography which have been confused or even identified with the Freudian but which have nothing in common with the psychoanalytic. I do not mean, however, to speak disrespectfully of Gamaliel Bradford and Lytton Strachey, authors of highly individual books whose distinguished characteristics are well known.

Numerous psychoanalytical biographies and studies have been made of English, French, and European writers.

The reader will note that in the old edition of this book there is no mention of Freud's book *The Ego and the Id* for it had not yet been published. Some have thought that the old principles which Freud advanced as to the relations between psychoanalysis and literature had now to be abandoned, because of the changes in some of his psychoanalytical opinions; that these invalidated the literary conceptions advanced by him and consequently those of his followers. But Freud did not repudiate those literary principles which he first set forth in 1908 in "Creative Writers and Day Dreaming" and which he elaborated in his *Delusion and Dream* and his *Leonardo da*

Vinci, and which he summed up on pages 327 and 328 of
A General Introduction to Psychoanalysis. In fact he repeated
them after he published his new views on psychoanalysis,
which really did not substantially differ from the old modifying
and clarifying, as he thought, by his new terminology, but in
the opinion of some critics merely confusing. However, whether right or wrong in his new views—and let us assume they are
right—he repeated his old theories of the relation of the
artist to the neurotic in his "A Short Account of Psychoanalysis: Exploring the Hidden Recesses of the Mind" published in
These Eventful Years in 1923. He wrote as follows:

> We have traced the convoluted paths, that lead from
> the urge of the unconscious wish to its realization in a
> work of art on the observer, and in the case of the artist
> himself we have made clear his internal kinship with the
> neurotic as well as his distinction from him, and we have
> pointed out the connection between his innate disposition,
> his chance experiences and his achievements.

Freud returned to the subject of the relation of psychoanalysis to literature the following year in his *An Autobiographical Study.*

This work appeared in a later edition in 1938, and we again
have to conclude that he saw no reason to change his views on
literature and art, for he retained the following restatement of
his old views:

> The artist like the neurotic, had withdrawn from an
> unsatisfying reality into [the] world of imagination; but,
> unlike the neurotic, he knew how to find a way back from
> it and once more to get a firm foothold in reality. His
> creations, works of art, were the imaginary satisfactions
> of unconscious wishes, just as dreams are; and like them
> they were in the nature of compromises, since they too
> were forced to avoid any open conflict with the forces
> of repression. But they differed from the social, narcisstic
> products of dreaming in that they were calculated to
> arouse sympathetic interest in other people and were able
> to invoke and to satisfy the same unconscious wishful
> impulses in them too.

In *The Erotic Motive* these views are expanded. Freud's
summaries showed he did not change his art views and hence
there was no need for me to change my views and bring in the

Ego, the *Id*, Castration Complex, penis envy, death wish, return to the womb, and other features modified or developed in later years. I know that critics since have introduced these concepts in literary studies, but I think often with unhappy results.

It is not true, then, that earlier psychoanalytical biography and criticism labored under the disadvantage of not having Freud's later views.

Eventually Freud saw that there were exceptions to his wish-fulfilment explanation of dreams. He discovered that war-shocked patients returned in their dreams to the very painful episodes that brought about the neuroses. They sought to reconstruct the unfortunate situation, Freud realized, so as to meet it in full and thus cure themselves. In short he found here no wishful fulfilment—no pleasure principle was invoked or involved—but here was an aspect of dream beyond the pleasure principle. Some critics thought that he ought to be true to the title of his book *Beyond the Pleasure Principle* and change his views on the relation of poetry to dreams.

This was not necessary. Creative writers had all along been doing what the war patients did—returning to the scenes of painful memory, dwelling on them, in an unconscious effort to rid themselves of their neuroses—if you will. I give the example of Dickens. His father spent some time in Marshalsea Prison for debt and Charles also lived there a short time. In his novels he returns not only to Marshalsea, but to prisons in general. I am indebted to Edgar Johnson's masterly life of Dickens for a list of the numerous references to prisons in Dickens' novels. The prison is the theme in *Pickwick*; it figures in *Barnaby Rudge*; it is the dominating symbol in *Little Dorrit*; it is a symbol in the *Tale of Two Cities*; it appears in *Great Expectations* and *Our Mutual Friend*. Dickens visited prisons in Philadelphia, in Lausanne, and in Paris. Surely he was not writing of episodes that could be compared to wishful events. Most of his literary life he was doing what war patients do, going back in his dreams and in his literary creations to painful scenes that aroused emotions in him that were akin to neuroses. And he was, without knowing it, thus seeking to get rid of the pressing burden. Many writers go back to painful scenes: Walt Whitman to the hospitals in the Civil War, and others to painful episodes in youth, of poverty and disappointment in love. Tennyson harped on the death of Arthur Hallam; for seventeen years he worked at the composition of *In Memoriam.*

The acceptance by such creative writers as Havelock Ellis, Arthur Schnitzler, Stephen Zweig, Arnold Zweig, Thomas Mann, and Georg Brandes has given the psychoanalytic approach great prestige. Of course I am glad to have a new edition of this book which has been out of print so long. Requests for it are often made, and it is at a premium. In my revisions I have corrected an error here and there, choosing a different word, toning down statements that were too positive and even adopting a suggestion or two from some of my hostile critics. I have also added some notes explanatory or corroborative of matter in the text and introduced new sections, one on Coleridge's "Ode to Dejection" and another on Swinburne's "Dolores." Two new sections on Byron have replaced the analysis of his work in the first edition. I have also added a new section on Poe, containing some criticism of the treatment by Princess Marie Bonaparte of his stories "The Black Cat" and "Loss of Breadth." A new section on some episodes in Shakespeare's personal life is pure speculation.

ALBERT MORDELL

Chapter 1

Introduction

1

THIS work is an endeavor to apply some of the methods of psychoanalysis to literature. It attempts to read closely between the lines of an author's works. It applies some principles in interpreting literature with a scrutiny hitherto scarcely deemed permissible. Only such suggestions have been set down whose application has been rendered fairly unimpeachable by science and experience.

In studying literature thus, I aim to trace a writer's books back to the outward and inner events of his life and to reveal his unconscious, or that part of his psychic life of which he is unaware. I try to show that unsuspected emotions of the writer have entered into his literary productions, that events he had apparently forgotten have guided his pen. In every book there is much of the author's unconscious which can be discovered by the critic and psychologist who apply a few well tested infallible principles.

This unconscious is largely identical with the mental love fantasies in our present and past life. Since the terms "unconscious" and "erotic" according to psychoanalysis are almost synonymous, any serious study of literature which is concerned with the unconscious must deal impartially with eroticism.

Every author reveals more than he intended. Works of the imagination open up to the reader hidden vistas in man's inner life just as dreams do. As the psychoanalyst recognizes that dreams are the realized repressed wishes of the unconscious, so the critic may discover in literary performances ideal pictures inspired by past repressions in the authors' lives. And just as anxiety-dreams spring largely from the anxieties of waking life, so literature describing human sorrows in general takes its cue from the personal griefs of the author.

A literary work is no longer regarded as a sort of objective product unrelated to its creator, written only by compliance with certain rules. It is a personal expression and represents the whole man behind it. His present and past, pleasurable and painful have gone into the making of it, and it records his secret aspirations and most intimate feelings; it is the outcropping of his struggles and disappointments. It is the outlet of his emotions, freely flowing forth even though he has sought to stem their flux. It dates from his apparently forgotten infantile life.

We know that a man's reading, his early education, his contact with the world, the fortunes and vicissitudes of his life, have all combined to influence his artistic work. We have learned that hereditary influences, the nature of his relations to his parents, his infantile repressions, his youthful love affairs, his daily occupations, his physical powers or failings, enter into the coloring and directing of his ideas and emotions, and will stamp any artistic product that he may undertake. Thus with a man's literary work before us and with a few clues, we are able to reconstruct his emotional and intellectual life, and guess with reasonable certainty at many of the events in his career. Georg Brandes has been able to build up a life of Shakespeare almost from the plays alone. As he said, if we have about forty-five works by a writer, and we still cannot find out much about his life, it must be our own fault.

Again we may deduce what kind of literary work would result if there were given to us not only the hereditary antecedents and biographical data of an author, but full accounts of his day dreams, ambitions, frailties, disillusionments, of his favorite reading, intellectual influences, love affairs and relations to his parents, relatives, and friends. I do not think it would be difficult for us to deduce from the facts we have of Dante's life that he naturally would have given us a work of the nature of the *Divine Comedy*.

Literature is a personal voice the source of which can be traced to the unconscious.

But an author draws not only on the past in his own life, but on the past psychic history of the human family. Unconscious race memories are revived by him in his writing; his productions are influenced by the most primitive ideas and emotions, though he may not be aware what they are. Yet they emerge from his pen; for the methods of thought and ways of feeling of our early ancestors still rule us. Nor is the idea of unconscious race memories idle speculation or fanciful theorizing. Just as surely as we carry in ourselves the physical marks of our forefathers of which each individual has millions, so undoubtedly we must have inherited most of their mental and emotional characteristics. The manner and nature of the lives of those who preceded us have never been entirely eliminated from our unconscious. We have even the most bestial instincts in a rudimentary stage, and these are revived, to our surprise, not only in our dreams but often in our waking thoughts and also occasionally in our conduct. We carry the whole world's past under our skins. And there is a sediment of that primitive life in many of our books, without the author being aware of the fact.

Thus a deterministic influence prevails in literature. A book is not an accident. The nature of its contents depends not only on hereditary influences, nor, as Taine thought, on climate, country and environment, alone, but on the nature of the repressions the author's emotions have experienced. The impulses that created it are largely unconscious, and the only conscious traces in it are those in the art of composition. Hence the ancient idea of poetic inspiration cannot be relegated to limbo, for it plays a decided part in determining the psychical features of the work. Inspiration finds its material in the unconscious. When the writer is inspired, he is eager to express ideas and feelings that have been formed by some event, though he cannot trace their origin, for he speaks out of the soul of a buried humanity.

There is no form or species of literature that may not be interpreted by psychoanalytic methods. Be the author ever so objective, no matter how much he has sought to make his personality intangible and elusive, there are means, with the aid of clues, of opening up the barred gates of his soul. Men like Flaubert and Mérimée, who believed in the impersonal and objective theory of art and who strove deliberately to conceal their personalities, failed in doing so. Their presence is revealed in their studies; they could not hold themselves aloof. It is true we have been aided by external evidence in learning what methods they employed to render themselves impersonal; the real Mérimée and Flaubert, however, were made to emerge by the help of their published personal letters. It matters not whether the author writes realistic or romantic fiction, autobiographical or historical tales, lyric or epic poems, dramas or essays, his unconscious is there, in some degree.

But in a field which is largely new, it is best to take those works or species of writing where the existence of the unconscious does not elude our efforts to detect it. Therefore, much will be said in this volume of works where there is no question that the author is talking from his own experiences, in his own person, or where he is using some character as a vehicle for his own point of view. Such works include lyric poetry which is usually the personal expression of the love emotions of the singer. Burns, Byron, Shelley, Keats, and Swinburne have left us records of their love affairs in their great lyric poems. Most of these were inspired by frustration of love, and were the results of actual experiences. And though much is said in them, other facts may be deduced.

It is also a fact that nearly every great novelist has given us an intimate though disguised account of himself in at least one novel (note *David Copperfield* and *Pendennis* as examples), while other writers have drawn themselves in almost every character they portrayed, Goethe and Byron being two instances. An author gives us the best insight into himself when he speaks frankly in his own person. His records are then intensely interesting and informative about his unconscious. But even if the author identifies himself with a fictitious character he speaks hardly less firmly.

2

Very important is the consideration of some of the literature where authentic dreams or dreams having the appearance of authenticity have been recorded. The connection between poetry and dreams has often been noted. The poet projects an ideal and imaginary world just as the dreamer does. He builds utopias and paradises and celestial cities. He sees visions and constructs allegories. I have interpreted, according to the methods of Freud, some dream literature like Kipling's "The Brushwood Boy" and Gautier's "Arria Marcella." These tales prove most astoundingly the correctness of Freud's theories about dreams being the fulfillment in our sleep of unconscious wishes of our daily life.

A literary production, even if no dream is recorded therein, is still a dream; that of the author. It represents the fulfillment of his unconscious wishes, or registers a complaint because they are not fulfilled. Like the dream, it is formed of remnants of the past psychic life of the author and is colored by recent events and images. Freud in interpreting the dreams of his neurotic patients, learned the substance, the manifest content of the dream, as he calls it, and inquired about the events of the preceding days, and he evoked all the associations which occured to the patients. He learned something of their lives and finally after a course of psychoanalytic treatment frequently cured them of their neuroses by making them aware of the unconscious repressions or fixations from which they suffered. These were removed and the resistances broken down. As critics, we may interpret a book in the same way. A literary work stands in the same relation to the author as the dream to the patient. The writer has, however, cured himself of his emotional anxiety by giving vent to his feelings in his book. He has been his own doctor. The critic may see how this has been accomplished and point out the unconscious elements that the writer has brought forth in his book out of his own soul. The critic, not being able, like the physician and his patient, to question the author in person, must avail himself, in addition to the internal evidence of the literary product itself, of all the data that have been collected from the author's confessions and letters, from the accounts of friends, etc. After having studied these in connection with the writing in question, he learns the author's unconscious. Shelley's "Epipsychidion," for instance, is an autobiographical poem, Shelley's dream of love, and can be fully followed only when the reader has acquainted himself with the history of Shelley's marriages and love affairs.

I have interpreted a dream of Stevenson recorded in his "A Chapter on Dreams," and have found in it a full confirmation of the Freudian theory of dreams. Stevenson, recounting at length a dream of his own, tells us unwittingly more about the misunderstanding that existed between him and his father and the difficulties he encountered before he married (since the object of his affection was separated but not yet divorced from her first husband) than his biography does. When the essay and the biography are taken together, we see the testimony before us as to why Stevenson dreamed this dream.

William Cowper's poem on the receipt of his mother's picture is a remarkable document in support of one of the tenets that are among the pillars of Freud's system, the theory of the Œdipus Complex. As is well known, Freud traced the nucleus of the psychoneuroses to an overattachment that the patient had for the parent of the opposite sex, a fixation which was very strong in infancy but from the influence of which there had never been a healthy liberation. This fixation which is often unconscious plants the seeds of future neuroses. The victim's entire life, even his love affairs, are interfered with by this attachment. Any one who knows his Freud and has read Cowper's poem can see in it the cause of most of the latter's unhappiness and most likely his insanity. His mother died when he was a child, and many years later he was still writing to her, almost with passion.

Both Stevenson's essay and Cowper's poem are self-explanatory to the disciple of Freud. If we had known nothing about the authors' lives, we would have seen beyond doubt that in the one case there was in actual life a hostility to the father, revealed by the dreamer's murdering him; and in the other case we would have known that a hysterical overattachment to the mother existed and that the writer's life would have been neurotic and that he might possibly experience an attachment to some older woman who replaced the mother.

Further, just as there are typical dreams from which alone the psychoanalyst can judge the wishes of his subject without asking him any questions about himself, so there are literary compositions wherefrom we can learn much of the author's unconscious, without probing into the facts of his life. Typical dreams in which certain objects like serpents or boxes appear, or in which the dreamer is represented as flying, swimming or climbing, have a sexual significance. Freud has shown this after having investigated thousands of such dreams and noted the symbolic language and customs of our ancestors. Literary works also speak *per se* for the author when they abound in similar symbolical images.

3

We now come to another species of literature that is important for the psychoanalytic critic. This is a class of writing which delineates primeval and immoral emotions. It often shows us the conflicts between savage emotions still lurking in man, and the demands of civilization. Either force may triumph, but the real interest of these works is that they show the old cave dweller is not yet dead within us, and that civilization is achieved gradually by suppressing these old emotions; sometimes these needs are strong and must not be extirpated too suddenly; in fact in some specific cases must be granted satisfaction. Among some of the interesting books in recent years have been tales where primitive emotions have been depicted as conquering their victims. Note Conrad's "Heart of Darkness;" where it is shown how the old barbarian instincts and the cry of the forest are part of us and may be revived in us. Jack London's *The Call of the Wild* is an interesting allegory on the subject. It is well known that we are descended from forbears who were wilder than the most savage tribes of today. Naturally some of the emotions they felt are not altogether extinct in us. Civilization is after all but a veneer and slight causes may stir up brutal sensations in many people. They are still in our unconscious and form for the literary man very fascinating though often dangerous material. Shakespeare understood this when he drew Caliban.

Poe once said that no writer would dare to write truly all his inner thoughts and feelings, for the very paper would burn beneath them. What he meant was that all writers, even the bravest, suppress those unconscious elements in their nature that are related to immorality, indecency, degeneracy, morbidity and cruelty. It may not be advisable for writers continually to remind the reader of the remnant echoes and memories of our primitive state, which have fortunately been made quiescent but not been completely exterminated by culture. In the confessions of criminals, in the pathological disclosures of sexually aberrated people given to physicians, in the records of atrocities committed in time of war, we have illustrations of the atavisms of our day. Often a diseased literary man ventures far in baring his soul and we get the morbid and immoral material that provides food for the unhealthy.

As a rule the author's sense of propriety and his prudence act as a censor for him and hedge in his dormant savage feelings, so as not to allow them to find a direct voice in his art. Yet we can often pierce through the veil and observe exactly where the censor has been invoked and guess fairly accurately what has been suppressed.

Some authors who relax the censorship voluntarily and appear to be without a sense of shame, give us some of the immoral literature which the world publicly abhors, but which individuals often delight in reading in private. I do not refer to the really great literature which has been stamped "immoral" by prudish people, because its ideas are too far advanced for them to appreciate, and are different from the conventional morals of society. I do not refer to the hundreds of great works which give us true accounts of the natural man, books whose irresistibility cannot be evaded except by hypocrites. I do not include novels and plays wherein the authors have realized that we are exerting too great a sacrifice upon our emotions and that many souls are starved by lack of normal gratification on account of the harsh exactions of conventional society. But there is a real immoral (or rather indecent) literature where the author allows his savage instincts to come to the surface and trespass on those aspects of his personality which civilization should have tamed. He may suffer from the vice of exhibitionism and think he is frank, when he is merely showing he has no sense of shame; and he may cater to a market merely for money, in which case he acts like a mercenary harlot. He may try to gratify himself by sexual abandon in art because he has never had the craving for love satisfied in life. He gives vent to instincts that are still ruling him because of his own atavistic or neurotic state. Psychoanalytic literature puts in a new light immoral literature, which hitherto has been dealt with from a moral, and not a psychological, point of view. This literature should be explained and its sources traced; these will be found in the infantile love life of the authors. Such writings should not be condemned offhand just because they stir our moral indignation. They must be interpreted so that we may learn the nature of their authors.

I have also made a study of so repulsive a feature in the lives of our earliest ancestors as cannibalism. It is one of the most primitive emotions. The discoveries of archaeologists show that cannibalism prevailed in Europe before the dawn of history; Greek plays show its early existence in Greece; and we know that it still prevails among savage tribes today.

Many of the views here presented will be strange and novel to those unacquainted with or hostile to Freud's theories, or to those who wish to ignore the fact of the existence of primitive emotions in man. The ideas advanced here will displease the puritanical opponents of scientific research. But it should be borne in mind that a study of the unconscious must necessarily deal with much that is obnoxious in human nature.[1] A study of this unpleasant element leads to the attainment of a more natural and moral life. But we should also remember that the unconscious, besides containing the seeds of crime and immorality, also is the soil of all those finer sentiments that the church and the state cherish. Conscience, self-sacrifice, moral sense, love, are often unconscious sentiments.[2]

[1] The reader should also remember that such fearsome words as "sex," "incest," "homosexualism," "sadism," etc., include in psychoanalysis love, great affection between mother and son, father and daughter, brother and sister, etc., deep friendship, cruelty, respectively.

[2] Fritz Wittels in his *Sigmund Freud* (pp. 83-84) says that Freud in his latest book *Das Ich und das Es* (1923) (*The Ego and the Id*) recognized that there must be dreams of conscience. He quotes from the book, "Not only the lowest elements of the Ego, but also the highest may be unconscious." Wittels asks, "Why has this admission come so tardily?" and adds that we cannot fail to regret that the statement was not more emphatic. He calls Freud's adoption of this view a term for a treaty of peace after a ten years war. Thus Freud admits that the normal human being is far more moral than he is aware.

Freud himself wrote after explaining why he did not lay emphasis on the

In the literature of metempsychosis people are depicted as remembering past experiences, as in Kipling's tale "The Finest Story in the World," George Sand's *Consuelo*, and Jack London's *The Star Rover*. I personally do not believe in the transmigration of the individual soul. But there are affinities between the Buddhistic conception of metempsychosis with its doctrine of Karma, the scientific theory of heredity, and the unconscious in psychoanalysis. They are all dominated by the idea that the ways of feeling and manner of thinking of our progenitors are in some respects exercised by us. We carry their souls, not the individual, but the collective ones; we are products of their sins and virtues; we have the idiosyncrasies, mental makeup, and emotional tendencies that they had; we have stamped upon us features of our race, our nation, our religion. We cannot remember isolated events of past ages, but the effects, of happenings then are registered in our nervous system. No one has done more than Hearn to show this, and he is, both because of his life and work, one of the fittest subjects for psychoanalytic study. The only possible rival he has is Edgar Allan Poe.

If any one wishes to see an adroit application of the method of reading between the lines in a poem, let him read Lafcadio Hearn's interpretation of Browning's poem "A Light Woman" in the *Appreciations of Poetry*. Hearn had probably never heard of Freud, but in his lecture to his class, he showed that the unconscious of the author and the character could be discovered by probing carefully into the literary work. Hearn tells in prose Browning's story of the young man who stated that he stole his friend's mistress to save him, and on tiring of her pretended he had never loved her. Hearn shrewdly observes:

"Does any man in this world ever tell the exact truth about himself? Probably not. No man understands himself so well as to be able to tell the exact truth about himself. It is possible that this man believes himself to be speaking truthfully, but he certainly is telling a lie, a half truth only. We have his exact words, but the exact language of the speaker in any one of Browning's monologues does not tell the truth, it only suggests

---

moral element in the unconscious, while not denying it, "Now that we have embarked upon the analysis of the ego we can give answer to all those whose moral sense has been shocked and who have complained that there must surely be a higher nature in man. 'Very true,' we can say and here we have that higher nature in this ego ideal or super ego, the representation of our relation to parents." *The Ego and the Id, Complete Psychological Works of Sigmund Freud* Vol. XIX. p. 35-36.

the truth. We must find out the real character of the person, and the real facts of the case, from our own experience of human nature."

Psychoanalysis was applied to literature long before Freud. When biographers recounted all the influences of an author's life upon his works, or probed deeply into the real meaning of his views, they gave us psychoanalytic criticsm. Great literary critics like Sainte-Beuve, Taine, and Georg Brandes traced the tendencies of authors' works to emotional crises in their lives. Critics who study the various ways in which authors have come to draw themselves or people they knew in their books, are psychoanalytic. When biographers and critics dilate especially on the relations existing between the writer and his mother, and trace the effects on the work of the author, they employ the psychoanalytic method. Any profound insight into human nature is psychoanalytic, and I find such insight in Swift, Johnson, Hazlitt, and Lamb.

It is, however, Freud who first gave complete application of that method to literature. He first touched on it in his masterpiece *The Interpretation of Dreams* in 1900, when he saw the significance of the marriage of Œdipus to his mother in Sophocles' play *Œdipus*. He showed that it was a reminiscence of actual incestuous love that was practised far back in the ages of barbarism, and that the play shows horror as a reaction to such attachment to the mother. The first treatment of an aesthetic theme from the viewpoint of psychoanalysis was made by Freud in his book *Wit and the Unconscious* in 1905. The first sole application of psychoanalysis to a work of literature was undertaken by him in connection with Jensen's novel *Gradiva* in 1907, where he shows the similarity between the emotions of the hero and the psychoneuroses. (The novel and Freud's essay have been both translated into English.) * Freud also studied Leonardo da Vinci and showed the influences of the artist's infantile love life upon his later career and work. Psychoanalytic methods have been applied to music, mythology, religion, philosophy, philology and morals, and indeed to almost every sphere of mental activity.

The new method will help to explain the nature and origin of literary genius, though it is not pretended it will create it. Psychoanalysis will show us the direction that literary genius takes and will explain why it proceeds in a particular path. It will give the reasons why one author writes books of a particular color or tendency, why he entertains certain ideas. It

* *Delusion and Dream*, Moffat, Yard & Co.

explains why certain plots and characters are indulged in by particular authors. It explains why Schopenhauer became a pessimist, why Wagner dealt with themes like the woman between two men. In fact studies of these artists, employing Freud's methods, have already been published. Max Graf and Otto Rank each wrote about Wagner, and Edward Hitschmann has given us a monograph on Schopenhauer. Similarly the critic of the future will explain the fundamental tone of the works of writers who differ vastly from one another. We shall see more clearly why Byron gave vent to his note of melancholy, Keats to his passion for beauty, Browning to his spirit of optimism, Strindberg to his misogyny, Swift to his misanthropy, Ibsen to his moral revolt, Tolstoy to his religious reaction, Thackeray to his cynicism, and Wordsworth to his love for nature.

The author is more in his work than he suspects. To illustrate: There is a theory of projection, in psychoanalysis, which explains to us why hysterical people lean with great eagerness for moral support or consolation on some actual person they love or admire. Often he is the clergyman or physician, at other times he is a friend or relative. The same thing occurs in literature. The writer who has certain theories clings for support to some characters in history or fiction. He projects his personality on theirs. If he writes a biography he chooses a type most like himself and is really writing his own life. Renan's *Life of Jesus* is really a life of Renan and he makes Jesus have many qualities he himself had. I have compared Renan's autobiography to his *Life of Jesus* and shown the resemblance between Renan and the Jesus of his creation.

An author also identifies himself with his characters and draws unconsciously on himself when he creates them. I have discovered a personal note in an epic like the *Iliad*, usually considered impersonal. I have deduced that the master passion of the author of the Achilles-Patroclus story was friendship, and that he sang a private sorrow in Achilles' grief for Patroclus. I have been aided in this by a dream of Achilles.

Authors also often draw their villains from their unconscious. They indulge in exaggeration, disguise, and various other devices. Balzac's worst villain, the intellectual, wicked Vautrin, is the Dr. Hyde of Balzac himself let loose in a fictitious character. And we know Byron was even accused of having committed the crimes of his villains. This, however, does not mean that the creator of vicious types himself may not be the purest person in his personal life. We must not conclude that actual events of a fictitious work have happened to the author himself. And this brings me to the real danger of a critical study of this kind.

I have maintained a double guard over myself so as not to transcend the danger line. I have sought not to interpret as a portrait of the author's own life, his delineation of a character, when no reason warrants such a conclusion. It is absurd to conclude that isolated incidents in a novel happened in the writer's own life. It is only when a writer harps on one plot—one motive—continually and in several works, that one's suspicions are aroused that he is really writing about himself. It is only when there is a genuine ring to the cry of distress, that the reader suspects that the work is more than a mere literary exercise. The early readers of Heine, Alfred de Musset and Leopardi, saw that the poets were singing about real sorrows. No one ever doubted that Goethe, Ibsen and Tolstoy used fictitious characters as vehicles for their own ideas, and that Wilhelm Meister, Brand, and Levine were really the authors themselves.

No doubt, many literary men will be among the first to object to a theory of literary criticism which tends to reveal their personalities more closely to the public. They may hold that they are painfully careful to keep their own views and personalities from the public eyes. I do not think that anything derogatory to authors as a whole will result from psychoanalytic criticism. They should be the first to welcome this method. In fact the older writers gain by the process of psychoanalytic study. We become more liberal and admire them all the more. I can only speak from my own studies and say that my admiration for the personal character of some writers, the moral standing of whom has never been very high with the public, has increased since my studies of psychoanalysis, and my appreciation of their work has deepened.

The reader's indulgent attention is invited to the pages where the effect upon literature of the sexual infantile life of the author is treated. This involves a résumé of one of Freud's most important and most abused discoveries, that the child has a love life of its own, the development of which has most significant bearing upon his entire life. More particular indulgence is pleaded for the pages dealing with sex symbolism in literature.

In conclusion, I quote a passage from William James to show the significance of the unconscious in modern psychology.

I cannot but think that the most important step forward that has occurred in psychology since I have been a student of that science is the discovery, first made in 1886, that in certain objects at least, there is not only the consciousness of the ordinary field, with its usual centre and margin, but an addition thereto in the shape of a set of memories, thoughts and feelings which are extra-marginal and outside of the primary consciousness altogether, but yet must be classed as conscious facts of some sort, able to reveal their presence by unmistakable signs. I call this the most important step forward because, unlike the advances which psychology has made, this discovery has revealed to us an entirely unsuspected peculiarity in the constitution of human nature.[1]

[1] *Varieties of Religious Experience*, p. 233.

Chapter 2

Eroticism in Life

1

PSYCHOLOGY has in recent years investigated the unconscious day dreams which are now recognized as part of our imaginative life. No matter how religious or moral we may be, erotic fancies are always with us. This mental life has often been described in medieval literature in the accounts of sensual visions which tempted saints. The authors who aimed at inculcating moral and religious lessons thus gave vent to their own erotic fancies in the alluring and enticing verbal pictures they drew. Many instances thus appear in puritanical and aescetic literature, of immorality and exhibitionism.

We are learning to deal directly with a phase of our lives, whose influence upon our happiness can scarcely be over-estimated. We must first admit the reality of the fantasies that occupy so much of our existence. Out of them bloom as a flower the emotions which are associated with the noblest sentiments in human nature—love. How these fancies may be sublimated into higher purposes, like beautiful deeds and works of art, how they may be directed into various channels, how they may be partly gratified without impairing the finer instincts of man, are problems which are being made the subject of serious study. It is also being realized that these fancies increase in vividness, number and variety where, for economic and conventional reasons, means of normal love life are cut off. It is also being admitted that much of the mental misery and physical debility of many people is due to the absurd asceticism forced upon us in sex matters by our modern civilization.

We must learn to discuss, in a sincere manner, the nature and tendencies of the erotic in our lives.

Let us examine the word "erotic" itself. Unfortunately it has assumed an unsavory meaning, although it means "related to love" and is derived from the Greek word "eros"—love. It has been used to designate the perverse and the immoral in sex matters; it has been made synonymous with lust, abnormality, excess and every unpleasant feature in regard to sex matters. Pater once complained that he did not like the use of the word "hedonism" because of the misapprehension created in the minds of the people who did not understand Greek. The same objection may be brought against the use of the word "eroticism." Properly speaking all love poetry is erotic poetry; in fact the greatness of poetry and literature is its eroticism, for they are most true then to life, which is largely erotic. To call a great poet like Paul Verlaine erotic is a compliment, not a disparagement. Nor is he nearly as erotic as the author of *The Song of Songs*. Since there is no word in English to specify love interest in its widest sense, we must cling to the use of words "erotic" and "eroticism." We should restore to the word "eroticism" its original and nobler meaning.

Any literary work that lays an emphasis on the part played by love in our lives is erotic. Literature could not exist without dwelling on the love interest. The stories of Jacob and Rachel, of Ruth, and of David and Uriah's wife, are all beautiful examples of eroticism in the Bible.

Man is adverse to admitting certain facts about his mental love life. People are often shocked by the immorality of the dreams which reveal their unconscious lives. A man, however, will often confess in intimate circles the existence of sensual fancies within himself. People show indications in many ways of the parts played by the love and sex interests in their mental lives. Some witness suggestive plays; others indulge in telling and hearing lewd jests, indecent witticisms and improper stories. Any one who has listened to the conversation of men in the club or smoker, in the factory or office, in the bar-room or sitting room, cannot be blind to the fact that the erotic interests rule us far more than we wish to admit. He who thinks that the wealthy are too much absorbed in accumulating more riches and the poor too much worn out by the struggle for existence, to be occupied with erotic fancies, is mistaken. A day spent in a factory or an evening at a club will show one that the millionaire and the pauper are brothers under their skins.

Man's nature is erotic to its very foundations; he was erotic, in infancy, in his own way; he carries within him all the erotic instincts of millions of ancestors for thousands of years back. His eroticism extends to many sensitive areas of his body like his lips, the palms of his hands, his chest and back. Eroticism often is hidden in an interest in many subjects which are apparently unrelated to it, an interest which is a compensation to one for his lack of love. Man's first real combined physical and emotional suffering commences at puberty when he hears new and strange voices calling for a reply to which there is no answer. He discovers that society is so constituted that he must spend his youth, when the passions are at their height, in unnaturally curbing or misdirecting them. He often discovers later that even marriage sometimes is not a full satisfaction for his love instincts.

Though some critics have refused to concede the importance that the erotic has played in life, poets did not conceal the truth, for the words in which their emotions were couched betrayed them.

The "purist" today is often the one who revels most (in private) in obscene literature; while many people find in such literature the only means they have of indulging their ungratified love life.

The mere interest, however, in a virile and unhypocritical literary work like a novel by Fielding or Smollett, does not indicate abnormal eroticism in the reader. In fact, it is often a sign of some unhealthy tendency or starvation in human nature when a person shrinks from honest and frank literature. The schoolboy or college student who reads in stealth Defoe's novel *Roxana*, instead of *Robinson Crusoe*, who turns from his Greek version of Aristophanes to the translation of *Lysistrata*, or who wearies of Chaucer's Prologue to the *Canterbury Tales* and tries to read in spite of the old English "The Miller's Tale" or "The Reeve's Tale," is not an immoral youngster. The adult who reads them is not an indecent or abnormal person.

Pierre Bayle whose *Dictionnaire Historique et Critique*[1] abounds in many risqué stories, defending himself in an excellent essay called "Explanation Concerning Obscenities." He said very aptly:

> If any one was so great a lover of purity, as to wish not only that no immodest desire should arise in his mind, but also that his imagination should be constantly free from every obscene idea, he could not attain his end without closing his eyes and his ears, and the remembrance of many things which he could not choose but see and hear. Such perfection could not be hoped for, whilst we see men and beasts, and know the signification of certain words that make a necessary part of our language. It is not in our power either to have, or not to have, certain

[1] Vol. V p. 850—English Translation, 1738.

ideas, when certain objects strike our senses; they are imprinted in our imagination whether we will or not. Chastity is not endangered by them, provided we don't grow fond of them and approve of them.

2

Men may be engaged in philanthropic or political movements; they may love their work intensely; they may be consummating an ambition; they may make sacrifices in performing their duties; but withal their minds are pondering on some particular woman, or on women in general. We hold imaginary conversations with women we have known, whom we know, or whom we would like to know. We think about the feminine faces we meet in the streets, and experience a passing melancholy because we are unacquainted with some of the girls we see. Undue interest in the opposite sex is of course also characteristic of women. They adorn their persons and choose their styles in dress with the object of physically attracting the male.

Those who are unhappy in love or marriage do not find themselves compensated for their misfortune by the fact that they may possess great wealth, or have a name that is respected or crowned with glory. The careers of Lord Nelson and Parnell show that national saviors and leaders may be engulfed in a grand passion whose fortunate outcome may be to them possibly as momentous as the welfare of their counrty. The fact that Mark Antony was a general on whose move the saving of his country depended, did not make him the less interested in Cleopatra. The fact that Abelard was a philosopher did not make him hold his studies higher than he did Heloise. There was really nothing abnormal about these men. Modern writers have been attracted to them. Shakespeare chose Antony as the hero of his play, and Pope's "Eloisa to Abelard" shows his interest in Abelard. The amorous adventures of great military leaders like Caesar and Napoleon are well known.

The love affairs of many literary men make us almost conclude that they were more concerned about their loves than their art. Recall Stendhal's famous cry about his perishing for want of love or Balzac's eternal ambition to be famous and to be loved. Goethe once exclaimed that the only person who was happy was he who was fortunate in his domestic affairs. He made every one of his love affairs the basis of some poem, novel, or play; and not to know anything about his love for Charlotte Buff, or Frederica or Lili, or Frau von Stein, is to limit oneself in being able to appreciate Goethe, in being able to understand *Werther, Faust, Wilhelm Meister*, and other works by him.

And we love these poets and writers who naïvely confessed that they did not care for aught in life but love, and who sang of their troubles frankly. Who does not find Catullus and Tibullus sweet? Who that has read them does not cherish the lyrical cries of the Troubadours or the poems of the Chinese poets of the T'ang period? Can any one help thinking of Burns or Musset without affection and sympathy? And there are some who would not surrender the great body of sonnets and lyrics of England's poets for one of her colonies. And why is this? Because these poets are ourselves speaking for us and saying what we feel but are unable to express. The cry of the medieval Persian or Japanese poet is our own cry. His joy is ours and he is we and we are he. Once a poem has left its author's pen it is no longer a mere personal record, but becomes an enduring monument of art in which millions of men discern a grief or gladness that they too have known. In a measure, literature is more real and eternal than life itself. It makes the past live and it holds emotions that can sway millions of people for ever and ever. As Cicero said in his speech for Archias the poet: "If the *Iliad* had not existed, the same tomb which covered Achilles' body would also have buried his renown."

Sometimes a poet conceals all traces that would lead one to suspect an erotic basis for his poem. Sometimes he has actually inserted erotic passages and subsequently removed them. Coleridge did both in the "Ode to Dejection." It gives a greater delineation of a saddened person's inner emotions than Shelley's poem on the same theme and similar poems by Burns and Byron. At one time it was not considered an erotic poem even though a Lady is addressed three times. It was held to be solely a lament for the loss of creative powers, but paradoxically it became a poem showing creative genius.

It was, as we now know, definitely inspired by the unfortunate love felt by Coleridge for Sara Hutchinson, sister of Mary who soon married Wordsworth. We have evidence of this in the early version, where the name of Sara had appeared instead of the word Lady, and where a considerable portion of the poem is devoted to expressing love for her.[1]

[1] This version was first published in 1937 by Ernest de Selincourt in *Essays and*

The "Ode to Dejection" was written in 1802 and entitled "A Letter to Azra," and the manuscript is in Dove Cottage, Grasmere. The final poem has nearly one hundred and forty lines while the original is more than twice as long. I am not concerned whether Coleridge improved the poem by condensing it, and have no criticism to make of him for concealing the fact that it was originally a love poem. There were no lines in the later version like "But thou dear Sara!—Dear indeed thou art, My comforter! (O Heart within my heart)." It is not necessary to quote other verses to show that a large part of the poem dealt with his love disappointment and that it was this which inspired the dejection. In the later and final version he threw readers off the track as well as critics by stating that it was only the conviction that he had lost his creative powers that brought about the dejective mood. It is not to be denied that to some extent this is true. But we have now the evidence that an erotic motive first instigated the poet to write the poem. A fine critic like Richard Garnett, not knowing of the early version, was led astray when he said that Coleridge substituted for Wordsworth to whom he had originally addressed a poem under the name of Edmund, an "imaginary Lady." No, the lady was not imaginary, she was very real. The motive for the poem was a love affair and Coleridge did not ruin the poem, as Garnett thinks, by enforcing numerous changes to the detriment of the poem.

Coleridge's explanation that he had lost his poetic gifts because he now gave himself to "abstruse research" was accepted. As a matter of fact, two of his best poems were published when he was past fifty, "Youth and Age" and "Work Without Hope." Although he wrote most of his great poems before he was thirty, he composed his best prose—his literary criticism, and some essays after this age. I am not sure but that the *Biographia Literaria* and some of the letters he wrote after 1802, the date of the ode, are not as important creative literature as some of his early poems. Surely great prose may also be regarded as evidence of creative genius.

I therefore maintain that an erotic motive may inspire a poem where it seems not to exist.

Studies XXII and reprinted by him in 1947 in *Wordsworth and Other Studies*. See also *Coleridge*, the Clark Lectures, 1952-1953 by Arthur Humphrey House (British Book Centre).

3

A comprehension of the erotic in ourselves will help us discern many false ideals connected with the treatment of love in literature. I refer especially to the ideal of a first and only love (regarded by the lover usually as Platonic) which has been spread by deceptive authors and which has produced much affectation and insincerity in literature.

In real life people do not generally marry their first loves; they often cherish contempt for persons once loved; they do not as a rule go through life always maintaining that they loved once and that they would never love again. On the contrary, they usually marry and settle down and even forget about their early affairs, although in many cases these have lasting influence.

If poets, however, were to speak in a prosaic manner of their early loves, their works would be less admired. The public loves loyalty and hence it encourages love literature that is over-sentimental and false. No doubt when a man contracts an unhappy marriage or does not succeed in winning love later in life he looks back upon an early love affair with tenderness. And while it is true that the past always rules us, we are often satisfied as to the manner in which it shaped our futures. Robert Browning had an early sad love affair which influenced his "Pauline" and indeed many of his later lyrics, but he was happy in the love of the poetess Elizabeth Barrett. Mark Twain's married life was ideal and happy, in spite of an early love affair of his which ended because of the accidental nondelivery of a letter. On the other hand Byron, who was unhappily married, cherished the love of his early sweetheart Mary Chaworth for many years. Strangely and unjustly enough he has been accused of insincerity and posing.

There are two conspicuous instances in literature where a poet's love was thought by himself to have lasted for life, the cases of Dante and Petrarch. If the loves of these Italians for their mistresses are strictly investigated, I think it will be discovered that they have hoodwinked the world about their loves. They wrote their best poems about their beloved ones, after these had died, and death often makes a man unwittingly write falsely about the past. Oscar Pfister tells us in his *The Psychoanalytic Method* of a diseased man of fifty who lived apart from his wife in the same house, and who treated her brutally. After her death he always insisted that they were an ideal couple. Pfister relates another story of a widower who recalled only the happy part of his unhappy married life, and thought he never would marry again.

There has always been a suspicion among some people about the durability of the love felt by Dante and Petrarch, for Beatrice and Laura respectively. Symonds says of Laura: "Though we believe in the reality of Laura, we derive no clear conception either of her person or her character. She is not so much a woman as woman in the abstract. . . .The *Canzoniere* is therefore one long melodious monotony poured from the poet's soul, with the indefinite form of a beautiful woman seated in a lovely landscape." [2]

Petrarch was twenty-three years old in 1327 when he met Laura. She died twenty-one years later. Petrarch survived her twenty-six years, dying in 1374. Petrarch, it should be mentioned, had two illegitimate children born by a mistress before Laura's death; they were later legitimised. The poet probably at times felt the pangs of disprized love to the extent that he states he did in his sonnets; he may have experienced the grief he describes he suffered in his sonnets. But that he was in the constant throes of love for her for forty-seven years is doubtful. He probably was projecting that ideal of faithful love to please the public; he offered himself as the type of hero the public likes; a faithful, steadfast lover. It was this kind of ideal that made so great a genius like Thomas Hardy gratify the public taste by portraying so unswerving a lover as Gabriel Oak in *Far From the Madding Crowd*.

The case of Dante is an even more noteworthy example of literary affectation and self-delusion. His love is the most astonishing in history. He and Beatrice were each only nine years old when he saw her. He probably saw her once after that. She died in 1290, when the poet was twenty-five years old. Great as Dante's sorrow was, it did not prevent him from marrying two years later. Dante makes Beatrice the heroine of his *Divine Comedy*, or at least of the "Paradiso." His platonic affection for her is so unnatural that one feels he was doing what Petrarch did, unconsciously creating an ideal and depicting as permanent an emotion, that had really brief sway.

Although it is true that their past love affairs may have ruled them for life, neither Dante nor Petrarch were the faithful lovers they would have us believe they were.

[2] *Encyclopaedia Britannica*, Vol. XXI, p. 314.

Chapter 3

Dreams and Literature

1

FREUD discovered that dreams were the royal road to the unconscious, in that they portrayed our most daring and immoral wishes as actually fulfilled. It is not necessary that we actually have those wishes in our waking life; it is sufficient if they merely intruded themselves upon us against our wills sometime in the past. The dream will express our inmost thoughts. It will use symbolical language to let us still remain in the dark about our painful desires; but the psychoanalyst can learn what these are. As a result, when we have revealed to us what unconscious emotions are at the bottom of our nervous disturbances, we may be eased of them.

Many writers on dreams, in the past, understood that they referred to events of our daily life, but the exact relation was not seen. The ancients were especially interested in the phenomena of dreams. Many ancient histories and fairy tales abound in narrations and interpretations of dreams.

Modern literary men also have paid a great deal of attention to them. There are essays on dreams by Locke, Hobbes, Thomas Browne, Addison, Leigh Hunt, Dickens, Emerson and Lafcadio Hearn.

One English writer who gave almost complete expression to the views of Freud was William Hazlitt. In his essay "On Dreams" in *The Plain Speaker*, he stated the theory. It may come as a surprise to Freud—probably as a greater surprise than when he learned that Schopenhauer had written about repression—to read the following passage:

"There is a sort of profundity in sleep; and it may be usefully consulted as an oracle in this way. It may be said that the voluntary power is suspended, and things come upon us as unexpected revelations, which we keep out of our thoughts at other times. We may be aware of a danger that yet we do not choose, while we have the full command of our faculties, to acknowledge to ourselves; the impending event will then appear to us as a dream, and we shall most likely find it verified

22

afterwards. Another thing of no small consequence is, that we may sometimes discover our tacit, and almost *unconscious* sentiments, with respect to persons or things in the same way. We are not hypocrites in our sleep. The curb is taken off from our passions, and our imagination wanders at will. When awake, we check these rising thoughts, and fancy we have them not. In dreams, when we are off our guard, they return securely and unbidden. We make this use of the infirmity of our sleeping metamorphosis, that we may *repress* any feelings of this sort that we disapprove in their incipient state, and detect, ere it be too late, an unwarrantable antipathy or fatal passion. Infants cannot disguise their thoughts from others; and in sleep we reveal the secret to ourselves." [The italics are mine.]

Freud's work may also be called a commentary on this extraordinary passage of one of England's greatest critics.

Let us examine a few dreams, actual and artificial, in literature, and we shall note that they show method in their madness, that they are ways of expressing the person's unconscious desires.

In his astonishing essay, "A Chapter on Dreams," Stevenson has shown us how dreams influence authorship. He tells us how the "Brownies," as he calls the powers that make the dreams, constructed his tales; he often, however, had to reject some of these stories because of their lack of morals. As we remarked above, wicked dreams are dreamt even by virtuous people, since the material is drawn from the psychic life of our infancy and primitive ancestors. Stevenson relates how his famous tale *The Strange Case of Dr. Jekyll and Mr. Hyde* was suggested by a dream.

Stevenson, in his essay, relates a dream wherein unwittingly he lays bare much about some past experience in his life. He found it too immoral he says to make a tale of it. But he did immoral things in his dream; these were related to certain wishes in his waking hours. Those who are familiar with an episode in Stevenson's life, that relating to his marriage, and with Freud's theories, will find no difficulty in interpreting the dream and seeing how the dream and the events in his life which gave rise to it, tally with one another, when the Freudian method is applied. In fact the truth of Freud's views could be established alone by the interpretation applied to this dream.

Stevenson dreamed that he was the son of a rich wicked man with a most damnable temper. He (the son) lived abroad to avoid his parent, but returned to England to find his father married again. They met and later in a quarrel the son, being insulted, struck the father dead. The step-mother lived in the same house with the son, who was afraid she detected his guilt. Later he discovered her near the scene of the murder with some evidence of his guilt. Yet they returned arm in arm home and she did not accuse him. Once he searched all her possessions for that evidence she had found of his guilt. He asked her why she tortured him; "she knew he was no enemy to her." She fell upon her knees and cried that she loved him. Stevenson comments that it was not his tale but that of the little peoples, the brownies. Stevenson was mistaken; it was his tale. Everything that happened in that dream had a *raison d'être.* Let us see why he dreamt this immoral dream and interpret it in the light of its own facts and those his biographer relates.

In early youth Stevenson was an atheist and had difficulties with his father. In 1876, at the age of twenty-six, he met his future wife, Mrs. Osbourne, who was not yet divorced from her husband. The elder Stevenson was opposed to the match. Robert Louis had travelled extensively; he went to France before he took his memorable trip to California to be near the object of his love. Mrs. Osbourne obtained a divorce and married Stevenson in 1880. Thus after four years of suffering and the removal of three great obstacles, the married state of his beloved, the objection of his father and financial troubles, the novelist was happily united to the woman he loved. Mrs. Osbourne's first husband remarried and Stevenson's father died in 1887. Stevenson and his father had become reconciled, and on the latter's death, Stevenson was so shocked that he had many nightmares of which in all likelihood this dream was one. The essay containing the account of this dream was published in January, 1888, in *Scribner's Magazine,* and is included in the volume *Across the Plains* issued in 1892. When the dream occurred I cannot say; it may have been between the date of his father's death on May 8, 1887, and the end of the year, by which time the essay had been written. In may have been dreamed even before the marriage in 1880, or thereafter while the elder Stevenson was alive. The interpretation is not affected. The state of mind, however, which gave birth to the dream is that in which he was before his wife was divorced and while his father was opposed to him.

Two men were in the way of Stevenson's marriage—his father and his loved one's husband, Mr. Osbourne. Stevenson wanted these men out of the way; they were the obstacles to his happiness. He wished that Mr. Osbourne were divorced and he entertained bitterness toward his father for showing such animosity to the match. We are not accusing Stevenson of a crime when we say that unconsciously the thought may have come to him if one or both of these men were dead his road to marriage would be easy. The dream of the murder of the father by the son is understood by all Freudians. It is not an uncommon one, especially where there is ill feeling between son and father, or where an over-attachment exists for the mother. It has its origin psychically in infancy when the father was looked upon as a rival of the infant in the affections of the mother, and the dream is given additional grounds for its entry when the relations between father and son continue or grow strained. It represents just what it portrays, the wish of the child for the father to be out of the way, or dead. When the child wishes some one dead he means he wants him absent; he has no conception of death. The dream of murdering one's own father then is evidence of hostile feeling entertained by the dreamer to him either in infancy, where it is always entertained, or later in life. It represents a wish of the unconscious fulfilled, the removal of an obstacle to happiness. Needless to say it does not represent a conscious desire on the part of the dreamer in his waking hours to kill his father.

We know how strained Stevenson's relations with his father were. The elder Stevenson was hostile to his son because of his atheism and later he opposed him in his lovemaking. Two more serious oppositions to a young man, one to the inclinations of his intellect and the other to his love, can not be imagined. The novelist never realized what the feature of the murder of his father in his dream meant, and how it arose. If in this dream his father appeared as rich and wicked with a damnable temper, that is what Stevenson really thought his father was. In the dream the son lived abroad to avoid the father, and this Stevenson also actually did in life, and as a result, by the way, we have some of his early books of travel.

As we know, in dreams there is considerable distortion, and the person of our dream in an instant becomes another individual. This occurs in Stevenson's dream. No doubt the dreamer's father was actually made up of a combination of the elder Stevenson and Mr. Osbourne, both of whom Stevenson wished out of the way. But a more important distortion takes place, the merging of the second wife of the dreamer's murdered father with the married woman in real life whom Stevenson loved. We recall that in the dream the dreamer lives with his father's second wife in the house after the murder, but there is a barrier between them, for the dreamer is haunted by the woman's possible knowledge of his guilt. He loves her really and they return arm in arm from the scene of the murder. He did not want her to know that he had committed the murder because he wanted to marry her. He searches her possessions for the evidence of the guilt she found and then bursts out asking why she tortures him, he is not an enemy of hers; that he really loves her is implied. She also, it appears, had loved him and makes confession of the fact. This scene must be largely a picture of the proposal of Stevenson to his future wife. The situation depicted showing the feeling of guilt the dreamer has for his murder may be traced to his own guilty thoughts in actual life on account of his unconscious wishes for both husband and father to be out of the way. These feelings appear in the remorse of the murderer and in his suspicion of discovery by the woman he loves. We might trace the dream to much earlier material in Stevenson's life if we knew all the facts. We do know that he had an earlier love affair in youth in which he was disappointed and that he has left us poems celebrating that episode.

The dream concludes with the implication that the dreamer and the step-mother marry since they had confessed their love to each other; there are no longer any remorses or fears on one side or suspicions on the other, and the obstacles to the marriage, the objections of the dreamer's father, the legal ties of the husband to the beloved woman, have been removed. Stevenson wanted all this to happen in real life and later it incidentally did turn out that way. Both his father and the husband of Mrs. Osbourne were removed as barriers, the former by acquiescence and forgiving, the latter by divorce. The dreamer represents as fulfilled his wish to marry Mrs. Osbourne, with all opposition removed. The dreamer's father is both the elder Stevenson and Mr. Osbourne, the father and the husband respectively, made one in the dream; the second wife of the father, step-mother of the dreamer, becomes Mrs. Osbourne, Stevenson's love who became a wife a second time. Thus we have had what Freud calls condensation and displacement in the dream.

The dream sheds much light on the most important period of Stevenson's life; it fits in with the facts left us by the biographer. We see what his repressed wishes were in those days and how they appeared realized in his dream.

2

Freud first applied this theory of dream interpretation to fiction in 1907 in his study of Jensen's *Gradiva* (1903).

Freud might have analyzed Gautier's story "Arria Marcella" instead of Jensen's *Gradiva*, which was obviously suggested by the plot of Gautier's tale. "Arria Marcella" appeared in 1852, more than fifty years before Jensen's story. It gives one a good opportunity for studying Gautier himself and is an effective corroboration of Freud's theories on dreams.

Octavius sees in a museum a piece of lava that had cooled over a woman's breast and preserved its form. He falls in love with the original woman, though he knows she is dead. He is a fetich worshipper and is enamored of ancient types of women preserved in art; he has even been cast into ecstasy by the sight of hair from a Roman woman's tomb. He dreams of the "glory that was Greece and the grandeur that was Rome." He is a pagan and loves form and beauty. In his dream that night he is transported to the year of the eruption of Vesuvius and witnesses a performance of a play by Plautus in a Roman theatre. Here he sees the real woman whose shapely breast had preserved its form in the lava that killed her. She also sees him and loves him. Her slave leads him to her home. She is a Roman courtesan and her name is Arria Marcella. She tells him that she has come to life because of his desire at the museum to meet her. His wish in waking life is fulfilled in his dream. As a matter of fact, as the poet comments, art preserves alive all the beauty of antiquity.

Octavius realizes his wish and, soon, kisses and sighs are heard. But the charm is soon dispelled, for a Christian man comes in who reproaches her, even though she did not belong to his religion. She refuses to abandon Octavius, but the Christian, by an exorcism, makes Arria release Octavius, who awakens and swoons. He loved her for the rest of his life and when he married later, in memory he was unfaithful to his wife, for he always thought of Arria.

The meaning of all this is obvious. It is an expression of Gautier's favorite theory that Christianity is hostile to love and beauty, and has deprived the world of much of the greatness of paganism. But there is more here than Gautier himself imagined. First, the story is a wish-fulfillment of the unconscious. Not only the girl but the world of her time become a reality and Octavius lives in his dream in the pagan world.

There are the moments of anxiety where the Christian inter-feres and hinders the satisfaction of Octavius's love. Freud's theory is that an anxiety dream is formed when a repressed emotion encounters a strong resistance.

Octavius is Gautier, who makes a work of art out of the dream, preserves it for humanity and gives us a valuable thing of beauty. He makes up for the ugliness of today by pre-serving the beauty of the past. He satisfies his longing for the old pagan world now vanished by making his hero live in it and realize the love of one of its courtesans.

This story reveals the author as much as his *Madamoiselle de Maupin* does. We have the same Gautier for whom only the material world existed, the Gautier who was obsessed by sex, hated Christianity and worshipped art alone. The trained psychoanalyist who wishes to go deep into the unconscious of Gautier will, I think, find some perverse qualities like fetich-ism, revealed not only in this tale but in others.

Gautier pursues the motive of this story in several other tales. He lives constantly in his fantasies amidst the beauties of the ancient world. It is hard to believe that many of his tales of phantom love scenes laid in ancient times were not actually dreamed by him.

His novel, *The Mummy's Foot*, his stories, "The Golden Chain," "One of Cleopatra's Nights," "King Candaules," and two that are considered his best, "The Dead Leman" and "The Fleece of Gold," show the unconscious worshipper of physical beauty in Gautier. All these stories may be analyzed like dreams, for they are creatures of the author's imagination whereby he consoled himself for the loss of the pagan world. He was really a pagan transported into our time and he lived those times over in his stories.

3

Kipling's dream story "The Brushwood Boy" is a very good confirmation of Freud's theories. We shall analyze it psycho-analytically; it will be seen that the artificial dream in it is in-spired by the same causes as real dreams are. The story was published in the *Century Magazine*, December, 1895, and ap-peared in book form in 1901, a year after Freud's great work on Dreams had been issued. Kipling had no knowledge of Freud's theories, but he shows his hero suffering an uncon-scious repression; Georgie saw for many years visions of a girl he had met in childhood and apparently forgotten. He dreamed of her often, and these dreams give us an insight into the hero's anxieties and longings.

Georgie, the Brushwood Boy, dreamed at the age of three of a policeman. At the age of six he had both day and night dreams which always began with a pile of brushwood near the beach. There was a girl he saw at the pile of brushwood who merged with a princess he saw in an illustration of Grimm's *Fairy Tales*. He called her Annie-an-louise. At the age of seven he saw at Oxford, on a visit, a girl who looked like the child in the illustrations of *Alice in Wonderland*, and he flirted with her. He went to India as a young man. In his dreams he saw the old policeman of his infant dreams, who was saying, "I am Policeman Day coming back from the city of Sleep." One day in a dream he stepped into a steamer, and saw a stone lily floating on the water. He met the same girl of his early dreams at the Lily Lock and they took a pony on the Thirty Mile Road. He often dreamed of her and in his dreams was happy when with her and unhappy when away from her. When he returned to England he heard a girl guest at his house sing a song of Policeman Day and the City of Sleep, and he guessed that it was she who wrote the music and composed the song. Her name was Miss Lacy; she was the girl he met as a child at Oxford. He took a ride with her and each found that the other had dreamed the same dreams. She knew all about the Thirty Mile Road and she had once kissed him in his sleep. At that very moment he had dreamed that she had bestowed the kiss. Each had cherished the other as an ideal, now to be realized in marriage.

What is the meaning of this story? How did Georgie come to love a girl he had known apparently only in his dreams? Where does the Policeman come in and what is the secret of the dream journeys on the Thirty Mile Road? Georgie's dreams were the fulfillment of his unconscious desires in waking life. He had actually seen his love in his childhood, was attracted towards her but apparently forgot about her. But the love was there nevertheless; it was repressed. He neither knew why he dreamed of her nor did he believe she actually existed. He conjured her up in the books he read and identified her with the princess of a fairy tale. Like the neurotic patient he did not know the cause of his anxieties; he could not fit altogether in the scheme of life; he was dreaming inexplicable dreams which were having an effect upon him in his waking hours. In a case like this we know that the dreams have a reality that make them almost equivalent to events of the day.

When he took those trips with her in his sleep he was fulfilling the unconscious wishes of his waking life. He suffered nightmares when anything interfered to take him away from her. The anxiety dream as Freud has explained shows that there has been an interference with the satisfying of the love desire.

Policeman Day is the cause of terror because he represents the time when the dreams do not occur, day time, when he becomes the symbol of love unrealized, for in the day Georgie is no longer with his love. Policeman Day is consciousness opposed to unconsciousness, reality opposed to illusion. Miss Lacy also felt this when she sang the song with the refrain:

> *Oh pity us! Oh, pity us!*
> *We wakeful! Oh, pity us!*
> *We that go back with Policeman Day*
> *Back from the City of Sleep.*

She also was with Georgie in her dreams and dreaded waking. He also was present in her unconscious and she never really forgot the boy she had met as a child, although she had no conscious memory of him. Their infantile impressions were powerful and ruled them all the time till they met again. They dreamed they were with each other because they wanted to be with each other. He guessed she wrote the poem because she had felt as he did. The poem was an anxiety poem, voicing the unconscious desire to be with the loved one. It represents the state of mind of both lovers; he had also felt the sentiments of the poem, but she put them in words. When he came back to England he was unconsciously going to find the ideal of his dreams, the original Annie-an-louise. When he found her he was cured of his dreams and anxieties. Their meeting acted like a cure for their mysterious longings. All their dreams were made up of infantile fantasies and represented repressions. The marriage satisfies these repressions.

I dare say Kipling was his own model for the Brushwood Boy.

This disposes of any interpretations based on mere mental telepathy between George and Miss Lacy. They had the same feelings because they suffered the same repression and had met and loved each other in infancy.

Among other dream stories by Kipling, two of the best are "They" and "The Dream of Duncan Parrenness."

4

Brandes said in his book on Shakespeare,

As, knowing the life and experiences of the great modern poet, we are now generally able to trace how these are worked upon and transformed in his works, it is reasonable to suppose that in olden times poets were moved by the same causes, and acted in the same way, at least those of them who have been efficient. When we know of the adventures and emotions of the modern poet, and are able to trace them in the productions of his free fancy; when it is possible, where they are unknown to us, to evolve the hidden personality of the poet and—as every capable critic has experienced—to have our conjectures finally borne out by facts revealed by the contemporary author, then we cannot feel it to be impossible, that in the case of an older poet, we might also be successful in determining when he speaks earnestly from his heart, and in tracing his feelings and experiences through his work, especially when these are lyrical, and their mode of expression passionate and emotional.[1]

Just as we can build up a picture of a modern author from dreams he reports, we can do the same with ancient authors. I have tried to build up a portrait of the author of the Achilles-Patroclus episodes in the *Iliad*, from a dream repeated there—that of Achilles in the twenty-third book. It is remarkable that no portrait of Homer, or whoever was the author of the books dealing with Achilles, has thus far been constructed. Whether we assume that one man or more wrote the *Iliad*, we may draw one inevitable conclusion: That the parts of the poem in which Achilles figures contain the clue to the author of those sections. It is assumed generally that Homer wrote those sections. Homer sang his own troubles through his hero as a medium. Unconsciously his own traits and personality crept in. The great tragedy of Achilles' life was the death of of his friend Patroclus; his master passion was friendship. It does not require psychoanalysis to detect beneath the great grief of the warrior, Homer's own despair. The poet sings of the bereavement of his hero in too poignant a strain for any one to doubt that in Patroclus he was not bewailing some loss

[1] *William Shakespeare*, pp. 289-290.

of his own. We need not hesitate in saying, to judge by the manner in which the poet treats of friendship, and writes of it with his heart's blood as it were, that some friendship was the crown of Homer's existence. He no doubt also suffered a terrible crisis when he lost his friend, as is only too apparent, through parting or by death. When the blow befell him, he was drawn to the one incident of the many in connection with the Trojan war, the legend centering around Achilles and Patroclus. Why did he not choose some other feature of which there were so many and with which other poets dealt? The very choice of the subject apart from the internal treatment furnishes the proof he could not help but choose that which interested him most because of some experience in his own life. He had now an opportunity of registering his sorrows and adding personal matters while singing his tale. Life had become empty to him and his only consolation was to put his pangs into song. He even wished to die.

The key to these deductions is furnished by a section of the twenty-third book, of about fifty lines, of which John Addington Symonds says, "There is surely nothing more thrilling in its pathos throughout the whole range of poetry." Achilles sees Patroclus in his dreams, who recalls to him their youthful days and asks to be buried with him and foretells Achilles' own death. The warrior promises to grant his friend's request and pleads: "But stand nearer to me, that embracing each other for a little while, we may indulge in sad lamentation." Achilles tried in vain to touch him, and told his comrades afterwards: "All night the spirit of poor Patroclus stood by me, groaning and lamenting, and enjoining to me each particular and was wonderfully like unto himself." All this has too authentic and personal a touch for any one not to feel that Homer was reporting a dream of his own and was attributing it to Achilles. The poet had also spent restless nights and saw his dead friend before him "wonderfully like unto himself"; the dream was very vivid to him, and more so if as tradition reports he was blind.

No indeed, Homer was no mere spectator reciting Achilles' troubles in an objective manner. He had a great sorrow of his own and he did not go out of the way to counterfeit one. He sang his own loss; he told his own dream; Achilles was the medium through which he told the world of his own troubles. Patroclus' prophecy that Achilles would die soon shows that Homer after his loss had wished he too would die, and Homer must have dreamt that his own end would come soon, in accordance with the principle that we often dream as happening or about to happen what we wish to take place. He saw his friend in his dream just as we all do because we wish our friends to be still with us. This dream then is the clue to the tragedy of Homer's life.

Homer had loved a friend and suffered. Like Patroclus, he hoped his friend wanted to be buried with him; at least Homer wanted to have his own bones repose near those of his friend. What the nature of the friendship was we cannot say; it may have been homosexual, a love which was common among the later Greeks, I do not, however, insist on this. But it did have the element of passion. We know now the chief event of Homer's life. What the details were we cannot say. It is rather unsafe to guess. But there are a few facts that appear, whose import is significant. Achilles, we recall, resolved to fight the Trojans again only because they killed Patroclus. He was now ready to forget Agamemnon's wrong to him in depriving him of his captive woman. He knew that by his new resolve he would lose his life. He was willing to die for his friend. Homer's love for his friend was also so great that he too would no doubt have given up his life for him. This I believe establishes the passionate element in the friendship of both warrior and poet.

Again, Achilles blames himself for Patroclus' death. Had he not withdrawn from the fight, the Trojans would not have gained any victories and not have killed his friend. In short, he had been too sensitive, proud and sulky; he had been too easy a prey to anger and revenge. Now he was suffering remorse. This indicates that Homer had quarrels with his friend. We know by psychoanalysis that people who lose by death a loved one feel guilt stricken if in life they had hostile wishes against that person; in fact they attribute the death to these secret emotions. The remorse is a reaction to the hostile wishes, and it is possible, but I do not wish to press this point, that Homer's friend was either ostracized or shunned by many for some idiosyncrasy or event in his past life for which he was not to blame and hence the poet loved him the more. Patroclus reminds Achilles in the dream that as a child, he, Patroclus, had killed a playmate. This detail would not have been invented by a poet writing impersonally. Homer thought of some event in the life of his own friend.

But the real deduction nevertheless remains I believe unassailable, that the master passion of Homer's life was friendship, that Achilles contains much of the poet unconsciously and that many of the moods and passions given to him were Homer's own. Homer also suffered a terrible loss and sang of it by emphasizing the despair of Achilles at Patroclus' death which made him forget Agamemnon's wrong. The great warrior's calamity was to him a sadder blow than the loss of his captive woman, with whom he had fallen in love, proving that with Homer, as with Achilles, friendship was stronger than the love passion. The fact that so little of love appears in the *Iliad* has often excited comment. It is true the war was fought on account of a woman, but there is almost nothing of romantic love in the poem. That love as a tender emotion existed, we know from the lyric poems written not very long after Homer. Women figure more in the Odyssey; Samuel Butler tried to prove that the Odyssey was written by a woman. This is absurd, but some woman's influence made itself felt in the writing of that poem.

It is only right to conclude that the same motives and principles of singing which actuated later poets prompted the earlier ones. If Milton appears in Lucifer, Goethe in Faust and Mephistopheles, Shakespeare in Hamlet, there can be no question Homer has drawn himself in Achilles and an intimate friend of his in Patroclus.

5

There are thousands of dreams, actual and artificial, reported in literature and history. Many of these may be analyzed, but in most of them sufficient data are lacking to help us with the analysis. There are entire books cast in the form of dreams. There are Flaubert's *The Temptation of St. Anthony*, Hauptmann's *Hannele*, Strindberg's *The Dream Play*, Maeterlinck's *The Blue Bird*, and its sequel *The Betrothal*, William Morris's *The Dream of John Ball*. There are the artificial visions of Dante, Bunyan, and Langland. There are dreams recorded in Apuleius, Rabelais, Chaucer, Malory, Swedenborg; in the Bible and the Talmud; in the histories of Herodotus, Xenophon, Suetonius, Dio Cassius; in *Richard III* and *Cymbeline*, in *Paradise Lost*, and *Robinson Crusoe*, and *The Scarlet Letter*.

The dreams recorded in ancient and medieval literature are in many cases actual ones. Dreams were formerly regarded as being prophetic of the future, but they only rarely have such value. For this reason most of the interpretations put to them by ancient sages are worthless for our purposes. Cicero in his

On Divination has reported many dreams and given us arguments pro and con regarding their prophetic value. It is to be hoped that the scientific investigation of Freud into the interpretation of dreams will not give superstition a new weapon.[1]

[1] The first article in English on the Freudian theory of Dreams appeared in the first volume of a four volume anthology called *The Balzac Library* (1900) made up of current periodical articles etc. It was a translation from *Die Grentzboten*, March 15, 1900, Leipzig, and entitled "What Are Dreams?"

Chapter 4

The Œdipus Complex and the Brother and Sister Complex

1

FREUD opened up a new field of dream interpretation by his discovery of the significance of the remark of the chorus in Sophocles' *Œdipus* about men dreaming of incestuous relations with their own mothers. He saw this dream referred to the barbarous times in which such incest actually occurred, and to the infantile affection of the child for the mother. He saw that the counterpart of this dream was in the mythical material dramatized by Sophocles of a man murdering his father and marrying his mother. The dream means that one wants his mother's love. Herodotus reports a dream of Hippias who dreamt of incest with his mother. Plato's *Republic*, Bk. IX, says that in our dream our animal nature practices incest with the mother. Dio Cassius reports Caesar had such a dream.

The influence of the writer's attitude towards his father or mother appears in his literary work. Stendhal has left us a record of the intense child love he had for his mother; he hated his father. One can see the results of these conditions in his life, work, and beliefs. He became an atheist; people who throw off the influence of their fathers often cast aside also their belief in a universal father. This does not mean that they may not use reason for their nonbelief; or that those who love their fathers may not become atheists. This also explains largely the atheism of Shelley, whose relations with his father were not cordial. The essay on the necessity of atheism was the cause of Shelley's expulsion from Oxford University.

An extreme attachment to the mother is the nucleus of future neurosis. If the mother is intensely loved by her infant son or boy, and then she dies, he will still be looking for a mother substitute, as it were. Freud's deduction about the mysterious smile of the Mona Lisa is very plausible; it was in all likelihood the unconscious reproduction by the artist of his mother's smile which he rediscovered in another woman.

The best example of the Œdipus Complex in English literature is to be found, I think, in the poem by Cowper, "On the Receipt of My Mother's Picture." Very few more touching tributes to a mother have been written. Cowper's mother died when he was six years old. The poem was written in 1790, when he was fifty-eight years old. The poet never married and found a mother substitute in Mary Unwin, who ministered to his comfort; to her he wrote a famous sonnet and also the well known lyric.

Cowper wrote the poem celebrating his love for his mother "not without tears." On actually receiving the picture he kissed it and hung it where it was the last object he saw at night and the first that met his eyes in the morning. In the poem he becomes a child again. The intervening fifty-two years drop out of his life; he is back with his mother and he narrates his infantile impressions. The psychoanalyst who is aware that this child's affection for his mother is its first love affair, will observe that Cowper in his poem is giving us reminiscences of a childish fantasy that shaped the course of his whole life. His insanity and fits of depression, his sentimental and platonic attachments to old ladies, his religious mania, are apparent, in the germ, in this poem.

The poet recalls the affection and tenderness lavished upon him by his mother; he relates how he felt at her death, when he was deceived by the maids who told him that she would return. He again sees her in her nightly visits to him in his chamber. He mentions the biscuits she gave him, dwells on her constant flow of love, and on the way she stroked his head and smiled. He thus relives those days. One should remember these are the reflections of a man fifty-eight years old. In his troubles he still looks back to her for support. He contrasts his position then with his situation now. He is suffering from depression and the memory of many griefs. His dead mother is like a bark safe in port.

> But me, scare hoping to attain that rest,
> Always from port withheld, always distressed,
> Me howling blasts drive devious, tempest-tossed,
> Sails ripped, seams opening wide, and compass lost,
> And day by day some current's thwarting force
> Sets me more distant from a prosperous course."

It of course displeases people to have any association made between the noblest sentiment, mother love, and so repulsive a feature as incest. When Freud interpreted the marriage of Œdipus to his mother both from a historical and psychological point of view, and called attention to the dream in the play where the Chorus mentions the most obnoxious dream that sometimes visits us mortals, that of incestuous relationship with the mother, he opened up a new field not only in psychology but in medicine. Psychoanalytic treatment has cured many people whose neurosis arose from the early attachment to the mother from which they were finally freed. Cowper was a victim of the Œdipus Complex; it was buried in his unconscious and in this poem of his he shows that the seeds that were sown fifty-two years before were still bearing fruit. Literature rarely furnishes a better example of the influence of the Œdipus Complex throughout a lifetime.

In his poem Cowper put his hand unknowingly on the cause of all his troubles, but he never realized it. Had the poem been written in his twenties instead of his late fifties, the subliminal process of freeing himself by art from his Œdipus Complex might have made his life more pleasant. The fact that the poem was written so late shows that the unhealthy attachment clung to him all his life; it ruined him mentally and gave us his strange personality.

Freud has shown us that psychoneuroses, like hysteria and obsessions, have their origin in an infantile overattachment to the parent of the opposite sex, which remains unconscious but nevertheless is an active and disturbing element. It is perfectly natural that this condition should exist in infancy, but it disappears in the normal person. If it does not, one's entire life may be influenced by one's inability to overcome the too intense love for the mother or infantile hatred for the father. If a man has had an unfortunate repression in childhood such as the early death of a mother he loved intensely, his destiny in life may be affected. This fact has been understood by people from time immemorial. If an abnormal situation develops like a hatred in childhood for the mother, the child's life may be in the future shaped differently from that of most people. People especially are influenced in the way they react to the world and to love affairs by the frustration or repression of their earliest love. If they become writers their literary work is charged with a certain tone, depending on the nature of the author's relation with his parents.

By this discovery of Freud's literary criticism receives a new impetus. Many literary biographers unconsciously worked in accordance with this theory, for they always stated, where possible, the relations of the writer to his parents. Freud merely formulated and proved the truth of the theory.

Why were Schopenhauer and Byron such pessimists? Among the many causes that later in life contributed to impart the note of woe and despair to their work, was also the fact that both men were in unusually unhappy relations with their mothers and their quarrels with them are matters of literary history. Why are men like Lafcadio Hearn and Edgar Allan Poe the unhappy Ishmaelites in literature, with their morbid and weird ideas? They both lost in infancy or early childhood mothers to whom they were greatly attached, one by divorce, the other by death.

Facts like these have great significance. It is not maintained that other factors do not go into the making of the man, but his relation to his parents is the earliest cause in determining his mental, moral, and emotional make up. A man who hates his father sees in many of his future enemies the image of his father. One who is overattached to his mother looks unconsciously for her counterpart, among women, in seeking his mate. He sees a reminder of his father in those people who interfere with his plans, ambitions, and conduct. He sees the father in the rivals he has in love affairs, just as in infancy he found in his father his rival in the affections of his mother. This seemingly absurd and repellent view has been scientifically demonstrated by Freud and his disciples.

The influence of step-mothers has always been noted in ancient times and the amount of material in folk lore dealing with the effects of step-mothers on the lives of children is large. We are all familiar with the Cinderella story. Literature is rich in examples of writers whose step-mothers colored their lives for them. Strindberg's misogyny no doubt dates back to his early dislike for his step-mother.

All literary works show between the lines a writer's early attitude towards his parents. An interesting volume might be written on the relations of literary men to their mothers. We would find the mother unconsciously influencing literary masterpieces. We might find the misanthropy of Molière's *Le Misanthrope* due to the fact that as a boy he lost his mother.

The fact that the mothers of Coleridge and Dickens had almost no influence upon them is seen in their work.

The relation of the only child to its parents must be mentioned here. The studies of both Freud and Brill in regard to the later neurotic condition of the only child applies to literary men who were only children. John Ruskin, although subjected

to a strict education, was petted and spoiled nevertheless lik
the average only child. His precociousness made his parent
admire and worship him. He was attached to his "papa" an
"mamma" for the rest of their lives. He was not young whe
they died, and he preserved the attitude of the child toward
them. His mother lived to a great age. When he was separate
from his wife he returned to his parents to live. His later trag
edy, the unmanly love for Rose Le Touche, which forms
most humiliating affair in his life, shows he was a neuroti
from childhood. He was in the later part of his life subject t
periods of psychosis. In his actions he was eccentric; he woul
be invited to lecture on art and would give a talk on economics

His passions were love of beauty in the early part of his lif
and interest in economic reform in his middle and old age.

We must always remember he was an only child. In his auto
biography *Praeterita*, he refers often to his "papa" and "mam
ma."

Alexander Pope, the poet, was also a spoiled child, thoug
he had a half sister.

The seeds of Browning's optimistic philosophy were sow
in the normal and quiet affection that existed between him an
his mother. There was no mad attachment, no repression, n
ill feeling, and hence he never became an abnormal or morbi
poet. He had less neuroticism than any of the great Englis
poets of the nineteenth century. His optimism was also fos
tered by his happy marriage to Elizabeth Barrett.

Freud's theories about the relations of the child to the par
ents are borne out whenever we consider the life of a poet.

2

The birth of a new child also has an influence on the psychi
life of the child. There is also always something in the relatio
between brothers and sisters that affects their lives. Hence th
subject of incest in literature is of paramount import, repulsiv
as the theme may be.* It has been most exhaustively studied i
unconscious manifestations in fictitious characters by Otto
Rank in his *Incest Motiv* (1912) a work which should b
translated into English.

The only phase of the subject I wish to touch on here is th
close relationship that prevails in some cases between brothe
and sister among authors. The brother and sister complex, as i

* Edgar Saltus has touched on the theme in a few of his novels, notable *Th
Monster.*

may be called, shows its effects upon the literary work of the writer.

The extreme attachment of Renan to his sister Henrietta and of Wordsworth to his sister Dorothy had much to do with the nature of the literary work of these men. The attachment explained from the point of view of psychoanalysis amounts to this: the affection which each man has for his mother is transferred to the sister who is the nearest resemblance to the mother. This new fixation may remain too long and the man hence for a time loves no other woman. The affection is usually at its height in youth before the man marries another, in case he does marry. Both Renan and Wordsworth married after they were thirty. The incest idea was unconsciously present but repressed by the natural disgust the men felt as a result of education and training. In all likelihood had each of these authors been separated from his sister in infancy and met her years later in youth, he might have fallen in love with her.

The effects of this extreme brotherly and sisterly love have been studied but not yet exhaustively. No doubt much of the effeminacy of Renan, the gentleness, the moral tone, the kindliness we find in his writings was due to his attachment to his sister. He dedicated his *Life of Jesus* to her. As I show elsewhere he drew himself in this book, and his love for his sister was a great factor in his making Jesus somewhat effeminate. He has also left a tribute to her in his *My Sister Henrietta*.

The influence of Wordsworth's sister upon him manifested itself in several ways, one of which is the utter respectability of his poetry, and another the almost total absence of any reference to love or sex. His sister was largely responsible for the trend of her brother's mind. She gave him eyes and ears, as he put it, helped him to observe nature and was herself a great force in the evolution of the new poetry. Her influence has not been overestimated. Another reason for the absence of love poetry in Wordsworth may have been due to a guilty conscience, as he left an illegitimate daughter in France, not being able to marry the mother for sufficient reasons. Professor George McLean Harper first published the story.

As one might have expected, neither Henrietta Renan nor Dorothy Wordsworth ever married, though the latter is said to have been in love with Coleridge.

Charles Lamb, the Gentle Elia, owes probably much of his quality of gentleness to his sister Mary, "Bridget Elia." She appears in his famous essays and they collaborated together in writing poems and tales. His kindness was no doubt enhanced by his pity for her unfortunate fits of insanity and by the fact that in one of these fits she had killed her mother.

The love felt for their sisters by Byron and Shelley made the subject of incest a common topic of discussion between them. They went so far as to question whether the law or feeling against marriage between brother and sister was not a convention based on ungrounded prejudice.

That Byron entertained what might be called unconscious or even conscious incestuous feelings towards his half-sister Mrs. Augusta Leigh, and that they influenced him in writing his two great plays *Manfred* and *Cain* and some poems cannot be denied. That he ever had actual sexual intercourse with her is still a question. It had been settled in the affirmative by the publication of *Astarte* by Lord Lovelace, and the view had been accepted by the two leading biographers of Byron, Ethel Colburn Mayne and Andre Maurois. One Byron student, Professor Samuel C. Chew, was converted to the view (as he wrote to me). Maurois thinks it is an unimportant matter.

The proof that both biographers lean on is Byron's letters to Lady Melbourne; but the editor John Murray who first published these letters does not find there is ground in the letters and rejects the theory. The supposedly evidence is found in a letter dater April 25, 1814 in which Byron referring to the daughter born to Augusta says "It is not an Ape, and if it is, that must be my fault. However I will positively reform"; he adds, "But positively she and I will grow good and all that, and so we are now and shall be now these three weeks and more too." A monster was supposed to be the child of incest in the middle ages. The Puritans held a monster child was also due to other causes. In no previous letter to Lady Melbourne had Byron admitted that he had incestuous relations with Augusta. How could she have concluded that Byron meant he was the father of the girl Medora? He speaks rather tamely about reforming. If he was the father, the mischief had already been done, and reforming would not have made Medora legitimate.

It is not conclusive that they were guilty of incest because they lived at times in the same house. Again it is a matter of law that a father cannot disown a child born in wedlock, nor can its legitimacy be impugned unless a very long time has elapsed in which it can be proved that there was no access; legally Mr. Leigh was the father of Medora. Yet her illegitimacy has been accepted by several biographers as a matter of course. She was born April 15, 1814.

That not every student of Byron has accepted his paternity is shown in a recent book *The Late Byron* by Doris Langley Moore. She says that the only documentary evidence, the allusion to the "Ape," can yield a more innocent interpretation. Augusta herself never stated that Lord Byron was Medora's father.

In one of a series of letters that Lady Byron wrote to Augusta she said: "As you do not and never have attempted to deceive me respecting *previous* facts of which my conviction is unalterable, I rely the more on your assertion of having never wronged *me* intentionally.

Lady Byron in a statement also said: "Augusta made full confession of the previous connection—that any subsequent to my marriage being stoutly denied."

Lady Byron met Augusta shortly before the latter died in 1851. Augusta was anxious to meet Lady Byron to dispel a rumor that reached her ears that Lady Byron had said that she, Augusta, had prevented Lord Byron from entertaining kindly views about his wife. This was the only reason that she wanted to meet Lady Byron. When they did meet Lady Byron was disappointed. She asked if this was the only complaint that Augusta wanted to convey to her, namely, that she did not prevent Byron from entertaining kindly views about his wife, "Is that all"? Lady Byron was self-righteous and stated that she had done everything to contribute to Augusta's peace of mind, presumably in not bringing out in public any charges of incest. All that may be gathered from Augusta's reply was that she had been really disturbed about the charges that Lady Byron had brought against her of encouraging Byron's bitterness toward her. It seems that Augusta had nothing to apologize for. She said, "I had not, and never implied that I had anything to reveal to you to which you were not previously acquainted." We do not know what this was. To repeat, it seems Lady Byron had expected that in this meeting Augusta would confess and state definitely that she had been guilty of incest. She was disappointed that Augusta did not admit incest, and Augusta was very angry at Lady Byron for wanting her to make such a confession.

Ethel Colburn Mayne concludes that after Augusta had died as well as Medora, Lady Byron could publicly announce the scandal and this she did.

It is likely that Byron and his sister kissed each other or made love without sexual relations. If all the facts as we have them were placed before a jury, a judge would have instructed the members not to bring in a verdict of guilty if they had "one reasonable doubt." They might have had such a doubt.

Yet I am not taking any position in the alleged incest.

What I maintain is that from the point of view of psychoanalysis the actual act is not of importance in determining that incestuous fantasies did influence some of Byron's work. Psychoanalysis would not deny that *Manfred* and *Cain*, two great works of Byron, were influenced by his interest in the subject of a brother's love for his sister. We may admit that incest existed in his unconscious, nay, that he resorted to an imaginary indulgence of sex relations with Augusta. Therefore we must admit that we owe to her the characters Astarte and Adah, respectively, in these dramas. (It has also been maintained that Astarte was suggested by Byron's first important love Mary Chaworth.)

Of course there are not the slightest indications in the three poems addressed to Augusta that anything improper ever occurred between them. They are Platonic.

Augusta is said to have admitted to Lady Byron that the poem "I speak not, I trace not, I breathe not thy name," was addressed to her. Byron had sent the poem to Moore in a letter to him May 4, 1814, and he published it in 1830. It was written then about two years before a poem he wrote, his first "Stanzas to Augusta" when he was finally leaving England in April 1816. Can we say certainly that this poem "I speak not, I trace not, I breathe not thy name," so highly thought of by Maurois, is a confession of guilt because the word guilt is used? (Byron says there is grief in the sound, there is guilt in the fame.) This may merely mean that there are rumors of his relation with her which are not true. It is undoubtedly a love poem to her and when he says, "Oh! thine be the gladness, mine be the guilt," it may mean that he feels guilty for having made her fall in love with him.

One thing we have to concede then is that we owe to Augusta, because she appears as Aida in *Cain*, one of Byron's greatest intellectual poems. The love of *Cain* for his sister leads Georg Brandes to the conclusion that the play was formed by psychological elements which include the effect of incest. Brandes finds Byron's freeing himself from religious superstitions in *Cain*, and he regards the play as representative of thinking humanity, a humanity striving to produce a new and better Eden of knowledge.

It is admitted that the four stanzas beginning "The Castled Crag of Drachenfels" following the fifty-fifth stanza of *Childe*

Harold, Book III, are addressed to Augusta. It has been suspected—concluded—from the fifty-fifth stanza that Byron confessed to incest.

> *And there was one soft breast, as hath been said*
> *Which unto his was bound by stronger ties*
> *Than the church links withal; and though unwed,*
> *That love was pure and far above disguise,*
> *Had stood the test of mortal enmities*
> *Still undivided, and cemented more*
> *By peril, dreaded most in female eyes:*
> *But this was firm, and from a foreign shore*
> *Well to that heart might his absent greetings pour.*

Then follow the lines on the crag of Drachenfels.

It seems that the words "dreaded most in female eyes" referred to his wife and Lady Caroline Lamb who were jealous of Augusta and believed in her incestuous relations with Byron. But we cannot conclude that Byron here openly confessed his incest to Augusta, because she was still alive.

No one would think of charging Wordsworth and his sister with actual sexual relations because the last third of his great poem "Lines Composed a Few Miles Above Tintern Abbey" are addressed to her with the assertion that the woods, cliffs, and landscapes were more dear to him for her sake. He addresses her "Thou my dearest Friend," "My dear, dear Friend" and "My dear, dear Sister." There are unconscious incestuous feelings in the poem. One almost feels that Wordsworth is saying that he could not have enjoyed nature unless she were with him. One should no more look for proof of Byron's actual incest in his incestuous fancies than in Wordsworth's.

Shelley had a great affection for his sister Elizabeth and wanted his friend Thomas Jefferson Hogg to marry her. She returned to her father, and Shelley was broken hearted that she drifted away from his own influence. He thought she was not lost to him and wanted to take her with him to the west of Ireland in 1814. He continued to love her, and this influenced his work. In the first edition of the *Revolt of Islam* he made Laon and Cythna, who were brother and sister, lovers. The publisher made the poet regretfully change certain passages, mostly single lines. In the early preface the poet concluded he could not see why an innocent act like love of brother and sister for each other should arouse the hatred of the multitude.

In *Rosalind and Helen* he describes Helen visiting a spot where a sister and brother had given themselves up to each other and had a child who was torn by people limb from limb. The mother was stabbed while the youth was saved by a priest, to be burned for God's grace. Their ghosts visited the spot.

Chapter 5

The Author Always Unconsciously in His Work

1

"No MAN," says Dr. Johnson in his *Life of Cowley*, "needs to be so burthened with life as to squander it in voluntary dreams of fictitious occurrences. The man that sits down to suppose himself charged with treason or peculation, and heats his mind to an elaborate purgation of his character from crimes which he was never within the possibility of committing, differs only by the infrequency of his folly from him who praises beauty which he never saw, complains of jealousy which he never felt; supposes himself sometimes invited, and sometimes forsaken; fatigues his fancy and ransacks his memory for images which may exhibit the gaiety of hope, or the gloominess of despair, and dresses his imaginary Chloris or Phyllis sometimes in flowers fading as her beauty, and sometimes in gems lasting as her virtues."

The shrewd doctor displayed great insight into the psychology of authorship in these remarks. They form a good argument against those who deny the importance of the personal note in literature.

One objection that these critics make is that an author may deliberately conceal himself and that in fact writers have often done so. Thus a writer who is happily married may write a novel or play, seething with attacks upon the sanctity of the marriage institution and strict divorce laws. The author may say that book does not represent his own life. It does, however, in that it shows his reaction to seeing life of this kind lived by others; it means that he has been struck by the cruelty or injustice of it, and that unconsciously he reflected that he too might but for a chance throw of the dice of fate be in the same position. His attitude towards the lives of others is part of his own life. The fact that he has suffered pain by witnessing other people's lives, shows that his own psyche is affected. The life described has been lived by some of his friends or relatives, and some of his ancestors. The griefs of others often affect us, if not like our own, at least strongly enough to make us devote ourselves to mitigating them.

Investigation however will show that the great works voicing sorrows were experienced by those who wrote about them. It is an unhappily married writer like George Sand who has given us the novels that deal with the marriage problem. It is a disappointed lover like Heine or Musset who writes the saddest love poems. Life is made up of so many sorrows that writers do not have to go out of their way to invent them. The rich man does not imagine himself starving and write books where the pangs of hunger are described. Such literature is written usually by a man who has starved, a man like George Gissing. The financier who has never had any business troubles as a rule will not waste energy nor court pain by trying to figure how a bankrupt feels and put those feelings in art. Such feelings are usually delineated by a man who has himself been bankrupt like Balzac in his *César Birotteau*. Of course, no writer could have felt all the emotions he describes. Balzac, for example, never had the troubles of Goriot, for he never had children to be ungrateful to him. But even here there must have been some personal equivalent, for the author had suffered from ingratitude of some other kind and all ingratitude hurts.

The author again may write merely for amusement or commercial purposes. In these cases it is true the author's personality may not be in his work any more than an editorial writer's real opinions are in the editorial which he writes in accordance with the policy of his paper. A writer may study the demands of the public and try to comply with them. In such cases the reader may detect the insincerity. The works are not representative of the author and he can no more be judged by them, than a person who would invent or falsify his dreams in reporting them to a psychoanalyst. Certainly these would not reveal the unconscious. And I realize much "literature" is of this nature.

An author again may purposely conceal himself, but the key once discovered reveals him. Deliberate and continuous concealment by the author of his personality can often be detected. We know Mérimée and Nietzsche were personally entirely different from what some of their books would lead us to suspect. Mérimée was not cold nor Nietzsche cruel; one was too emotional and the other too genteel.

2

A good example of the follies that may follow by the refusal to adopt psychoanalytic methods in literature is seen in the case of Charlotte Bronte. Several similar motives appeared in her novels; the love of a girl for her school master, a married man; an intense craving for affection; and pictures of sad partings. It was known that Charlotte had attended the school of M. Heger, a married man in Brussels, that she had left it and then returned, and later departed finally. There were critics who suspected that Charlotte was really in love with her teacher and that various scenes in her novels had their counterpart in reality. Among these were Sir Wemyss Reid, Augustine Birrel and Angus Mackay. But other critics scoffed at the idea. So great a Bronte student as Clement Shorter said it would be the act of treachery to pry into the writer's heart. May Sinclair, especially, repudiated with indignation the possibility that Charlotte Bronte drew on actual facts for her novels; and her purposes in writing *The Three Brontes*, was to demolish the theory that Charlotte Bronte was in love with M. Heger. But shortly after this work appeared there were published in 1913 in the London *Times*, one of the "scoops" of the age, four pathetic love letters by Charlotte Bronte to M. Heger, written without pride, pleading for a little affection. The secret was out; there could be no doubt that the scenes of unrequited love in her novels were due to her own unreciprocated love for M. Heger and that Charlotte was Lucy Snowe and Jane Eyre in *Villette* and *Jane Eyre*, respectively. Miss Sinclair wrote an article attacking the publication of the letters which had disproved her theory.

An excellent study of the influences of Charlotte's sad love affair on her work was made by Mrs. Ellis H. Chadwick in her *In the Footsteps of the Brontes*. It is really, to some extent, a psychoanalytical study for it traces the novelist's work to her repressions.

I just wish to point out a few of the influences of Charlotte Bronte's love affair upon her work. She published *Jane Eyre* in October, 1847, and wrote in 1848: "Details, situations which I do not understand and cannot personally inspect, I would not for the world meddle with. . . . Besides not one feeling on any subject, public or private, will I ever affect that I do not really experience."

After she left Brussels on December 29, 1843, she wrote that she suffered much and that she would never forget what the parting had cost her. This departure inspired the description of the flight from Thornfield (which is Brussels in *Jane Eyre*), the part of the novel which she told her biographer appealed to her most.

In her letters to Heger which were published she begs for sympathy as a beggar for crumbs from the table of the rich man. In the second letter written in 1844 she tells how she waited six months for a letter and she sent that one through friends. In *Villette*, in the twenty-fourth chapter, she wrote how Lucy Snowe studied to quench her madness because she received no letters. "My hour of torment was the post hour." She wrote that in all the land of Israel there was but one Saul, certainly but one David to soothe him. Heger was the David, she says symbolically, to soothe her. (In the novel Heger is called Paul Carl David Emanuel).

Villette is the most autobiographical of her novels. It appeared at the beginning of 1853 and had occupied the author the previous two years. It cost her great effort and she recalled in it the sleepless nights in Brussels about which she told Mrs. Gaskell; her anxieties were caused by her hopeless love for M. Heger. She knew that the novel would be recognized by the Hegers, and she printed in it a statement that the author reserved the rights of translation, as she feared M. Heger would read it if it were translated into French. She first had wanted to publish it anonymously. She also refused to make a happy ending which was wanted by the publishers; she would not have Paul and Lucy marry, for such was not the case in real life. (Jane Eyre, however, married Rochester.) The book is full of the Hegers; even their children are in it. Madame Heger is not portrayed in a favorable light; one could hardly expect a girl to admire the wife of the man she loved herself.

The interval between the first and last of the letters published in *The Times* is about two years, which covers the saddest period of her life from the time she left Brussels finally on December 29th, 1843, to the end of 1845. She had gone to Belgium originally in February, 1842; she was then twenty-six and Heger was seven years her senior. She left in November, 1842, when her aunt died, and returned in January, 1843. Heger wanted her to return and Charlotte was only too eager to do so, though she could have received a better position. She describes this second trip in *Villette*. She left finally because Mme. Heger really did not want her services.

Charlotte's brother Branwell also fell in love with a married woman, the wife of his employer.

Charlotte Bronte drew herself as a man in her first novel, *The Professor*. She calls herself William Crimsworth who loves his teacher Mlle. Reuter. The account she gives of the parting of the student with his teacher is again reminiscent of her memories of parting from M. Heger. She portrayed herself only once in the rôle of the male lover.

"The principal male characters," says Mrs. Chadwick, "to be found in Charlotte Bronte's great novels were those drawn from M. Heger: M. Pelet, Rochester, Robert Moore, Louis Moore and Paul Emanuel."

Hence we may conclude as a rule that when a motive appears often, or a note persists continually, in a writer's work, there were reasons in his personal life. Charlotte Bronte was no exception to the rule.

She married in 1854 but did not love her husband as much as she had M. Heger. All her youth she had craved love and wanted to marry and to be a mother. She betrays herself in a dream reported in the twenty-first chapter of *Jane Eyre*. Had she known that dreams are realized unconscious wishes she might never have recounted this dream, a frequent one among women, both married and unmarried, who have no children:

. . . . During the past week scarcely a night had gone over my couch that had not brought with it a dream of an infant, which I sometimes hushed in my arms, sometimes dandled on my knee, sometimes watched playing with daisies on a lawn, or, again, dabbling its hands in running water. It was a wailing child this night and a laughing one the next; now it nestled close to me, and now it ran from me; but whatever mood the apparition evinced, whatever aspect it wore, it failed not for seven successive nights to meet me the moment I entered the land of slumber.

Literature can scarcely present a more personal confession in disguised form. That dream of Jane Eyre's was Charlotte Bronte's who wanted children by M. Heger.

3

The value of the study of an author's works in connection with his life is also seen in the case of Dickens. An excellent book by Edwin Pugh, *Charles Dickens Originals*, really applies the psychoanalytic method, to a great extent, to Dickens' work. Some of the main influences in Dickens' life and work were due to two girls, Maria Beadnell, his boyhood sweetheart who rejected him and Mary Hogarth, his wife's sister, who died young. These women were respectively the models of Dora in *David Copperfield*, and Little Nell.

The story of Dickens' early love became known when his letters to Miss Beadnell were published. He was eighteen when he loved her, and when she finally rejected him he wrote to her saying he could never love another. Not long afterwards he married. In 1855, when he was nearly forty-four years old, he said in a letter to his future biographer, John Forster, that he could never open *David Copperfield* "without going wandering away over the ashes of all that youth and hope, in the wildest manner." He was thinking of his love for Maria, for the reference in the letter is to Dora, of whom Maria was the prototype. She also appears as Dolly Varden in *Barnaby Rudge*. He again draws her in Estella in *Great Expectations*, and describes the sufferings that Pip, who is himself, had undergone on account of her.

In 1855 Maria Beadnell, who had become Mrs. Henry Winter, wrote to the author, and he agreed to meet her clandestinely. He was unhappily married but not yet separated from his wife. The separation came a few years later. Dickens was disillusioned when he met Mrs. Winter; he found her homely, stout and silly. He was cruel in his portrait. He describes his disillusionment in *Little Dorrit*, where Mrs. Winter is Flora Finching. "Flora whom he had left a lily, had become a peony." And then he gives way to a personal pathetic cry. He could no longer love his first love, he was not in love with his wife; with all his fame and wealth he had missed the greatest pleasure in life. "That he should have missed so much, and at his time of life should look so far about him for any staff to bear him company upon his downward journey and cheer it—was a just regret." He looked into the dying fire by which he sat and reflected that he too would pass through such changes and be gone. Thus we can trace the childwife Dora and the sufferings of Pip to Dickens' first love.

Mary Hogarth, who helped to shape Dickens' ideals of women, was a younger sister of his wife, and she died as a girl. Dickens was so shocked by this that he could not go on for a while with his *Pickwick Papers* and *Oliver Twist*. This was about 1837, when he was twenty-five. He has left a number of records of the great and lasting effect upon him of the grief he felt. He describes a dream where he sees her; he thinks of her when in America. She was his model for Little

Nell and he wrote that old wounds bled afresh when he wrote this story. But she was responsible for all those pure, bloodless girls, lacking in individuality, which fill his pages. She died when she was innocent of worldly guile, and unconsciously was the type before him when he drew women. He could not understand the modern intellectual woman, and he owes this literary deficiency to his misfortune. "And so he presents to us," says Mr. Pugh, "that galaxy of amazing dolls variously christened Rose Maylie, Kate Nickleby, Madeline Bray, Little Nell, Emma Haredale, Mary Graham, Florence Dombey, Agnes Wickfield, Ada Clare, and Lucy Manette. . . . Modern criticism has exhausted itself in scathing denunciation of these poor puppets. And yet there is perhaps something to be said in defence of the convention that created them. Dickens was never a self-conscious artist. He had indeed no use for the word 'Art'." His female types were the result of his faith in the perfection of woman as he saw it in Mary Hogarth.

Two women who did not influence his work are his mother and his wife. He entertained no affection for either. He had no pleasant memories of his mother because she was indifferent to his sufferings when he worked as a boy in the blacking factory. She is drawn in Mrs. Nickleby. David Copperfield's mother may also have been an idealized portrait of Dickens' own mother, but Mrs. Copperfield resembles more the Little Nells and other characters based on Mary Hogarth in her colorlessness, and her goodness. Dickens' own wife scarcely, if ever, served as a model for any of his female characters. They lived apart for the last twelve years of the author's life.

Dickens' greatness lies in his portrayals of male characters. He was poor in his female characterization because Mary Hogarth unconsciously influenced him into drawing spineless women and he kept the painful memories of his love affair with Maria Beadnell suppressed except to caricature her in Dora and Estella and Flora. When we think of Dickens we have memories of men like Sam Weller, Micawber (Dickens' father), Uriah Heep, Pecksniff, and others. Why he especially excelled in characterization of these types familiarly known all over the world, and how he was led to that peculiar "exaggerative" portrayal of eccentric creatures is a theme which can be explained by psychoanalytic theories and the application of Freud's theories of the comic, and a study of the originals and the types Dickens met in his life. It should also be remembered that this style of character portrayal was common in Dickens' youth, and he also imitated other writers.

4

Swinburne has been usually regarded as an impersonal poet, though some of his critics have tried to see in the accounts of derelictions from the path of virtue in the poems, records of actual experiences. The poet has himself written something on the subject. In the Dedicatory Epistle of 1904 to the collected edition of his works he wrote:

> There are photographs from life in the book (*Poems and Ballads*, 1865); there are sketches from imagination. Some which keen-sighted criticism has dismissed with a smile as ideal or imaginary were as real and actual as they well could be; others which have been taken for obvious transcripts from memory were utterly fantastic or dramatic. . . . Friendly and kindly critics, English and foreign, have detected ignorance of the subject in poems taken straight from the life, and have portested that they could not believe me were I to swear that poems entirely or mainly fanciful were not faithful expressions or transcriptions of the writer's actual experience and personal emotion.[1]

The poet does not tell us which poems were fanciful and which were not. He does let us know that some of the poems were the record of his own experience. I propose to show that many of the poet's best known poems had a personal background and thus to differ with the theory usually prevalent that Swinburne, instead of having sung his own soul, was but a clever manipulator of rhyme and metre. The clue to the investigation is furnished by our knowledge that one of his greatest poems in the *Poems and Ballads*, "The Triumph of Time," was inspired by the one love disappointment of his life. It was written in 1862 when he was twenty-five years old and "represented with the exactest fidelity," says Gosse, his biographer, "his emotions which passed through his mind when his anger had died down, and when nothing remained but the infinite pity and the pain." The young lady gave the poet roses and sang for him. She laughed in his face when he proposed. He was hurt grievously and went up to the sea in Northumberland and composed the poem. The poet told Gosse the story in 1876.

[1] *Poems and Ballads,* 1865.

The poem is a cry of a wounded heart; one of the most powerful in all literature. The poet recounts all his emotions and foresees that this affair will influence his life. Many lines in it are familiar to Swinburne lovers, such as "I shall never be friend again with roses," "I shall hate sweet music my whole life long." It is one of Swinburne's masterpieces.

One may now see that the terrible declamation against love, one of the lengthiest and best choruses in his play *Atlanta in Calydon*, rings with a personal note. The lines beginning "For an evil blossom was born" constitute one of the most bitter outcries against love in literature. Unconsciously, memories of his lost love were at work and the chorus must have been written about the same time as "The Triumph of Time." The play itself was published in 1864. Swinburne is the Chorus and thus chants his own feelings in the Greek legend he tells.

Swinburne may have had other love affairs though Gosse tells us this was his only one. I find memories of the unfortunate episode throughout the entire first volume of *Poems and Ballads*, and note recurrences to the theme in later volumes. In one of his best known poems, "The Foresaken Garden," written in 1876, he dwells on the death of love. The idea of love having an end is repeated with much persistency throughout many of his poems; he so harps on the same note, that the suspicions of critics should have been roused before we learned about the romance of his life. No doubt the reason he was attracted to the love tragedy of Tristram of Lyonesse, published in 1882, was his own tragic experience; and in the splendid prelude (written, Gosse tells us, in 1871) we see the effects of his love affair.

We have evidence of Swinburne's grief in two of the greatest poems of the *Poems and Ballads*, where it was least suspected, in "Anactoria" and "Dolores," poems whose morality he had to defend. He pours some light on the subject in his *Notes on Poems and Reviews*, published as a reply to his critics after the issue of his *Poems and Ballads* in 1865. Of "Anactoria" he said: "In this poem I have simply expressed, or tried to express, that violence of affection between one and another which hardens into rage and deepens into despair. . . . I have tried to cast my spirit into the mould of hers (Sappho), to express and represent not the poem but the poet. . . . As to the 'blasphemies' against God or gods of which here and elsewhere I stand accused—they are to be taken as the first outcome or outburst of foiled and fruitless passion recoiling on itself."

In other words he was singing his own grief through Sappho. The rage and despair were Swinburne's own and the "blasphemies" were his own reaction to frustrated love.

On "Dolores," the poet says: "I have striven here to express that transient state of spirit through which a man may be supposed to pass, foiled in love and weary of loving, but not yet in sight of rest; seeking rest in those violent delights which have violent ends in free and frank sensualities which at last profess to be no more than they are."

The poet gave himself up to light loves as a result of his disappointment. But the point here to be remembered is that the poem is by his own confession a result of a state of spirit through which a "man foiled in love" (the poet himself) may be said to pass and through which Swinburne did pass.

Let us examine some of his lyrics, chiefly those in his first volume where we can see the result of the love affair.

In "Laus Veneris" he breaks off from his story to say:

> *Ah love, there is no better life than this;*
> *To have known love, how bitter a thing it is,*
> *And afterward be cast out of God's sight.*

He spoke here from personal memories.

After he tells the story of "Les Noyades," of the youth who was bound to a woman who did not love him and thrown into the river Loire, the poet ends abruptly, and addresses his own love, regretting that this could not have happened to him. He re-echoes the sentiment in "The Triumph of Time" where he wishes he were dead with his love. Swinburne was drawn to this tale by his unconscious, by the fact that he had lost his love. The following concluding lines were personal and addressed to the kinswoman of the Simons:

> *O sweet one love, O my life's delight,*
> *Dear, though the days have divided us,*
> *Lost beyond hope; taken far out of sight,*
> *Not twice in the world shall the gods do this.*

His address to the spirit of Paganism, the "Hymn of Proserpine," which should not necessarily bring up thoughts of his love tragedy, nevertheless begins, "I have lived long enough, have seen one thing, that love hath an end," and later on he complains that laurel is green for a season, and love is sweet for a day, but love grows bitter with treason and laurel outlives not May. I fear that the poet deserves more sympathy than he has hitherto been accorded. He had accused his love of having encouraged him; hence he knew what he meant when he sang those sad words "love grows bitter with treason."

Two other pathetic poems are "A Leave Taking" where he constantly reiterates "she would not love" and he turns for consolation to his songs; and "Satia de Sanguine" where he says, "in the heart is the prey for gods, who crucify hearts, not hands."

In "Rondel" he begins:

These many years since we began to be
What have the gods done with us? what with me,
What with my love? They have shown me fates and fears,
Harsh springs and fountains bitterer than the sea.

In the "Garden of Proserpine," he sings,

And love, grown faint and fretful
With lips but half-regretful
Sighs, and with eyes forgetful
Weeps that no loves endure.

This poem shows his longing for rest after his sad experience; he is tired of everything but sleep.

In "Hesperia" he again refers to his troubles:

As the cross that a wild nun clasps till the edge of it
*   bruises her bosom,*
So love wounds as we grasp it, and blackens and
*   burns as a flame;*
I have loved over much in my life; when the live bud
*   bursts with the blossom*
Bitter as ashes or tears is the fruit, and the wine
*   thereof shame.*

Even in "The Leper" he gives us an inkling of his great love by describing the devotion of the lover for the smitten lady. "She might have loved me a little too, had I been humbler for her sake."

All these poems appeared in his first volume and were written within at least two years after his sorrow. He can scarcely write a poem or chant about a woman or retell an old myth or legend, or venture a bit of philosophy but he unconsciously introduces his aching heart. The burden is always that love has an end or lives but a day.

There are other poems in the first volume where the personal note is present and yet very little attention has been called to this.

The poem "Félise," with its quotation from Villon, "Where are the Snows of Yesterday," is I believe a personal poem, based on an actual or desired change between him and his lost sweetheart, that is, if this poem refers to her. Some day new data may appear to tell us whether the facts of the poem had any basis in reality. It seems that a year after the poet's love was rejected by the girl, she wished to win his love back and that he now scorned her. The poem was written, Gosse conjectures, in 1864, but 1863 is most likely the date from the internal evidence, as she rejected him in 1862. Swinburne refers to the change a year had brought:

> *I had died for this last year, to know*
> *You loved me. Who shall turn on fate?*
> *I care not if love come or go*
> *Now, though your love seek mine for mate,*
> *It is too late.*

He exults cruelly; in the new situation he is revenged: "Love wears thin, And they laugh well who laugh the last."

He concludes:

> *But, sweet, for me no more with you:*
> *Not while I live, not though I die.*
> *Good night, good bye.*

If she ever sought a return to the poet's affections, he refused to receive her. He had hoped she might seek to return; read the following lines from "The Triumph of Time," where he takes the same stand that he does in this poem.

> *Will it not one day in heaven repent you?*
> *Will they solace you wholly, the days that were?*
> *Will you lift up your eyes between sadness and bliss,*
> *Meet mine and see where the great lane is,*
> *And tremble and turn and be changed? Content you,*
> *The gait is strait, I shall not be there.*

No, never would he take her back. Whether the incident of her asking to be restored to his affections happened or not is unimportant, relatively. Sappho prayed to Aphrodite to reverse the situation of her love and make the rejecting lover come to her suppliant; a situation that every suffering lover wants, and as we know, very often happens.

One of the finest poems inspired by his love, "his sleek black pantheress," is the poem called "At a Month's End," published in 1878 in the second series of *Poems and Ballads*. He recalls the old days and his grief is not now so maddening. He sighs:

> *Should Love disown or disesteem you*
> *For loving one man more or less?*
> *You could not tame your light white sea-mew,*
> *Nor I my sleek black pantheress.*

> *For a new soul let whoso please pray,*
> *We are what life made us and shall be.*
> *For you the jungle, and me the sea-spray*
> *And south for you and north for me.*

Edward Thomas was certainly in error when he concluded that Swinburne did not directly express personal emotion and that few of the pieces could have been addressed to one woman and that he never expressed a single hearted devotion to one woman except in "A Leave Taking." We need not insist that one woman was always in his mind, but one woman inspired most of his love passages. New information may show that other women inspired some of his love verse.[2]

Another phase in studying the poet that has interested readers is whether he actually figured in the light and lewd loves he sang. The poet says in his notes in reply to critics that "Dolores" and "Faustine" are merely fanciful. Gosse has been censured for not having written an honest biography and for having passed over certain episodes in the poet's life. It had often been rumored that the poet did lead, occasionally, a dissipated life. In the late seventies he was rescued by his friend Watts-Dunton from the effects of a presumably long dissipation. After that time the poet's life was normal and the publication of the early poems of passion became a source of regret to him. He never again returned to that strain and incidentally rarely wrote work that was equal to his first period. It may then

[2] Among recently published posthumous poems of Swinburne is one called "Southward," written no doubt with his love still fresh in mind.

be true that some light loves and immoral women inspired poems like "Anima Anceps," "A Match," "Before Parting," "Rocco," "Stage Love," "Interlude," 'Before Dawn," "Faustine," "Dolores," "Fragoleeta," "Aholibah," etc.

Swinburne then, who of all lyric poets was the one deemed least to have drawn on his personal life for material, has done so in great measure.

His "Thalassius" gives us his spiritual autobiography. At the age of fifty-five he recurred to his childhood scenes and gave us memories of them in his drama *The Sister's* (1892) where he drew himself in Clavering. His *The Tale of Balen*, published a few years later, is also personal.

The poet who gave us such rich verse wrote from the unconscious. The first stanzas of "A Vision of Spring in Winter" were composed in sleep. He awoke at night and penned the verses he had composed. His "A Ballade of Dreamland" was written in the morning without a halt. Swinburne worked from impulse.

Swinburne's affinity to Shelley calls for special comment. He was attracted to him, because Shelley too, like Swinburne, hated monarchy and the church, because he had a mastery over melody in verse, because he was persecuted. He wrote to his youngest sister:[3]

> I must say it is too funny—not to say uncanny—how much there is in common between us two; born in exactly the same class, cast out of Oxford—the only difference being that I was not formally but informally expelled—and holding and preaching the same general views in the poems which made us famous.

This is a good illustration of the process of projection in literature. Swinburne was attracted to Shelley because he was most like him.

The influence of his mother, Jane Swinburne, was a determining factor in his life. She guided his reading and took care of him, and he was mentally a good deal like her. He was very much attached to her and no doubt she unconsciously is present in much of his work. She died in 1896 when eighty-seven years old, and her death left him a changed man and was the tragedy of his later life. When she came to live with him before her death, he wrote a poem of welcome to her, "The High Oaks," and when she died he wrote "Barking Hall."

[3] Disney Leith: *Swinburne*, p. 221.

From letters published for the first time recently we have learned that Swinburne had a morbid interest in flagellation, was not opposed to flogging boys on their bare buttocks in the public schools and wrote with a sort of delight about bleeding as a result of flagellation. In short he was in the full sense of the word both a sadist delighting to inflict pain and a masochist experiencing pleasure from seeing pain inflicted. He harked back to the days when he himself was flogged at school. We know that flagellation is a perverted form of sexual activity and is concluded with orgasms. Whipping produces a satisfaction sexually in both the person whipped and the whipper.

It would be extraordinary if we did not find an unconscious reflection of Swinburne's monomania on the subject of flagellation in some of his poetry. We can now give a new interpretation of the famous "Dolores," Our Lady of Pain, a poem that is drawn out into 55 stanzas of eight lines or four hundred and forty lines.

For my purpose I again cite Swinburne's own explanation of and excuse for the poem:

> I have striven here to express that transient state of spirit through which a man may be supposed to pass, foiled in love and worry of loving, but not yet in sight of rest; seeking rest in those violent delights which have violent ends in free and frank sensualities which at least profess to be no more than they are."

He does not use the word flagellation, nor does he use it in the poem "Dolores," but he does so in his letters. The poem however has revealed him.

The poem which is at times vague and obscure is addressed to a prostitute whom he turns into a lady of pain. But she, as we shall see, is a symbol of the birch. He asks that her lips bite hard to make his heart spring up in pleasure; they are curled snakes that are fed from his breast. We have the famous or infamous lines about her lips making men change in a trice "The lilies and languors of virtue For the raptures and roses of vice."

He then speculates upon the possibilities of new sexual pleasures that are not normal:

> There are sins it may be to discover,
> There are deeds it may be to delight

> *What new work wilt thou find for thy lover,*
> *What new passions for daylight or night?*
> *What spells that they know not a word of*
> *Whose lives are as leaves overblown?*
> *What tortures undreamt of, unheard of,*
> *Unwritten, unknown.*

He then asks, "Shall no new sin be born for men's trouble, No dream of impossible pangs?"

He calls her sanguine and adjures her to respond from her altars by the

> *Cruelty deaf as a fire,*
> *And blind as the night,*
> *By ravenous teeth that have smitten*
> *Through the kisses that blossom and bud.*

He calls her Our Lady of Torture and says that into her worship, "I have passed from the outermost portal To the shrine where sin is a prayer."

Her people, her chosen children are "marked cross from the womb and perverse."

He talks about blood. Her serpent will nestle in the lips of love, her cruelties thrive in its hands. He prefers the pagan days and the poets of old who revered whores and indulged in perverted loves. "Come down and redeem us from virtue, Our Lady of Pain," he cries.

Then unconsciously Swinburne in describing the Lady of Pain gives a picture of a flogged person's back:

> *Thy skin changes country and color*
> *And shrivels or swells to a snake's,*
> *Let it brighten and bloat and grow duller*
> *We know it, the flames and the flakes*
> *Red brands on it smitten and bitten*
> *Round skies where a scar is a stain,*
> *And the leaves with thy litanies written*
> > *Our Lady of Pain.*

The poet recalls the old poets who outsang and outloved us especially Catullus who makes mouths at our speech, and Swinburne refers to the orgiastic rites under Cybele.

He concludes with a eulogy to "Dolores," really to the birch.

> *We shall know whether hell be not heaven*
> *Find out whether tares be not grain*
> *And the joys of thee seventy times seven*
> *Our Lady of Pain.*

Little wonder the poem shocked, but people would have been even more shocked had they known what was in the poet's unconscious mind. His explanation was only half true. He wanted to say that he does not "really approve of an immoral or perverse life, that he has his narrator indulge in it temporarily till he frees himself from the grief caused by an unfortunate love."

It is no pleasing task to deduce the interpretation given above. But the symbols are there; the very title chosen is indicative. And yet it is a great poem. One can forget that Swinburne was thinking of the pleasures and pains caused by whipping, just as one forgets that some of the ancient poems of Greece and Rome, great love poems, were addressed by men to men.

In an able and well balanced article Dr. Louis J. Bragman had the courage to give us the first extended psychoanalytical interpretation of poems and fiction by Swinburne from the point of view of flagellation and emphasized the poet's extreme admiration for the Marquis de Sade and his novel *Justine*.[4] Dr. Bragman had access to the facts before the full letters on the subject were recently given to a wide public. The conclusion was inescapable to him that Swinburne was both a sadist and a masochist. The seeds were already planted, says Dr. Bragman, in *Lesbia Brandon* in which he attached pleasure to pain. One able Swinburne biographer, Harold Nicolson, in 1926, already had expressed his fears that some day writers might explore the poet's intricacies of nonexistent(!) sexual repression and trace depressing and essentially erroneous analogies to Masoch and Marquis de Sade. He already recognized that "Dolores" was "a sadist jingle." But the sexual repressions did exist; they were not released by the poet's visits to loose women; they were the result of desire for one he loved and could not attain. Dr. Bragman mentions the frequent references to the birch in *Love's Cross Current* and Swinburne's raptures over the birch in *The Sisters*. He notes how in *Rosamond*

[4] "The Case of Algeron Swinburne" *Psychoanalytic* Review Vol. XXI, January 1934, Number 1 pp. 59-73.

Swinburne has Hugh beat Arthur with a switch. He mentions that the poet's earlier writings, a drama written at Eton, and later plays were sadistic. Dr. Bragman does not dilate on all the poet's poems as he says sadistic references are too frequent, but he refers to three of his famous poems in the poet's first volume *Poems and Ballads*. In "Laus Veneris," he says there is a reference to the pleasures deduced from pain; in "Anactoria" there is a sadistic tone, and in "Dolores" with its "sadistic jingle" we have a perverse litany, a reiterated paean to the mystic and sombre Lady of Pain.

Chapter 6

Unconscious Consolatory Mechanisms in Authorship

1

THERE is a large body of popular literature that may be called the literature of self-deception. The author makes statements that are false, but which he wants to be true. He is aware, too, that most people like these sentiments, and he gives a forceful expression to them so that they have a semblance of truth. Dr. Johnson once said that all the arguments set forth to prove the advantages of poverty are good proof that this is not so; you find no one trying to prove to you the benefits of riches.

The literature of self-deception, which is nearly always optimistic and consolatory, derives its value as a defence mechanism. It is based on a lie but is efficacious nevertheless. Of this species Henley's famous poem ending with the lines "I am the Master of my fate, I am the Captain of my soul" is a good example. Of course no one is master of his fate. To this class belongs much of the consolatory advice found in the stoical precepts of Epictetus, Marcus Aurelius, and Seneca. Most religious poems and works like *The Imitation of Christ* may be included here.

Many writers whose lives have been bad, have written works that buoyed them up. They have affected to learn much from their calamities, although they unquestionably would have preferred not to have been victims of these misfortunes. They have pretended to exult over the failures of their ambitions when at heart they would have wished a more successful termination to them. Naturally literature of this kind is popular, although any vigorous intellect can see through the fallaciousness of the reasoning in a poem like "The Psalm of Life."

All the literary works wherein the precious and valued things in life are decried, wherein asceticism and death and celibacy are vaunted, are usually unconsciously insincere. The writer cannot have certain things and he bolsters himself up by pretending he is better off without them.

65

In examining a literary work we should always find out what the author's real thoughts must be, and not assume that they are what he holds them to be.

Eulogies of pain and the praise of the advantages of misfortune are forced, and though the literature abounding in such sentiments may aid some, it will only irritate those who think.

It would be interesting to collect passages from the works of writers who give us such ideas and inquire what motive prompted them. It is not very difficult to unravel the unconscious in these cases, especially if we know something of the writer's life.

Take the following lines from "Rabbi Ben Ezra" by Browning: "What I aspired to be, And was not, comforts me."

No doubt these lines, put in the mouth of the Rabbi, were a consolation that Browning administered to himself in his days of obscurity. It could not be possible that he really meant it. He wanted his work to be read and he wanted to have recognition as a poet. While it is not to the credit of a poet to seek popular applause by trying to do commonplace work, still a poet of value is anxious to be recognized as such by his peers. He is not comforted that he does not attain this end; on the contrary, he is disappointed. And while it is always best to do one's utmost and to be resigned if one fails, it does not follow that the man should be satisfied with his misfortune. The lines of Browning are a confession of regret for failure.

Then the various passages in the same poem seeking to show the advantages of age over youth merely tell us that after all the poet was really bemoaning his lost youth. Love and recognition came to him late in life, and as his youth was embroiled with some unsatisfactory love affairs and as he was not recognized as a great poet, we cannot say that Browning had an altogether happy youth. He would have preferred to become young again but to spend his youth more happily than he had done. He also no doubt had unconsciously before him the praises sung by poets of youth, and recalled Coleridge's beautiful plaint for his own departed youth, in the fine poem "Youth and Age." Browning really agreed with the sentiments of that poem, but after all what was the use of regrets? One might as well pretend that age was the better period of life, and one would then possibly be able to enjoy it. He wrote then, when past fifty, to counteract his real feelings, the lines:

Grow old along with me!
The best is yet to be,
The last of life for which the first was made.

Much of Browning's optimism was forced.

The most famous example of consolation for the miseries of old age is Cicero's discourse *On Old Age* addressed to Atticus when they were both about sixty-three years old. Cicero puts his own arguments about the advantages of old age into the mouth of Cato who is eighty-four years old. Cato tries to prove beneficial the four assumed disadvantages of old age; these are that it takes us away from the transactions of affairs, enfeebles our body, deprives us of most pleasures and is not very far from death.

Cicero really tried to console himself for the loss of his youth. Most assuredly he would rather have been young. The objections that he finds against old age are not satisfactorily removed by him and he does not state them all. Even though he does show old age has its pleasures, we read between the lines that he is aware that his body is subject to ailments, that he is shut off from certain pleasures, that he has not the energy or health or zest of life he had in youth and that he dreads death; we perceive all his arguments are got up to rid himself of these painful thoughts. People as a rule do not write on the disadvantages of youth; its advantages, in spite of struggles, are taken for granted. Rich and successful men who are old would generally be young again and give up some of the advantages of old age. Not that many people have not been happier in age than in youth, not that age is not free from those violent passions to which youth is subject, but youth still is preferable to old age and all the arguments in favor of it will not make a man want it to be reached more quickly.

Carlyle was the author of many statements meant to salve his own wounds. One of his famous hobbies was to attack people who seek happiness, no doubt because that is the very thing he himself sought his whole life long. He told them to seek blessedness. Let us examine the following passage from one of the most famous chapters of *Sartor Resartus*, entitled "The Everlasting Yea."

I asked myself: What is this that, ever since earliest years, thou hast been fretting and fuming, and lamenting and self-torturing, on account of? Say it in a word; is it not because thou art not happy? . . . Foolish soul!

What act of legislature was there that *thou* shouldst be happy? . . . Close thy Byron; open thy Goethe . . . there is a man a Higher than love of Happiness: he can do without happiness, and instead thereof find Blessedness.

We can discern under all this Carlyle's despair because he is not happy. Teufelsdrock, who is Carlyle's picture of himself, had a sweetheart who was stolen by a friend. One may be sure that Teufelsdrock would have given up his ideal of blessedness if this misfortune could have been prevented. No doubt, like Carlyle, he had dyspepsia, was poverty-stricken, and had a hard path to travel to success. Of course he would have wished to have had a good stomach, to be free from money troubles, and to be recognized. All these fortunate circumstances were not his. He had to say to himself, "Away with them. I am better off without them." But it is certain he could not have really felt this way. We learn from Carlyle's recently published letters, written to his future wife in his courting days, that he was unhappy for personal reasons; because she coquetted with him or jilted him, because he was unsuccessful, because he was poor, etc. He whined too much, although no doubt he had reason. He is full of the Byronism which he affected to despise.

It is likely that Browning and Carlyle at the time they were writing believed what they said. But psychoanalysis teaches us that we frequently do not know our own minds. We may think we are honest when we really are deceiving ourselves.

A writer may seek an effect which is attained by lauding a moral sentiment. Did not Shelley profess to believe in immortality of the soul in his elegy on Keats, "Adonais," while we know from a prose essay of his that he did not believe in immortality?

We should try to learn the whole truth from the fractional part of it (or the unconscious lie) that authors give us. We shall find a personal background for all their theories, a past humiliation or a personal need, which will explain the origin of the ideas professed.

When we read in his *Autobiography* that Herbert Spencer ascribes his nervous breakdown to hard work, if we are Freudians we may think that Spencer may not have told us the whole truth. We know that most cases of breakdown have had a previous history, usually in some love or sex repression. We are aware that Spencer was a bachelor who never had his craving for love satisfied. This may have led to his nervous troubles. This is merely one instance where by the aid of psychoanalysis we may read more than the author reveals.

Literary critics who never heard of psychoanalysis still have often applied its principles. In his essay on Thoreau, Stevenson dilates on his cynical views of friendship. When Stevenson included the essay in his *Familiar Portraits of Men and Books*, he wrote a little introductory note in which he shows he penetrated the secret of Thoreau's views. Thoreau was simply seeking to find a salve for his own lack of social graces. His strange views and personality made him almost an impossible friend except to Emerson and one or two others.

2

Even a great writer like Goethe deceived himself, as one can see by a famous passage in his autobiography explaining why Spinoza appealed to him. In the fourteenth book he says that his whole mind was filled with the statement from the *Ethics* that he who loves God does not desire God to love him in return. Goethe says that his question, "If I love thee, what is that to thee?" was spoken straight from his heart.

Great as Goethe's intellect was, he could not perceive that his partiality for this passage from Spinoza was due to the consolation he found in it for unreciprocated love. This particular sentiment from the profound work of that philosopher was probably inspired unconsciously by Miss Van den Ende's rejection of him when he hoped to marry her. The *Ethics* was finished when the author was about thirty-three. Spinoza, who led the life of a celibate, sublimated his repressed love into philosophic speculation. When he wrote the passage in question he was unconsciously consoling himself for loving a girl who did not care for him. The mechanism was: "I am not such a fool after all, because I love a girl who does not love me; why should I even want her to do so; don't we love God, and yet don't want Him to love us in return.[1] Goethe, having gone through the harassing experience that led to the writing of *Werther*, repeated the mental processes that Spinoza must have gone through in creating the sentiment about our not desiring God to love us in return.

Goethe imagined that love could be disinterested, and this is really not so. The lover seeks a return of his love, for that is

[1] I am aware that this sentiment of Spinoza may be interpreted as meaning that we must accept the laws of nature as they are, and must not expect them especially to favor us. And I do not intend any adverse criticism of him or of Goethe.

just what love means. Those novels where sacrificing lovers turn over the women they love to rivals, as in George Sand's *Jacques* and Dostoevsky's *The Insulted and Injured*, do not show disinterested love but merely obedience to an abstract idea with which the whole individual's psychic and physical constitution is not in harmony at all. Goethe tried to be different from what he really was. The question, "What is that to thee if I love thee?" with its corollary that the love need not be returned, did not come, as Goethe thought, straight from his heart. His interest in Spinoza's sentiment was a self-curative process for grief. All psychoneuroses are unsuccessful efforts to purge one's self of repressed feelings.

As a matter of fact, there is no warrant for Spinoza's assumption that man does not desire that God love him in return. All religion is based on the principle that God loves us and cares for us more than he does for other animals, or more than he does for other tribes or religious sects. Prayers are made to God to make us happy and prosper and satisfy our wants. This is tantamount to saying we want His love. If God, or Nature, as Spinoza understood Him, was only a malevolent force and gave us undiluted pain, we would not love Him. Again, man does not love God or Nature in the sense that he loves a woman, so even if Spinoza were right that man does not desire to be loved by God or Nature in turn, it is because that love does not promise the pleasure derived from the returned love of the woman.

The truth is that both Spinoza and Goethe would have preferred to have had their love returned, and had such been the case, they would not have occupied themselves with this idea.

3

Then there is the reaction-impulse and the infantile regression in writers. Many books are written by their authors to counteract certain impulses. They feel that their course of conduct or thought was reprehensible, and they try to make amends for this. They become fanatical converts; they show a regression to a fixed period in their own lives and return to the religion of their parents. Writers who in spite of being unable to believe in religious dogmas, miracles, ascetic notions of morality, nevertheless return in later life to the religions advocating these, belong to this class. The leading of a wicked life, but often the influence of childish memories of a religious household, are responsible for such conversions. The converts feel young again; pleasant recollections of the mother or father and delicious memories of school days play a part in the process. Many free thinkers who have had a theological training never really outgrow this.

Tolstoy's conversion was due to the wild days he spent as a young man. He was a proud aristocrat, and gave play to all his instincts; he was an atheist and pessimist, he was a gambler and a rake. He shows us his evolution in his various novels and autobiographical works. He finally came to deify ignorant peasants and advocated extreme nonresistance. He worshipped poverty, practised self-abnegation, and derogated sex. But, after all, his latter views are but the reactions to the life he led in youth, and a regression, with some changes, to views he was taught in childhood.

The same is true of Strindberg, who as a young man was an atheist, and a believer in free love; through the sufferings brought about by his three marriages and his attacks of insanity, he "turned." He looked with disapproval upon his early ideas, attributed much of his misery to his entertaining them; hence he discarded them, and returned to the religious views he held as a child. But his greatest work belonged to the period when he held liberal ideas.

Dostoevsky was at heart a devout orthodox Christian, even in his early revolutionary days. His great suffering in Siberia chastened him, and made him find a welcome religion in the religion of suffering, a guide in Christ who suffered. He is always at pains in his later novels to prove the existence of a personal God—a fact which makes one suspect that he had his own doubts, and that he tried to rid himself of them by his writing. Being also an epileptic, he would, particularly in these attacks, digress to infantile fixations and they would lead him to worship his sublimated "Father in Heaven."

There are many who naïvely insist that these men, when they went back to the belief of childhood days, had at last come to see the truth. The point of view taken is dependent on whether a man considers belief in the dogma of a religion a fetter or an asset.

In English literature we have as examples of reactions, both in religion and politics, the Lake School of poets, Wordsworth, Coleridge, and Southey. All of them later turned away from the republican, deistic, and pantheistic ideas of their youth. The reason Southey fought so bitterly against free thinkers like Byron and Shelley, is that in youth he, like them, also was attached to the ideas of the French Revolution. He became a

Tory of Tories, showed disapproval of all the leading thinkers of the time, of men like Hazlitt, Lamb, and Hunt. Liberal ideas, it is well known, have no greater enemy than a renegade liberal. Southey was sufficiently pilloried by Byron in the *Vision of Last Judgment*, and the psychology of his reaction has been drawn in the portrait of him by Hazlitt in *The Spirit of the Age*, while the gentle Lamb has administered to him a rebuke in the immortal *Letter of Elia to Robert Southey*.

When one reads the theological works of the gifted Coleridge, such as *The Aids to Reflection* and some of the *Table Talk*, and ponders on the spectacle of this former Spinozist and Unitarian, speaking in defence of dogmas that have not one logical argument in their favor, one is amazed. What a wreckage of the human intellect is often made by private misfortunes. Here was one of the greatest literary critics and one of the subtlest poets England ever had. But he wrote much nonsense in his theological essays. "The image of my father, my reverend, kind, learned, simple-hearted father, is a religion to me," he once said, thus giving us the key to his reaction. The elder Coleridge was a vicar, and died when the poet was nine years old. The poet became religious because of his repressed childish affection for a religious father who influenced him.

As for Wordsworth, he was sufficiently punished for his reaction, in that in later life he was often unable to do creditable literary work. And Shelley's poem, "To Wordsworth," and the lines of Browning beginning, "Just for a handful of silver he left us," generally thought to refer to Wordsworth, were deserved rebukes.

The reaction impulse plays a great rôle in shaping the destinies of literary men. It sometimes sweeps an entire age and gathers all before it. This happened in France in that period of French Literature which Brandes called the Catholic Reaction, when Chateaubriand, Joseph de Maistre, Louis de Bonald, and others were influential. It again occurred in the same country in the early nineties when leading free thinkers like Bourget and Huysmans went from the extreme radical position to Catholicism. Only great writers like Zola and Anatole France were able to keep their heads clear. Most of these converts really were always at heart religious. They never emerged from the associations of their religion even though their intellects would not enable them to believe some of its dogmas. Unconsciously Bourget and Huysmans were always Catholics in feeling.

Hawthorne wrote a story in which he imagines some of the dead English poets of the early decades of the nineteenth century continuing to live, and living a life in complete reaction to their youthful lives. He pictures the atheist Shelley becoming a Christian, a prediction that might have come true; for had Shelley died at seventy instead of thirty, he might have changed, as there was some similarity between his ideas of "perfectibility" and those of Christianity. This is, however, a mere surmise, as one of the last letters he wrote contains an attack on Christianity.

There are numerous instances of the reactionary impulse in literature. Shakespeare, who was of plebeian origin, often attacked the common people in his plays. He wrote favorably of nobility, and had little sympathy with democracy. Nietzsche, who was gentle personally and suffered much pain in his life, wrote in defence of cruelty, wished to do away with pity, sought to kill the finer emotions, and thought invalids should be left to die instead of being allowed to be cured. He was creating a system in philosophy whose ruling ideas were the very opposite to those which governed his private life. He could not even witness another's pain. Professor Eucken tells a story illustrating Nietzsche's gentleness. When that philosopher of the superman orally examined a student who did not answer correctly, Nietzsche would prompt him and answer the question for him, as he was unable to witness the student's discomfiture. Burns gave us some poetic outbursts against the crime of seduction, probably because he himself was guilty of it. Thackeray, who was hopelessly in love with a married woman, Mrs. Brookfield, and was rejected by her, affected to be very cynical at disappointed lovers and ridiculed them in his *Pendennis*. Cicero, who loved glory, wrote against it.

So men are often the very opposite of what they appear to be in their books, but this is unconscious, although sometimes the effort may be deliberate. Converts are fanatics. Reformed drunkards are the most convinced prohibitionists. The severest moralists and Puritans are often former rakes. The man who rails most bitterly against vice may often be suspected of struggling against temptation with it.

Similarly, the fact that professors in exact sciences and devotees to a philosophy of materialism, often become the most ardent exponents of spiritualism, may be due to an unconscious reaction on their part. No doubt the desire to believe that the dead can still communicate with us is the real basis of this belief. It would seem that scientists like Lodge, Crookes, Barrett, Wallace, and Lombroso, who have done so much to spread spiritualism, should be the last persons to embrace absurd beliefs so at variance with the principles which these men profess in their scientific work.

Chapter 7

Projection, Villain Portrayals and Cynicism as Work of the Unconscious

1

RENAN drew himself in his *Life of Jesus*, as one may see by comparing it with his *Memoirs of My Youth*. He projected himself upon Jesus and wrote a life of Renan instead. He portrayed in the volume his individual traits and gave his own characteristics to Jesus. His picture of Jesus is not a true one. Unconsciously he read into Jesus' life predominating features of his own personality, and also his sister Henrietta's. He emphasized Jesus' love of flowers, his indifference to the external world, his obsession with a utopian ideal and a mission in life. He found in Jesus a love for the simple and common folk, and a partiality towards women and children. He admired his exaltation of beggars and sympathized with his making poverty an object of love and desire. He saw no external affectation in Jesus, who was bound only to his mission, and who was a revolutionist besides. Jesus had only some of the qualities Renan attributed to him.

"Never did any one more loftily avow that disdain of the 'world' which is the essential thing of great things and great originality," said Renan of his Master. Thus was he describing himself unconsciously and presenting the plan of life which he, Renan, had followed.

If we read the analysis of Jesus' character and teachings in the last three chapters of the *Life of Jesus* and then turn to Renan's analysis of his own character in his autobiography, we shall see that the author had projected himself upon Jesus, as it were, and identified himself with the Master he worshipped. He finds in himself, he tells us in his autobiography, love of poverty, indifference to the world, devotion to his mission, affection for the common people, esteem for simplicity, contempt for success and luxury, dislike for the world of action, mercantile life—in short, he dwells on all the meek and lowly traits that he has, and arrogates to himself Jesus' practices, and attributes to his Master idiosyncrasies of his own. In an unguarded moment he forgets his customary modesty and gives us the clue to himself in these words: "I am the only man of my time who has understood the character of Jesus and of Francis of Assissi." In this bit of self-portraiture lies the whole secret of his *Life of Jesus*. Critics were attacking him for drawing a false picture of the founder of Christianity, but it did not dawn on them why the portrait was distorted. "Jesus has in reality ever been my master," says Renan.

How strongly Renan identified himself with and projected himself upon Jesus may be seen from the fact that the memoirs written at the age of sixty are in the same tone as the *Life of Jesus*, published twenty years earlier. He also tells us in the memoirs how the *Life of Jesus* originated. From the moment he abandoned the church, he says, with the resolution that he should still remain faithful to Jesus, the *Life of Jesus* was mentally written.

A few more traits that may be mentioned, which he felt he had in common with Jesus, were his aversion to incurring intimate friendships. There is reason to believe that Jesus did have friends, but Renan, who did not cultivate friendship (though he had a good friend in Berthelot), tried to persuade himself that Jesus was also like him in this regard. Again Renan deemed himself a dreamer, like Jesus, who was, however, also a man of action. Renan also saw his own effeminacy and kindliness in Jesus, who, however, vented himself of vigorous utterances.

Renan also fancied he found in Jesus his own inherent hostility to Jewish culture; his own anti-Semitism. As a matter of fact, Jesus owed much to Jewish culture, though he wanted the Jews to abandon some of their customs and to revise the Mosaic laws; the feeling among Jews was that Jesus, instead of being anti-Semitic, wished to be their leader and Messiah and King. Renan reads into Jesus his own anti-Semitism. Those who are familiar with Renan's writings are aware of the many slurring and contemptuous references he makes to the Jews. In fact, one of the paradoxes of his life is that with his liberality and gentleness, with his abandoning of all Christian dogma, he entertains a bitter feeling towards the people who gave him his ideal man, the people who originated, even by his own admission, many of Jesus' maxims. Renan states that Jesus profited immensely by the teachings of Jesus, son of Sirach, of Rabbi Hillel and of the synagogue. Renan unjustly made Jesus have his own failing, anti-Semitism.

Strangely enough, Renan's treatment of the story of Jesus

(outside of his giving Jesus traits of his own) has been very largely a Jewish one. It is for this reason that all devout Christians were offended. Renan treated Jesus as a man and refused to credit all the legends connected with him. Renan did not believe that Jesus was born without a human father; that he was a member of a Trinity; that he could perform supernatural miracles. In short, Renan did not accept Jesus as a son of God, though giving him traits almost divine and free from human frailties. The picture of Jesus in the life is an idealized Jewish portrayal.

Renan serves as one of the best examples of a free thinker remaining a devotee of his faith, though discarding all the tenets on which it rests. His early religious training had a permanent influence on him, and he was a Christian all his life, even though he differed with the church. In one of his last and most profound essays, the "Examination of the Human Conscience," he gives us a confession of his faith. Here he appears as a pantheist, but ventures incredible conjectures that there may be a supernatural. His church mind plays havoc with his Spinozism, and we sees his early infantile influences. Intellectually at times he stands high, higher it may be said without irreverence than his master Jesus, since he had at his command a knowledge of science and philosophy with which Jesus was unfamiliar. The greatness of Renan appears in his *Philosophical Dialogues*, in his *Philosophical Dramas*, in his *Future of Science*, in the *Anti-Christ* and other essays and books. When he moralizes he is a monk; when he speculates on philosophic and scientific subjects, he is a thinker. Georg Brandes' "Renan as a Dramatist" is an excellent study.

Yet literature scarcely offers such an instance of a man projecting himself so closely upon a historical character. Such a projection is similar to the seeking, in an unusual degree, by nervous people of moral shelter and consolation in some other person. The reposing of Renan on Jesus gives us an insight into the birth of worship of religious founders. Pfister, a disciple of Freud, and himself a Christian pastor, says: "In the divine fatherlove, he, whose longing for help, for ethical salvation, is not satisfied by the surrounding reality, finds an asylum. In the love for the Saviour, the love-thirsting soul which finds no comprehension and no return love in his fellowmen is refreshed."

A complete psychoanalytic study of Renan, which this essay does not pretend to be, would make a fuller inquiry into his relations with his mother, his affection for his sister and her influence on him and his never-swerving admiration for the priests who were his early teachers. He has left tributes to all of them. They ruled his life. In his unconscious a fixation upon them was buried. His love for them kept him a Christian, when intellectually he was a free thinker. They are present in his *Life of Jesus*, and the psychoanalyst can see them guiding the pen of Renan. They are always with him. Had they not loved him and he them so intensely, had he not inherited so strongly those meek, effeminate, and kindly traits, his temperament might have been as unchristian as his intellect.

We see why the extreme liberal and the orthodox Christian were offended by his *Life of Jesus*, and why hundreds of pamphlets and articles were written against it. It was really a portrait of the author, and the unconscious Christian in him puzzled the radicals, while his conscious intellect seemed like blasphemy to the devout followers of dogmas. He gave his own idealized traits to his hero, and the free thinkers complained Renan made Jesus a god anyhow, while it seemed an insult to the Christians that mere moral virtues instead of divinity should be thrust upon Jesus, who they felt did not need Renan's compliments.

2

Authors also draw on the unconscious for their immoral characters. In *Le Père Goriot* Balzac drew himself in Eugene Rastignac, but the author is also present in the villain of the novel, Vautrin or Jacques Collin, who appears likewise in *Lost Illusions* and *The Splendors and Miseries of Courtesans*. Vautrin, it will be recalled, tries to persuade Eugene to marry a girl whose father will leave her a million francs, if Eugene consents to have her brother, the more likely heir, despatched by a crony of Vautrin's. Thus Eugene would become rich immediately, instead of being compelled to struggle for years. Vautrin wants a reward for his services. Vautrin's words are really the voice of Balzac's unconscious; Eugene's inner struggles are Balzac's own; and though the young student rejects the proposition, he takes up Vautrin's line of reasoning unconsciously, even though to drop it. Vautrin's Machiavellian viewpoint was at times unconsciously entertained by Balzac himself, though never practised. We know Balzac always sought for schemes of getting rich to pay his debts, and was always occupied with thoughts of his aggrandisement and ambition. He no doubt unconsciously entertained notions that riches, love, fame might be attained by violating the moral edicts of society; these ideas may have obtruded but a few seconds to be immediately dismissed. But once they made their appearance they were repressed in Balzac's unconscious, and emerged in the characters of Vautrin and other villains who are part of the author's unconscious.

Balzac understood that vice often triumphed and that the way of virtue was often hard. "Do you believe that there is any absolute standard in this world? Despise mankind and find out the meshes that you can slip through in the net of the code." Vautrin here gives Balzac's inner unconscious secret away. The author was not aware that he drew upon himself unconsciously in depicting Vautrin. This, of course, does not mean that Balzac agreed with Vautrin. We remember Eugene shouted out to Vautrin, "Silence, sir! I will not hear any more; you make me doubt myself." The author merely got his unconscious into one of his leading villains, just as Milton did in Satan, as Goethe did in Mephistopheles.

Vautrin is Lucien de Rubempré's evil influence also, his Jacques Collin. Balzac saw how disastrously he himself might have ended his life had he heeded his unconscious.

Since literature is often depicting struggles and conflicts with our evil instincts, it deals directly with the material of the unconscious; for the unconscious that psychoanalysis is concerned with is that which springs from repressions forced upon us by society as well as by fate. In literature the unconscious appears under various symbols and disguises, just as it does in dreams. The devil, for example, is but our unconscious, symbolized. He represents our hidden primitive desires struggling to emerge; he is the eruption of our forbidden desires. His deeds are the accomplished wishes of our own unconscious. We are interested in the devil because he is ourselves in our dreams and unguarded moments.

The fascination that the villain has for us is because our unconscious recognizes in him a long-forgotten brother. True, our moral sense soon prevails, and we rejoice when the rascal is worsted, but he represents the author's unconscious as well as our own. Any one who has read of the thoughts and conduct of Raskolnikoff in *Crime and Punishment*, or of Julian Sorel in *The Red and the Black*, or of George Aurispa in *The Triumph of Death*, will see that much of the authors themselves, or rather their unconscious selves, is drawn in these criminals. Dostoevsky, Stendhal and D'Annunzio all said to themselves in writing: "I too might have ended like these characters. I did think their thoughts and a slight circumstance could have led me to the crimes they committed."

The man who hates a vice most intensely is often just the man who has something of it in his own nature, against which he is fighting. The author sometimes punishes himself in his novel by making the character suffer for engaging in the course of life that the author himself followed. There is always a suspicion, when a writer raves most furiously against a crime or act, that he has committed that deed in his unconscious.

It is gratifying to find the views in this section also stated by a creative writer who arrived at them independently. Somerset Maugham in *The Moon and Sixpence* writes:

> It may be that in his rogues the writer gratifies instincts deep-rooted in him, which the manners and customs of a civilized world have forced back to the mysterious recesses of the subconscious. In giving to the character of his invention flesh and bones he is giving life to part of himself which finds no other means of expression. His satisfaction is a sense of liberation.[1]

Maugham's novel was published about the same time as my book, and of course he could not have been indebted to me. We both separately arrived at the same conclusions. It is likely he also knew something about psychoanalysis, though this was not necessary to arrive at his conclusion, but he does mention the word subconscious. One must conclude that his natural insight into the unconscious which most creative writers have guided him.

3

The reason La Rochefoucauld, author of the *Maxims*, is called a cynic is that he reveals the unconscious, at the bottom of which is self-love. He knows that there is great egotism, nay something akin to depravity, at the root of our emotions. He shows us much in our psychic life that many of us never suspected was there. When he brings it forth we grow indignant and yet say to ourselfes, "How true!"

Let us examine a few of these maxims at random and note the insight into the unconscious that the author displays. He understood that repression was at the basis of our unconscious.

[1] Chapter XLI, p. 102.

Take the following sentence: "Wit sometimes enables us to act rudely with impunity." This saying anticipates Freud's analysis of wit in his *Wit and the Unconscious*. The Frenchman digs up in a sentence the hidden strata of the unconscious. La Rochefoucauld recognized that we must curb our primitive instincts, repress our private wishes, and leave our innermost thoughts unexpressed in order to adapt ourselves to people. The world moves by concealing for charity's, and often decency's, sake its unconscious. "Men would not live long in society," say the *Maxims*, "were they not the dupes of each other."

He knew that our primitive instincts could be subdued only when they were not too strong, and that virtue was practised when it was not difficult to do so. "When our vices leave us we flatter ourselves with the idea we have left them." "If we conquer our passions it is more from their weakness than from our strength." "Perserverance is not deserving of blame or praise, as it is merely the continuance of tastes and feelings which we can neither create nor destroy."

He understood the great part played by vanity in the unconscious. The most modest of us are, in our unconscious, vain. "When not prompted by praise we say little." "Usually we are more satirical from vanity than malice." "The refusal of praise is only the wish to be praised twice."

La Rochefoucauld was aware of the unconscious "immoral" instincts in virtuous women. Though we may dislike him for some of his remarks, he, however, gave utterance to a truth when he asserted that women do not want their love or sex feelings repressed any more than men do. "There are few virtuous women who are not tired of their part." "Virtue in woman is often love of reputation and repose." Freud went a step further and showed that women usually have neurosis from repressed sex.

The Frenchman also understood the rôle played by the unconscious in friendship, and that is the reason he made his well-known statement, "In the adversity of our best friends we always find something which is not wholly displeasing to us." He might have been less brutal had he stated his meaning directly in words to the following effect: When we strive for the same goal as our friend and he reaches it and we do not, his success hurts our vanity and we would almost prefer that he too had failed. We are pleased by his success only if we would profit thereby.

La Rochefoucauld's statement, "It is well that we know not all our wishes," will be appreciated by students of psychoanalysis.

To conclude, La Rochefoucauld always read between the lines. He fathomed the hidden motives of our conduct. Note the great powers of observation he displayed in the following: "Too great a hurry to discharge an obligation is an ingratitude." "The gratitude of most men is but a secret desire of receiving greater benefits."

He recognized that life is often possible only by a process of self-deception, but that too much of such deception is responsible for individual and social evils. There are times when the truth about our unconscious must be told, no matter how painful.

Chapter 8

Works of Genius Directed by the Unconscious

1

IN studying the psychology of authorship by means of psychoanalysis we learn something about the unconscious growth of an author's book; this phase of its process has not been universally admitted. We are often told certain incidents gave rise to the writing of a volume, but they were only the precipitating factors. The book had shaped itself unconsciously in the author's mind long before; it only gets itself projected in an endurable form. So though Stevenson tells us that the shape of a map of an island took his fancy and gave birth to *Treasure Island*, we know as a matter of fact that he had, as a boy, for many years been leading mentally the life of the treasure hunters. Stevenson himself relates how the brown faces of his characters peeped out upon him from unexpected quarters. The map just set him in action.

Let me sum up briefly the growth of a literary performance from a psychoanalytical standpoint. Let us assume that the author at some time of his life was placed amidst circumstances the reality of which jarred on him, offended his sense of beauty, wrecked his happiness and frustrated his most cherished desires. Deprived of a world that he wished to inhabit, he built one in his fantasies and day dreams, one that was the very opposite of that in which he was constrained to dwell. If he was toiling in barren labor he pictured himself at congenial work, or leisure; if he dwelt in squalor and was deprived of necessities, he mentally placed himself in beautiful surroundings, rolling in luxury, and in possession of property he prized most. If he had no one to love he formed an ideal for himself, with which he lived. If the loved one did not return his love, he depicted himself as wed to her.

That literature is influenced and created by the wishes of the character or author may be seen readily. A tale of Ernest Renan sheds light on this theory, and also serves as a valuable illustration how neurotics and insane people contract their illnesses from unfulfilled love desires, and how they build phantasies where those wants are satisfied. Pleasant pictures appear in day dreams, but these often assume such reality that the victim cannot tell the fanciful from the actual. In the first sketch in his autobiography, called "The Flax Crusher," Renan relates a pathetic story of the daughter of a flax crusher who lost her mind because her love for a priest was unreturned. She unconsciously carried out her wishes in her actions and thoughts. She would take a log of wood and dress it up in rags and rock and kiss the artificial infant and put it in the cradle at night. She imagined that this was her child by the priest. Thus she stilled the maternal urge. She fancied that she was keeping house for him. She would hem and mark linen, often interlacing his and her own initials. She finally was led to commit theft from his home. This story was taken from real life. The artist who is frustrated in love acts like this girl; he imagines that his love is being fulfilled and that he is living with the loved one.

A classic example of fantasy building is Charles Lamb's *Dream Children; a Reverie*. Rejected by the sweetheart of his youth, Ann Simmons, he pictured himself married to her and surrounded by their children and talking to them and entertaining them. He projected a world as it might have been, and as he desired it for himself; he wakes up from his day dream —the children were merely those of his imagination.

Day dreams then constitute the beginning of literary creation. In them we create a world for ourselves, and we make real people fit into it. After continuous living in a fictitious realm, a writer seeks to express himself and to give his expression artistic form. If the dreamer dwells too long in one imaginative abode he may lose the faculty of distinguishing the real from the ideal. He may become subject to hallucinations and utterly unbalanced like Renan's flax crusher's daughter.

The literary man often saves himself from neurosis by putting his dream into artistic shape; writing of their dreams and troubles has not prevented even artists from going mad, nor continuing to brood over the troubles that had already inspired their works. But the point of difference is clearly established between the neurotic and the artist. One dreams on till he is rescued by a physician's help, if possible; the other partly cures himself by self-expression, and at the same time gives the world a work of art or literature; this work consoles many, because they too have either experienced similar troubles, or considered themselves possible victims of such tragedy.

Very few English writers understood the mechanism of day dreams better than Dr. Johnson as is shown in the chapter "The Dangerous prevalence of Imagination" where Imlac speaks of the imagination's domination over reason.[1]

One of the best illustrations of the psychoanalytic theory of authorship detailed by the writer himself occurs in a once-famous English novel, Kingsley's *Alton Locke*, published in 1850. Alton Locke tells us how he began to write poetry. The chapter entitled "First Love" recounts the process, and we learn how because he led a life of drudgery, he created a far more pleasant one in his imagination and then unconsciously sought to make a record of this life.[2]

2

Psychoanalysis is always interested in learning exactly how literary masterpieces are born. Just as it seeks to know through dreams some of the hidden secrets in the unconscious, so it tries to discover what unconscious life made the writer project his vision.

Two of the most famous love stories of the eighteenth century which had a personal background, and whose evolution has been told by the authors themselves, were Rousseau's *La nouvelle Heloise* (1760), and Goethe's *The Sorrows of Werther* (1774). They were the predecessors of the entire field of auto-biographical love-lorn lugubrious literature that pervaded Europe in the early decades of the nineteenth century. Georg Brandes has shown how Chateaubriand, Madame de Stael, Senancour, Byron, George Sand, and others owed much of their methods of recording their love troubles to these two novels. We today scarcely realize the great vogue that these tales at one time had.

[1] *See* Chapter XLIV, *Rasselas.*

[2] Otto Rank has done me the honor of citing my references to *Rasselas* and *Alton Locke* in his new edition of *Das Inzest-Motiv in Dichtung und Sage Grundzuge einer Psychologie des dichtereschen Schaffers* in 1926, page 18, *Ganzahnlich versteht Dr. Johnson die "Gefahrlichkeit des Tagtraumes" in seiner Abhandlung* "The Dangerous prevalence of imagination in Rasselas." *Auch der bekannte englische* Novelist Kingsley *erzahrt* in "Aton Loche" *wie er aus der unbefriedigenden Wirklichkeit zum Tagtraumen und dann zum Schreiben Kam"* (Zit nach A. Mordell: *The Erotic Motive in Literature,* New York, 1919 S.110.)

Probably Dr. Rank saw no reason for looking up both these books. Had he done so he might have added what I add here that Imlac was voicing Dr. Johnson's opinion and was specifying that there was a domination of the imagination over the reason.

The authors have given us accounts of the birth of these novels. Both of these geniuses had been frustrated in their loves; as a result they created mental fantasies and lived in a more pleasant world of their own creation, and finally, bursting with desire for expression, produced their novels. The unconscious life buried in them came forth and was crystallized in art. Rousseau's *Confessions* and Goethe's autobiography, *Poetry and Truth*, tell us how the novels came to light.

In the ninth book of the *Confessions*, Rousseau informs us that when he reached the age of forty-five, he realized that he had really never enjoyed true love. As a result he bgan living in a fantastic world where his craving was satisfied. He realized his wishes in his day dreams. "The impossibility of attaining real beings," he says, "threw me into the regions of chimera, and seeing nothing in existence worthy of my delirium, I sought food for it in the ideal world, which my imagination quickly peopled with beings after my own heart." He tells us how he valued love and friendship, and that he created two female friends according to his taste, that he gave one of them a lover, who was also the platonic friend of the other lady; that in this friend and lover he drew his own portrait. He imagined that there were to be no rivalries or pain. These fictions, he continues, gained in consistence. He then had an inclination to put on paper this situation of fancy. "Recollecting everything I had felt during my youth, this, in some measure, gave me an object to that desire of loving which I had never been able to satisfy, and by which I felt myself consumed." Here we have the secret. He sought in art what he had not in reality. At first he wrote incoherent letters, just as his feelings prompted him, and he thus completed the two first parts of the novel (which is in the form of letters) without a conscious effort to make a connected work.

At this time Rousseau, who was a married man, fell in love with the wife of D'Holbach, Sophia D'Houdetot. He loved her madly. He says, "It was not until after her departure that, wishing to think of Julia (his heroine), I struck with surprise at being unable to think of anything but Madame D'Holbach." He then identified the real with the ideal; he found the woman of his dreams. But now his troubles began. Union with his beloved Countess was impossible. New emotions rose within him, as material for his novel. The work really wrote itself. He originally formed an ideal because he was not loved by any one who fulfilled that conception. When he discovered such a person and she was beyond his attainment, he imagined himself as her lover. All the misery he recorded had its counterpart in his personal experience. Without the unconscious reveries which he indulged in as a result of his needs and tribulations, the novel would not have been written.

After the story was published, women worshipped the author. It was recognized that he was the hero of the book, and it was generally believed that the characters were not fictitious. The novel gives us an account of the real Rousseau at least as fully as the *Confessions* themselves, where facts are not always truthfully reported.

Goethe has recorded just as minutely the origin of his *Sorrows of Werther*. He traces the book back to his love for Charlotte Buff, the betrothed of a friend of his. He resolved to give free play to the idiosyncrasies of his inner nature. He describes how he had day dreams and how he held mental dialogues with different people. He then was led to record these fancies on paper. The substances of his novel "were first talked over with several individuals in such imaginary dialogues, and only later in the process of composition itself were made to appear as if directed to one single friend and sympathizer." He became weary of life, and had suicidal thoughts. He then heard of the suicide of his friend Jerusalem, who had been in love with a married woman. Goethe saw that he was really in the same position as his friend; his loved one belonged to another. "On the instant," Goethe goes on, "the plan of Werther was formed, and the whole drew together, and became a solid mass. I was naturally led to breathe into the work I had in hand all the warmth which makes no distinction between the imaginary and the actual." He wrote the book in four weeks. "I had written the little volume, almost unconsciously like a somnambulist." As a result he freed himself from his suffering. The artist stepped in and cured the man. Goethe illustrates the theory that artistic creation acts as a self-cure of a developing neurosis. "By this composition," Goethe wrote, "more than by any other, I had freed myself from that stormy element in which . . . I had been so violently tossed to and fro. I felt as if I had made a general confession and was once more free and happy, and justified in beginning a new life."

The public thought that the book was solely the history of young Jerusalem's tragic love affair, and did not altogether understand that the cry was Goethe's own. His mental dialogues and the longings of his inner spirit found expression in this novel. His sufferings were undecipherable by the public, he tells us, because he worked in obscurity. He also gave the attributes of several women to Lotte, and hence several ladies claimed to have been the original models.

Thus we see how two great love stories were created almost unconsciously by the authors. Day dreams and actual love; the longing for reality, for lack of which imaginary situations were created; and the putting down in the form of letters and dialogues the ideas and emotions that burst forth, all led to the shaping of the literary product.

3

Psychoanalysis sheds some light on the nature, or rather the direction of genius, and especially literary genius. But it does not define it within hard and fast lines.

Literary works are largely the result of repressions that the author has suffered; he has been led as the result of them to cry out his grief or to depict ideal situations where such grief does not exist. He must write so that people who have had similar repressions, (or who can imagine them), will find a personal appeal in his works. But the situations described must also, besides evoking an emotional appeal, stir the readers intellectually, so that they sympathize where the writer counted on sympathy. When the author writes only of his joys, the unconscious may also be at work.

The writer also must be a master of his art, so that he does not violate fundamental rules of composition and commit outrages of common sense.

Especially when the author has discovered new features of his unconscious life, or has been led to present original and profound ideas as a result of such discoveries, particularly when he moves the reader with intensity and evokes a passionate response, does the writer begin to merit the name of genius. When we say that a genius is a man who discovers a new truth or depicts beauty, we often mean that he is a man who, having experienced a repression, has been led as a result to draw conclusions that society has not wished to accept; he is a great artist when he gives an effective delineation of that repression; he is a great thinker when he discovers ways by which that repression may be avoided, and he is a humanitarian when he informs the world how to attain a form of happiness that had been denied him.

We thus do away with the very pernicious doctrine that genius is a form of degeneracy or insanity. Geniuses sometimes are sufferers from neurosis, or describe characters suffering from them; they are not degenerates, as Lombroso and Nordau would have us believe. A neurotic person and a degenerate one are not the same. The term "degenerate" is not the proper name for men like Ibsen or Tolstoy no matter how repugnant their ideas might be to people. Nor does it follow that because poets like Villon, Verlaine, and Wilde had spent time in jail for crimes, their poems are to be stamped as degenerate products. While it is apparent that some of the author's insanity appears in works by Swift, Rousseau, Maupassant, Nietzsche, and Strindberg, their masterpieces are noble works of art.

The faculty of literary genius is possessed by a few; but many people possess some of its qualities. Intelligent or sincere lovers have often written love letters that never got into print which were stamped with the qualities of genius. Highly gifted people in private life often utter thoughts which if collected and published would constitute works that show genius. There have been many people who have uttered sentiments as wise as some in Boswell's *Life of Samuel Johnson*, or Eckermann's *Conversations with Goethe*, but the ideas were not reduced to writing, either by the speaker or a friend. Goethe once said that every genius has in his lifetime been acquainted with men who were obscure and unproductive, but who possessed greater intellects, more originality than those geniuses themselves.

There is no dividing line between the genius and the talented or even average person, any more than there is a marked boundary between the normal and the abnormal.

The genius, however, always has something of the pioneer in him; even after his work is no longer new, he retains the title of genius, though there are people who can write better works than he or even advance greater ideas than he.

The world has agreed on some geniuses. Most people are ready to admit that a few men of letters like Shakespeare, Molière, Cervantes, Goethe, and Balzac were geniuses of the first order. But when we are concerned with literary men who have done good work, it is not easy to say whether they were geniuses, though we are ready enough to concede that they had the qualities that make up genius.

The genius must be able to do more than write of the repressions which he has actually experienced; he must be a master of technique and means of expression. He must be able to describe with force and imagination, those repressions he has witnessed others suffer. The more use he makes of his unconscious, the nearer he gets to truth, and it has often been the lot of genius to depict those very emotions which society wants to be kept in the unconscious; and the more he draws on his unconscious, the less use he has for actual experience.

Yet the ability to present works of human interest that appeal to the public does not alone constitute genius; otherwise many of the thrillers of the movies would be works of genius. Nor does the writing of sad tales or depicting ideal pictures make genius. There must be an important idea, or the presentation of the emotion in a particularly compelling manner. Then there is something cumulative about genius; we expect from it a repetition of literary feats that is beyond the power of most writers; we are not contented with an isolated literary effort. Still, there are poets and novelists who are regarded as geniuses though they have produced but one or a few pieces of importance.

The literary genius then has a keen insight into the psychology of the repression of the emotions and can beautifully express this repression and make valuable intellectual deductions therefrom. He can vary this work for many years, and move people not only to feel but to think.

Chapter 9

Literary Emotions and the Neuroses

1

THE emotions that literature often deals with bear a close analogy to symptoms in the neuroses or nervous diseases. Every emotional conflict, every repressed love is an incipient neurosis, and the sufferings described in books sometimes are full-fledged cases of neuroses. The author may unintentionally draw characters suffering griefs which the physician can recognize as analogous to the cases he has observed in practice. The writer may show how the character cures himself of his neuroses by being made aware of the unconscious forces struggling within him, or how the sufferer effects a recovery by sublimation, or how he succumbs to his disease.

Some authors like Rousseau in his *Confessions*, or Strindberg in his *Confessions of a Fool*, give us detailed accounts of their neuroses, though they may not always exactly fathom the causes. Poets have in their collections of lyrics told us of the sufferings that they have personally gone through, and the trained scientist can see to what neuroses the symptoms described are related. Other authors have in the guise of fictitious characters described what are analogous to the neuroses they have been suffering. Byron in his *Manfred*, Hauptmann in his Heinrich in the *Sunken Bell*, Shakespeare in *Hamlet*, Goethe in *Faust*, have told us of love repressions that were their own, and these characters can be studied by critics as neurotic patients are analyzed by physicians.

The author may even purposely draw himself in the guise of a character who is utterly insane, as Cervantes did in *Don Quixote*. One feels that the author was his own knight; in fact, he to had a sneaking fondness for books of chivalry, and the familiarity that his hero shows with them is good evidence that Cervantes was a careful student of that kind of literature. He too had been bruised by windmills; he too found that the real did not coincide with his ideals. It is most likely that Don Quixote developed his mental illness by his abstinence from love, by living in fancy with the high dames he read about, and by cherishing an affection unreciprocated for the peasant girl he called in his madness Dulcinea del Toboso. At least these factors cannot be ignored in the insanity he developed from reading books of chivalry. It is not improbable that Cervantes drew on a real woman for Dulcinea; he too had wasted affection on some woman, ignorant and coarse, whom he took for a lady of high degree. We do know that in the year he married, in 1584, at the age of thirty-seven, he had an illegitimate daughter. There is also a tradition that he had a few years previously a daughter by a noble lady in Portugal, and though this story is discredited, it must have had some basis in reality. However, Cervantes, though not, like his knight, suffering a mental ailment, must have had a neurosis on which he drew for the material of this novel; it was no doubt caused by his worship of a Dulcinea del Toboso.

Writers like D'Annunzio and Dostoevsky have given us cases of neuroticism; they described themselves in their books. Since the line between the normal and the neurotic condition is hard to draw, and we all daily or at different crises in our lives overstep the limits, the works of literary men as a rule are concerned with those cases where the neurotic and normal merge. Freud said that no author has avoided all contact with psychiatry. And he is assuredly right. Dickens' eccentric characters, Balzac's heroes and villains in the grip of great passions, semi-neurotics like Bunyan, Thomas, a'Kempis and Pascal, whose repressed love perhaps made them religious fanatics; Iago, Richard the Third, Macbeth, Hamlet, Antony, and Timon of Shakespeare; the leading characters of Ibsen, the unhappy Heine, Musset, Baudelaire, Verlaine, Leopardi, Carducci, Burns, Byron, Shelley, Keats, Poe and Hearn, all—both characters and their authors—can to some extent be studied like patients who suffer from neuroses. In fact all characters in fiction who suffer are in a small degree related to neurotics, for sex and love are usually the cause of their troubles. Though the author usually deals with mild cases of neuroses, and the psychiatrists with severe ones, their provinces are often the same. The writer details his case with art, and lays stress on the emotional phases and deduces ideas, while the psychiatrist gives us bare scientific analyses. "The author," says Freud, "cannot yield to the psychiatrist nor the psychiatrist to the author, and the poetic treatment of a theme from psychiatry may result correctly without damage to beauty." [1]

[1] Delusion and Dream.

Characters with conflicts resembling neuroses frequently lend themselves to literary treatment. Think of the women sufferers in literature like Madame Bovary, Hester Prynne, Anne Karenina, Hedda Gabler, Magda; you can always trace their troubles to love repression. Fictitious characters who have not had a natural outlet for their love and have been abstinent, or have had a love disappointment or have suffered from a trauma in their infantile life, present phases of neuroses.

Freud has studied Jensen's novel *Gradiva*, and shown how the leading character has troubles analogous to the psychoneuroses, and cures himself unconsciously by the methods of psychoanalysis.

Literature records some fully developed cases of neuroses. A story like "The Fall of the House of Usher" presents a complete case of neurosis. Characters in literature who commit suicide, like Werther and Hedda Gabler, are really victims of neurosis; sex is usually at the bottom of their difficulties. This fact is sufficient for the layman to know without making a deep inquiry into the nature of neuroses and attempting to classify them. Here the work of the physician begins and a penetrating insight into the real neuroses described in literature can be made only by the psychoanalyst.

Nevertheless, there are some cases that the layman may recognize if he has familiarized himself with the Freudian views of the neuroses.

Freud divides the neuroses into two classes, the true or actual neuroses, and the psychoneuroses.

The true neuroses are neurasthenia and anxiety neurosis, which formerly was included under neurasthenia, but which Freud set off as a separate class. He calls these true neuroses because there are present abnormal disturbances of the sexual function, not necessarily due to heredity. Neurasthenia is due to excessive physical abuse, and the anxiety neurosis results from abstinence or unsatisfactory gratification. All agencies which prevent the psychic utilization of the physical excitement lead to anxiety neurosis. Literature gives us cases of true neuroses, but they are not as frequent as the other class, the psychoneuroses.

The psychoneuroses are due to repressions but date back to infancy; the influence of heredity is important; unconscious factors are at work. The child's relation to his parents and his infantile sex life have great influence on his future. The crisis comes when a love repression in later life breaks out. The psychoneuroses are hysteria, compulsion neurosis, and mixed cases, especially anxiety hysteria.

In hysteria the patient suffers from reminiscences, and his recent experiences are unconsciously attached to infantile sexual impressions. Instead of solving his love difficulties he builds fantasies. Certain mental impressions remain fixed. The early painful effects struggle to consciousness, but instead are transformed into uncommon inhibitions, by a process known as conversion.

In compulsion or obsessional neurosis we also have unconscious sexual factors at work since infancy, but the effect of the painful idea affixes itself to other ideas, producing obsessions. These are transformed reproaches which have escaped the repression. Morbid fears, doubts and temptations are the result.

The most common form of neuroses in life, and hence most described in literature, is anxiety hysteria. They partake of the nature of hysteria and the true neurosis, anxiety. "In these cases," says Dr. Hitschmann, "the anxiety arises not only from somatic (physical) causes but from a part of the ungratified libido which embraces unconscious complexes and through the repression of these gives rise to neurotic anxiety." The excitation is phsychic as well as physical.

Literature does present cases of psychoneuroses and anxiety neuroses.

The author who is recalling old griefs on which he still broods, looking upon them as if they had happened yesterday, almost makes one think that he is suffering from hysteria. Incessant complaints about early love disappointments in which are again revived all the incidents; constant memories of the mother and of childhood days; and obstinate clinging to ideas and pictures that were uppermost in early life, are remotely related to hysteria. Lady Macbeth, however, as Dr. Isadore Coriat has shown, was really a victim of hysteria.

We see obsessions at work in characters like Ibsen's Brand who aims at all or nothing. In short literature records the neuroses of human beings; the psychoanalyst does not put them there. And hysteria is suffered by men as well as by women, as Freud finally proved after encountering great opposition to this view.

2

The details of Lord Byron's life and the accounts of his love affairs have become more familiar than those of any other poet. In his poems and letters he has himself aided future biographers. Were we studying his poetry as a whole we should have taken into consideration his noble ancestry and many external events of his life, but we wish to discuss the origin of what is known as Byronism and to show the effects of his first disastrous love affair with Mary Chaworth upon his poetry. We must however, touch on his relations, as psychoanalysis would demand, with his father and mother.

Byron never knew a father's care; Mad Jack Byron died at the age of 36 when his son was three years old. He had before his marriage seduced a married woman and then married her. She was the mother of Augusta. He then married Catherine Gordon. He ran through her fortune and deserted her. Byron's mother was an erratic person. (The story of her chase after him with a poker is familiar.) He never loved her, although he became hysterical when she died.

Byron unconsciously sought a substitute for the mother love he never had, in his love affairs. We may mention briefly the two earliest loves of his childhood, one with his cousin Mary Duff at the age of nine; even at the age of sixteen he fell into convulsions when he heard of her marriage. Then at the age of twelve he was seriously in love with Margaret Parker who inspired his very earliest love poems, and who died from consumption two years later.

But it was Mary Chaworth with whom he fell seriously in love at the age of fifteen in 1803; she encouraged him, then repudiated him, denying that she had loved him, as he learned when he heard her remark about not loving that lame boy. She married John Musters, Lord Melbourne, in June 1805 when Byron was in his seventeenth year; it was a marriage that turned out unhappily and Mary became insane later. Byron continued in love with her till he left England in the summer of 1809; but the memories of it still haunted him even several months after he returned from his trip in the summer of 1811. These memories were particularly revived after two disasters, one his separation from his wife and the other, Mary's insanity, which led him to write his great poem "The Dream" in 1816. He had a chance to meet her early in 1814, for she wrote to him asking this. He wrote to Lady Melbourne he was no longer interested in her as a lover, though he did not deny that seeing her might revive his love.

What interests us here is the effect of this love upon his poetry for eight years from 1803 to 1811. Naturally she was the subject of some of the poems in his first book *Hours of Idleness* published in 1807. He had spent only six weeks in her company in 1804 but he was deeply smitten and on hearing of her marriage he wrote the fragment ending with the lines that the hills of Annesley would no more be a heaven to him as he would no longer see his Mary smiling there.

The pathos of some of the poems in his early book should have softened the hardened heart of the Edinburgh reviewer who attacked it. There is something really sad in the stanzas of the poem "The Tear."

> *Though my vows I can pour to my Mary no more,*
> *My Mary to love once so dear;*
> *In the shade of her bower I remember the hour*
> *She rewarded these vows with a Tear.*
>
> *By another possessed, may she live ever blest!*
> *Her name still my heart must revere;*
> *With a sigh I resign what I once thought was mine,*
> *And forgive her deceit with a Tear.*

The story of his lost love figures in many poems, some with her name and some with another name substituted. One of the best of these is the poem "To a Lady" beginning with the line, "Oh! had my fate been linked with thine."

This not altogether immature volume foreshadowed a writer of excellent poems that have become part of English and world literature dealing with the emotions of disprized love.

Byron's love poems concerned with Mary's rejection continued until he left for the continent in the summer of 1809. The poem "When We Two Parted" and the poems published in 1809 in John C. Hobhouse's *Imitations and Translations*, "Remind Me Not"; "When Man Expelled from Eden's Bowers"; "Well, Thou Art Happy"; "And Wilt Thou Weep I Am Low" and "There Was a Time I Need Not Name" are well known in English literature. On leaving England he wrote the poem "Stanzas to a Lady on Leaving England" and reiterates at the conclusion of each stanza that he can love only one.

Shortly after he returned to England he wrote on October 11, 1811 the poem "Epistle to a Friend" (Francis Hodgson) in answer to some lines exhorting the author to be "Cheerful and to banish Care." He commemorates here a meeting with Mary and states the effect upon him in seeing her child. "I've seen my bride another's bride," he announces, "I'll whine no more, nor seek again an eastern shore." This seems to imply that he had made that pilgrimage of two years before to forget Mary.

The love for Mary had been thought by some students of Byron's work—including myself—to have lasted all his life, but this cannot be true, for after Byron's great poem "The Dream" in 1816, she does not appear directly although her name "Mary" is mentioned by him as one that he loved. Even John Murray believed, and I mistakenly followed him, that the poem "Stanzas to the Po" (1819) was addressed to Mary Chaworth and not as we now know to Countess Teresa Guicciola, Byron's last love. I disagree with Ethel Colburn Mayne who treats the affair with Mary lightly as if it were of no significance in the poet's life.

One of the reasons that Byron gives for his wanting to marry Mary was that some old wounds would be healed, since an ancestor of hers was run through the body in a duel in 1765 by his grand-uncle William, the Fifth Lord Byron, called "The Wicked Lord." Byron the poet was the Sixth Lord. The duel was over a trifle and William, Lord Byron was found guilty of manslaughter and finally escaped punishment. His brother, grandfather of the poet, was the Admiral John, "Foul Weather Jack," who died before the poet was born.

A story is told of Byron's great love for Washington Irving's sketch "The Broken Heart" and his weeping two months before his death, after an American read it to him at his request. What is singular is that this poet who had his own heart broken in youth ruthlessly broke the hearts of several women, Lady Caroline Lamb, his wife, and two mistresses, Mariana Segati and Margarita Cogni, both married women. Caroline Lamb and Margarita Cogni tried to commit suicide when he abandoned them. He fathered an illegitimate child of Clare Clermont before he finally left England in 1816.

His real love affair was with the Countess Teresa Guiccioli during the last five years of his life. Her influence was a very conscious one and I do not go into this.

My purpose has been to show that Byronism originated in the poet's rejection by Mary Chaworth and in his unconscious choice of her as a substitute for the mother love he did not have. True, poems about rejected love have been written by the hundreds of people from time immemorable, but Byron gave his a new note, one perhaps not altogether commendable, a whining one with a hostility towards the world and contempt for humanity. His influence was responsible for some very bad poetry produced by disappointed women. However it also inspired some very excellent love poetry, notably Heine's and Musset's.

I think we may dispense with the theory that Byron was a poseur, that his passion was unreal, and that he was only rhetorical. His melancholia was genuine. He really suffered from semi-hysteria, which had its origin in lack of mother love and in the repression of his first three loves, especially the one with Mary. One thing we can say of nearly all his love poems, they awoke responses in the hearts of thousands; we must concede that they were genuine.

A critic has demanded of me proof that the poet's Byronism was the result of the ill-treatment he received from his mother and his rejection by Mary Chaworth. It seems to me that the unconscious quest for a substitute for mother love and an early and deep lasting repression are proof enough, if Freud's principles are valid at all. By writing poems lamenting his sorrows he finally did (to some extent) cure himself of the malady of Byronism, as it has been called, from which he suffered; he sublimated, as Goethe did before him, his love into artistic lyrics and so purged himself. He finally won a completely satisfying love in Countess Guiccioli, and Byronism disappears from his late work altogether. The artist had developed the mature man.

3

Freud has told us that the idea of repression is the main pillar on which the theory of psychoanalysis rests. There has been at some time in the patient's life a serious inhibition of some desire. There are different kinds of repression, the most serious of which have a sexual basis. But the denying oneself of the play of any emotions that seek an outlet, constitutes a repression.

Sex with Freud means love in its broadest sense. The most common repression is the inability to satisfy one's love, either because the person has not met any object upon whom to lavish his affection, or if such an individual is found there is no reciprocation, or if the love is given it is later withdrawn. All these factors act in a repressive manner upon a person. For it must be understood that not only the stinting of sexual satisfaction, but the interference with all those finer emotions associated with it, cause a repression in the subject. When the emotions have been satisfied for a long time, and then there is a sudden cessation through change of heart or infidelity or death of the beloved one, the repression is very serious. It is this kind of repression that has produced most of the literature of the world.

But repression includes the stinting or uprooting of any emotion. Great grief as the result of the death of any one we love of either sex, whether friend or relative, is a repression. The death of a loved one puts the sufferer in a worse position than the man who has been stinted in a great love passion. And the great elegies in literature have been cries of poets because of the death of fellow writers. *Lycidas, Adonais, In Memoriam* and *Thyrsis* are examples. The authors here suffered repressions in the loss of brother poets.

The grief which seems to be the greatest of all, that following on the death of a beloved child, is an instance of the most intense repression on the part of a parent. Here there is nothing really sexual, but the death of a child and the consequent agony to the parents is a far greater repression than any purely sexual one. Hugo's famous elegies on the death of his daughter which appear in *The Contemplations* are among the greatest poems of this kind. In America we have had a few poems by Lowell, and a famous elegy by Emerson, "The Threnody," in which the loss of children is mourned.

If there were no repression, there would be little literature.

The varieties of repressions are as numerous as the emotions to which we are subject. For the inability to satisfy any emotion is a repression; the deprivation of an emotion long gratified, the conquering of a habit or the struggle for activity of a partially extinct emotion, are repressions. The feeling of loneliness or homesickness, which has given rise to much good literature, shows repressed emotion. The wish to wreak revenge or to punish evil or to do away with injustice or to devote oneself to the following of an ambition or the pursuit of a certain kind of labor, are all symptoms of repressions.

4

Psychoanalysis starts with the assumption that the entire past in a man's life, beginning with the first day of his birth, is always with him and is really never forgotten. That which has seemed to pass out of the haunts of memory, has become part of our unconscious, and is often revived in dreams. Nothing is really ever forgotten. De Quincey understood this and discourses on the subject in his *Confessions of an Opium Eater* and thus anticipates an important modern psychological discovery.

Longfellow said, "Let the dead past bury its dead." Ah, if it only could! Ghosts of sorrows and griefs that we thought laid away still revisit us even in our waking hours. They stalk before us and open up closed wounds and we learn that these are not yet healed. They awaken memories of agonies that again smite us; they make us hearken back to unkind words dealt us, to suffering inflicted, to injustice done. Shocks which time had made obtuse are revived; we reap the harvest of anxieties garnered in our hearts; and we discover that the old despair has not altogether vanished but still occasionally gnaws us.

The dead rules the living; forgotten incidents, soul-wrecking mistakes, chance misfortunes still dominate us. We recall the mortification of a decade or two ago and as its details are resurrected, we again live through the madness of past years. Prejudices are thus built up, unreasonable indeed. We become averse to a face that reminds us of a countenance belonging to a person who troubled us.

The old poverty still haunts us in our present prosperity; memories of unpleasant toil in the past may make us shrink in terror in our newly found leisure or congenial labor. Mark Twain describes how in his prosperity he would dream that he had to return to the hated lecture platform or that he was again a pilot on the Mississippi River. Past solitude may still send its roots down to the present and leave us lonely in society. He who has known a starved body or many unfulfilled desires, he who has been the victim of ridicule or persecution or never before been encouraged or sympathized with, remembers the past only too well, even when the world honors him with recognition.

Impressions are strongest in youth and hence molest us in old age. The finer our nerves, the less easy is it to forget. The mother who has lost a child cannot forget the misfortune even after other children are born.

It is life's grimmest tragedy that we carry within us ghosts of our old days—ghosts which take us by surprise with their vigor. They mock us at their will; we are tormented unawares; we travel about with them and cannot shake them off. They stand beside us when we love; they take the savor out of our food; they dangle at our footsteps when we go to the house of mirth; they trail us in ghastly pursuit long after we have emerged from the house of mourning. Hence when the poet sings and the philosopher speculates, when the storyteller gives us a tale, unconsciously those old ghosts are with him and get between the lines of his writings. An unseen spirit seems to move his pen and he tells more than he had desired and he gives voice to emotions that he had sought to suppress or regarded as long since buried in a sepulchre that was impenetrable. But the dead passions and tear-stained griefs come gliding forth and pierce all barriers and dictate to him. They even wish to be remembered, to be made as enduring in art as in life. They never weary of uttering their sentiments; they pursue the human race to eternity. And when we read of the troubles of man whether in the Bible or the *Iliad*, they are familiar often to us because they are our own. The author cannot escape the past and he always opens up more channels of his heart than he has suspected. His work shows that his old sorrows rise up like the phoenix from its own ashes. The fires that were thought smouldering are lighted and we as readers are caught in the flames and are purged in them.

Psychoanalysis tries to rid us of the evil influences of the past by making us aware of the unconscious disturbances.

Chapter 10

The Infantile Love Life of the Author and its Sublimations

1

THOSE who are familiar with the theories of Freud are aware that one of his most important discoveries is that the child before the age of puberty has a sex or love life of its own. As he puts it, it is absurd to imagine that sex enters suddenly at the age of puberty just as the devils in the New Testament were supposed to enter the swine. Freud regards the child's sucking of its thumb as a manifestation of infantile sexuality. In his *Three Contributions to the Theory of Sex* he studies the sexual life of the child. The studies of Moll, Havelock Ellis, and Helgemuth confirm Freud's views.

The theory shows that the nature of our later emotional and especially our love life is far more dependent upon the nature, aberrations, inhibitions, sublimations, developments and transformations of our infantile sex life, than we ever in our wildest dreams imagined it to be. Here in childhood are laid the seeds of our future emotional life. Early repression or seduction or bad training influences our later lives. These facts are recognized by many trained parents who refuse to overfondle their children or to do anything that may awaken sexual activity too prematurely.

Freud's idea is of value to the literary critic for it shows that the characteristics of an author's work may be traced back to his infantile sex life. As a rule we know little about the lives of literary men when they were children, but we can often judge what the infantile sex life must have been from the traits appearing in the writers' literary performances.

Inversion or homosexuality can be traced to the child's love life. As infants we are bi-sexual in our pre-dispositions. Children display sentimental friendships for members of their own sex, as we all know. Even in later life in each sex there are remnants of the other stunted sex, breasts on the man and hairy faces on women. Freud has given us a very interesting but by no means full explanation of the origin of inversion.

The abnormal development is favored by the disappearance of a strong father in early childhood, and by the over-attachment to the mother at the same or earlier time. The love for the mother is soon repressed and the boy identifies himself with her and loves other boys like himself. He returns to that self-love which is a second stage after auto-eroticism in the infant, and is known as narcissism. He wishes to love those boys as his mother has loved him. He may like women but he transfers the excitation evoked by them to a male object, for they remind him of his mother and he flees from them in order to be faithful to her. He repeats through life the mechanism by which he became an invert.

The fact then is that homosexualism is an abnormal development from the infant's love life. It is the germ in all normal people, especially in those capable of intense friendships. It is naturally abhorrent to us when it vents itself in any abnormal relations.

The sublimated homosexualism which we find in literature is that which gives way to outbursts of friendly devotion, and intense and passionate grief at the loss of a friend; it is at the root of the idea that a man should lay his life down for his friend. Then there is the real inversion which the world rightly stamps as immoral.

A few examples of literature where the homosexualism of the author's unconscious is present are Shakespeare's *Sonnets* and Whitman's *Calamus*. These works show what capacities their authors had for friendship. But they do not indicate homosexual practice. Whitman wrote to John Addington Symonds in response to an enquiry about the "Calamus" poems that he would prefer never to have written them if they gave any one the inference that he either practised or tolerated homosexualism.

Two poets of recent years who, we know, practised homosexualism, each of whom also served jail terms, were Paul Verlaine and Oscar Wilde. There were critics who saw that certain passages in Wilde's novel *The Picture of Dorian Gray*, published about five years before he went to jail, pointed to the homosexual proclivities of the author. His curious interpretation of Shakespeare's sonnets also shows these. It is possible that some of the love poems written by Verlaine and which are supposed to be addressed to women were really written to Arthur Rimbaud, the poet he loved. This is a practice indulged in by homosexual poets to avoid suspicion.

The classic stories of ideal friendship are those of David and

Jonathan, and Damon and Pythias; the most widely known essays in ancient literature discussiong homosexual love as a legitimate pursuit are in the dialogues on love by Plutarch and by Plato. Theocritus and the *Greek Anthology* authors refer to homosexual love. Homosexualism was a blot upon Greek as well as Roman civilization.

The only interest the subject has for the psychoanalytic critic of literature is in tracing the connection between the works of authors where homosexual remnants in the form of extreme friendships are present and their infantile sex life.

Freud's monograph on Leonardo da Vinci is the best study we have of a homosexual artist.

It appears then that the bisexual tendency which is in infancy in all of us, in later life may lead, where it does not become absolutely normal, to actual homosexuality, or to a sublimation of this early inverse tendency; one of the manifestations of this sublimation being literary products in which friendship is exalted.

2

There are other perverts whose vices in later life can be traced to the infantile sex life. These are sadists, masochists, exhibitionists, and voyeurs. The child's sex life takes place through the pleasures which it creates for itself in the erogenous zones, which are sensitive areas in any part of the body. It gratifies itself mainly on its own body; it is autoerotic. But grown up as the youth, it derives pleasure through other persons as sexual objects. There are also components or partial impulses, which are: for causing cruelty to others (sadistic), for deriving pleasure from pain to itself (masochistic), for showing itself shamelessly (exhibitionistic), and for peeping at others in a nude state (the voyeur's instinct). As a rule these impulses are sublimated very early, but if they persist the perversions govern the individuals for the rest of their lives. Where they are sublimated we have as a result some of the most essential features of our modern cultural institutions.

The child who continues shameless for a few years may become very vain, and as an author write indecent literature. The child who was cruel may later in life love contests and competitions, and write books where cruel scenes or virulent abuse of people abound. The infant who derived pleasure from pain inflicted on it may be interested in solving intricate problems that as a man annoy him with a demand for solution, and he will torture himself in solving them. He also may be a conformist and find pleasure in crucifying himself upon the rack of the church and the state and the home; or become a martyr for an idea. As a writer he would depict martyrs or indulge in self-commiseration.

Literature shows sublimations of these impulses and also gives evidences of the authors' perverse tendencies where these impulses have not been sublimated; they may contrive to exist or be buried in the unconscious.

There are many literary men who have been perverse in their tendencies in later life without knowing it. Often the man who merely thinks he is fighting Puritanism in art when he shows a tendency to describe the nude only, or to describe people in compromising positions, is both an exhibitionist and voyeur. These impulses have been suppressed in him by civilization and he finds an outlet for his unconscious by his art. Such literature is not so much immoral as indecent. A literary man may become an exhibitionist in his work so as to give play to an impulse he cannot otherwise gratify. A writer may write exhibitionistic books for money or to attract attention or for fun, but his work shows that psychologically he has never completely suppressed the exhibitionistic or peeping tendencies of his childhood. Like the child he is without shame. The feature of the cheap and lascivious literature that is written merely to pander to certain tastes is in these traits.

But the traits of the exhibitionist and voyeur are found more or less in much of the good literature of the world. In the cases of works, however, like the *Arabian Nights*, Rabelais, Chaucer, the novels of Sterne, Fielding, and many others where great genius, intellect, and honesty are displayed, the liberal minded critic is willing to smile and pass over these exhibitionistic blemishes. In the cases of the older works these are due to the general looseness in speech of the times.

The application of psychoanalytic methods puts then in a new light much of the so-called immoral literature. In much of the indecent comic literature, like the Restoration dramatists, Balzac's *Droll Tales*, Boccaccio's *Decameron* and La Fontaine's *Tales*, the object is to arouse laughter by making a person accidentally exhibit himself. The author still finds an outlet for his repressed exhibitionalism. There is a distinction between this literature and the "immoral" literature of a writer like Ibsen, who merely differs with the current morality and questions it, and who therefore seems immoral to the conventional man.

Again there is a distinction between exhibitionism in literature and real immoral literature, where an author tries, for example, to defend sexual crimes like rape or seduction.

Exhibitionism then as we find it in literary men points to infantile practices that were never completely suppressed and are finding an outlet. It is true, other motives may enter into the work. There may be a disgust on the part of the writer at his fellowmen's hypocritical and prudish standards of modesty and shame, and he may write to counteract these. But the exhibitionism of writers like Apuleius and Petronius, does not interfere with the artistic value of their works.

Another form of sublimation of exhibitionistic traits leads to works in which the author is always boasting or showing off, directly or indirectly. Sometimes the sublimation process is not complete and we have examples of the exhibitionistic traits alongside of the egotism. The reader will at once think of Montaigne's *Essays* and Rousseau's *Confessions*, two of the greatest works in the world's literature. Among ancients two of the vainest men were Cicero and Caesar, whose writings show that exhibitionistic traits of their infancy were strong.

We here may consider the effects of infantile sexual investigation. Freud says its activity labors with the desire for looking, though it cannot be added to the elementary components of the impulses. Many reader may refuse to follow Freud here, where he concludes that the great desire for knowledge in later life may be traced to this infantile sexual curiosity. But that there must be some connection cannot be doubted. A child who has never displayed any curiosity as to where it came from must be one in whom the desire for knowledge has not been and probably never will be strongly developed. The child is father of the student man. Freud asserts in his study of Leonardo da Vinci that there are three sublimations in later life of this curiosity, the most important and rarest being where a pure scientific investigation replaces the sexual activity and is not occupied with sexual themes. Thus he explains the scientific work of Leonardo and his chaste life.

3

Let us consider the other two partial impulses, sadism and masochism, noted by Freud, and note their effect on the literary work of a man in later life.

"The repression of the sadistic impulse," says Dr. H. W. Frink, "produces not its annihilation but merely its transfer from consciousness to unconsciousness. And there, withheld from the neutralizing influence of conscious reasoning, the impulse and the phantasies derived from it are not only preserved without deterioration but may even grow in vigor and intensity. Thus, despite the fact that in many instances the individual's conscious life is apparently singularly irreproachable, nevertheless this life is lived coincidently with an undercurrent of impulses of anger, hate, hostility and revenge and their corresponding phantasies." [1]

This would account for the tales of horror we find in Poe, Kipling, and Jack London. Today we do not always assault or kill our enemies. Literary men do so by depicting scenes in literature where this is done. Jack London describes fist fights in which he is always defeating his enemies. It is said that in real life he boasted of his abilities as a fighter.

Pfister, in his *Psychoanalytic Method,* formulates a law from an earlier work of his, as follows: "The repressed hate of certain individuals forms phantasies out of suitable contents of experiences, either actual or imaginary, according to the laws of the dream-work, by which procedure it creates for itself imaginary gratification. This gratification of complex comes about through the mechanism of a disguised wish, directed towards the injury of the hated person, being represented in the content of the waking dream as realized."

This explains the literature of hatred and how authors come to put their enemies in books and poems. Such works are traceable to the sex sadistic instincts of childhood. We find sadism in books reeking with curses. Ovid's *Ibis*, directed against the person who was to blame for his exile, is a good example; it is one of the most bitter invectives in literature. We also understand now the significance of the imaginary punishments inflicted by an author upon his enemies. The severe chastisement inflicted by Dante in his *Inferno* upon his enemies represents the poet's wishes carried out in his imagination to gratify him for his inability to fulfil his repressed hatred.

Literature abounds in hostile and satirical portrayals of the author's enemies. In ancient Greece we have many examples, the best known probably being the caricature of Socrates by Aristophanes, in the *Clouds.*

Elizabethan literature, especially the drama, gives us portrayals of fellow authors. Ben Jonson attacked the dramatists Marston and Decker in *The Poetaster* (1601), and they retaliated in *Satiromastix.* The most familiar example in English

[1] *Morbid Fears and Compulsions,* p. 291.

literature of an abuse of enemies is Pope's *Dunciad*. Then we have Byron's poem "The Sketch" directed at the maid he considered responsible for his wife's desertion of him, and Shelley's bitter diatribe "To the Lord Chancellor" against Lord Eldon, whose decree deprived the poet of his two children. Richard Savage's poem "The Bastard" against his alleged mother for neglecting him, her illegitimate son, is not as well known as it used to be. An author who was past master at the art of lampooning his enemies was Heine, and his attacks on Count Platen in the *Pictures of Travel* are among the most bitter in literature. All these attacks follow one principle; the author finds an outlet of his repressed hatred, and the desire for vengeance not being always possible in a physical sense, in modern times gives rise to phantasies of vindictiveness. The sadistic impulses of childhood are the sources of such literary works.

Take the portrayal of Thersites in the second book of the *Iliad*. This notorious character was surely some real person whom the author knew and despised and on whom he wreaked vengeance by drawing him. He was some man of Homer's own time, centuries after the Trojan War, and his type is as common today as it was in the days of Homer. The poet no doubt felt a grievance against some prattler and nonentity he knew, and pilloried the man for posterity; the personal note appears throughout the whole passage. Thersites is described as ill-favored beyond all men, bandy-legged, lame, round-shouldered, largely bald. He tries to rebuke his betters, and Odysseus admonishes him severely, calling him most base of the Greeks, telling him not to have the names of kings in his mouth and threatening to strip and beat him. Thersites received a welt on the back and sat down, crying. Then notice how Homer puts his personal feelings still more into the mouth of the Greek who laughed and said that Odysseus had done many great deeds but this is the best he had done in that he had stayed this prating railer. Homer thus punished some man he did not like. It is rather odd that those who maintain the theory of the impersonality of the epic poem do not apply a little knowledge of human nature in studying literature, as this is often of more value than scholarship.

Lists may be compiled of nineteenth century novels, where the authors drew their enemies as villains. Often these are fellow authors. Dostoevsky put Turgenev into *The Possessed* in an unamiable light, under the character Karmanzinoff. George Sand introduced lovers of hers with whom she had parted in her novels, and Chopin and De Musset have been drawn by her for us. Balzac righted his grievance against his critic Jules Janin by putting him in the *Young Provincial in Paris*. The motive of vengeance figures considerably in literature, though at times a malevolent mischievous instinct drives the author on, as when Dickens drew Leigh Hunt under the character of Harold Skimpole in *Bleak House*. Sadistic instincts are of course primitive, and where in ancient times a man might have put his enemy out of existence, today he can kill him only in imagination. The man does not have to be a personal enemy, but may be some character in real life who represents an idea or follows a course of conduct that the author thinks reprehensible. Demosthenes, Cicero, Milton, Swift, and the author of the Junius letters knew how to castigate their enemies. Hugo's attacks on Napoleon in his *Chatiments* and *Napoleon the Little* are among the most bitter in literature.

An excellent analysis of hatred is found in Hazlitt's *Pleasure of Hating*, where he shows hatred is a real instinct and needs satisfaction—it is a remnant of savage days. Hazlitt's attack on Gifford presents many opportunities for the study of the psychology of hatred.

There are cases of sublimated sadism in practically all literature where pain is described. The author displays a craving to see people suffer even where he sympathizes with them and he satisfies that craving by drawing them in their agonies. Take Flaubert's keen interest in describing the torture and sufferings physically inflicted on Salammbo's lover Matho. There is hardly anything more sadistic in literature than the conclusion of *Salammbo*.

Sadism is often sublimated into interest in contests. One of the most ancient examples we have of such sublimation is in some of Pindar's odes, where contests in Greek games are described and the victors praised. We have sadism, in fact, in all tales of competition where some one is vanquished.

The sadistic trait is the source of the glee with which people watch someone in a moving picture being beaten or hurt. It is the cause of the pleasure and interest we find in reading of executions, battles and physical suffering. There is nothing strange in tracing all this to the delight we had as children in torturing animals. This is a partial sexual impulse and is sublimated in most of us in later life and finds expression in our literature.

It is held that masochism is usually found side by side with sadism. Literature is also rich in sublimated masochism. Many authors are apparently only happy in their woe. They find delight in torturing themselves and in recounting their sufferings. Many of them were not as unhappy as they persuaded us to believe. The whole school of woe that had its origin in Rousseau and that was prominent in the early decades of the nineteenth century was full of sublimated masochism. Hence it has been called insincere. Byron and Chateaubriand were regarded, though not justly, as affecting woes they never really felt. Some of the sonneteers who imitated the Italians before and even during the Elizabethan period wrote about woes they never felt. This was, however, not the usual process, and the greatest Elizabethan sonneteers like Shakespeare, Spenser, and Sidney described real sorrows.

Another phase of sublimated masochism is the attempt to torture one's self to solve puzzles and problems, and vex one's self more for the sheer delight in unravelling difficult situations than for the pursuit of knowledge. Note how children like to solve puzzles in newspapers. Poe, who had the sadistic instinct in sublimation, also had the masochistic impulse. We are familiar with his interest in reading cryptograms and with his paper on the subject. We remember his essays on studying persons' characters from their autographs. His stories of ratiocination like "The Gold-Bug," "The Murder in the Rue Morgue," and "The Purloined Letter" are examples of sublimated masochism. His Dupin, the detective, is an example of a man who likes to annoy himself. Sherlock Holmes is the best known modern example. Indeed the interest in tales of mystery and detective stories shows the power of the masochistic instinct in human nature.

Still another example of sublimated masochism is found in stories and plays where the idea of self sacrifice and penance figures. Dante's *Purgatorio* is a good illustration of the author's masochistic tendencies as the *Inferno* is of his sadism. He who tortures himself whether to follow the laws of society or to fight them is masochistic. Hence the tales of martyrs and heroes and idealists all betray the sublimated masochistic impulse. Both the rebel and the conformist, because they embrace torture, one might say almost willingly (though they really cannot help it), are masochistic. All literature describing these types shows that the author has a keen interest in suffering, and is the result, if Freud is right, of the author's infantile delight in suffering, which became later sublimated.

Rousseau describes the pleasure he received from beatings, and this masochism is seen in his *Confessions*, where he tells us of his woes with apparent enjoyment.

All this is significant. Freud says: "Children who are distinguished for evincing special cruelty to animals and playmates may justly be suspected of intensive and premature sexual activity in the erogenous zones; and in a simultaneous prematurity of all sexual impulses, the erogenous sexual activity surely seems to be primary. The absence of the barrier of sympathy carries with it the danger that the connections between cruelty and erogenous impulses formed in childhood cannot be broken in later life." [2]

There is then a connection between the sadism and masochism of early infancy which is related to sex, and the sublimations in art of those impulses. People who can hate fiercely or are vindictive or have a tendency towards cruelty or who like to torture themselves have as a rule strong sex impulses.

4

There are other phases of infantile sexual life that rule a person for life. One of these is that stage between the first period of the child's sex life known as autoeroticism when it finds pleasure in its own body, and the period when it selects an object to love apart from itself. This stage is called narcissism because then the child loves itself. Many people never grow out of this; we are all more or less narcisstic. This narcissim is the basis of egoism in literature and is no doubt related to extreme individualism. Stirner, Nietzsche, and Stendhal, who rank intellectually among the greatest writers the world has had, are often narcisstic.

Walt Whitman would be a good subject for study of the manner in which infantile narcisstic sex life is sublimated in later life into individualism.

The following are passages from the "Song of Myself," showing that the narcisstic infantile life of Whitman was sublimated into good poetry and philosophy:

> *While they discuss I am silent, and go bathe and admire myself.*
> *Welcome is every organ and attribute of me, and of any man hearty and clean,*

[2] *Three Contributions to the Sexual Theory of Sex*—p. 54.

Not an inch nor a particle of an inch is vile, and none
  shall be less familiar than the rest . . . .
Having pried through the strata, analysed to a hair,
  counsel'd with doctors and calculated close,
I find no sweeter fat than sticks to my own bones. . . .
Divine am I, inside and out, and I make holy whatever I
  touch or am touch'd from,
The scent of these arm-pits aroma finer than prayer,
The head more than churches, bibles and all creeds.
If I worship one thing more than another it shall be the
  spread of my body, or any part of it,
Translucent mould of me it shall be you! . . .
I dote on myself, there is that lot of me and all so luscious.

His early narcissism did not lead him into selfishness but taught him self-respect.

He says in the "Song of Myself":

I chant the chant of dilation or pride;
We have had ducking and deprecating about enough. . . .
I am an acme of things accomplished and an encloser of
  things to be. . . .

In "By Blue Ontario's Shore, he writes:

It is not the earth, it is not America who is so great,
It is I who am great or to be great, it is you up there or
  any one. . . .
Underneath all, individuals,
I swear nothing is good to me now that ignores individ-
  uals. . . .
The whole theory of the universe is directed unerringly to
  one single individual—namely to You. . . .
I will confront these shows of the day and night,
I will know if I am to be less than they. . . .
I will see if I have no meaning, while the houses and ships
  have meaning.

The following lines from "I Sing the Body Electric" is another example:

O my body! I dare not desert the likes of you in other men
  and women, nor the likes of the parts of you,

*I believe the likes of you are to stand or fall with the likes
    of the soul (and that they are the soul.)*
*I believe the likes of you shall stand or fall with my
    poems, and that they are my poems.*

Where Whitman shows sublimations of these infantile
phases he deduces important and profound views of life to
make us happier. He questions whether the giving up of some
of the heritages we surrendered to cultural demands has not
made us also part with some valuable emotions and whether
we have not denied ourselves rights we ought to resume. He
makes egoism respectable, and deduces individualism from it.

5

I also wish to mention that sexual aberration, in which an
object unfit for the sexual aim is substituted for the normal
one, and is known as fetishism. We need not go into the causes
of it, but psychoanalysis has shown that smell plays a part. We
often find poets celebrating the eyebrows, the gloves, and other
objects connected with the women they love. Though a certain
amount of fetishism is normal in love, literature gives us instances where it amounts to an aberrated passion in the
author. There is much fetishism in Gautier's stories, where he
dwells on the fetichistic characteristics of his heroes in whom
he describes himself. Then those poems where the sparrows
and dogs of the beloved are described as if the author were in
love with them bcause of their associations, those tales where
too much attention is given to the dress of the heroines, all
have fetichistic traces.

A phase of sex life in the child that is significant for the
future is the sublimation that occurs in the sexual latency
period between the third and fifth year, when the sentiments
of shame, loathing and morality appear. These are reaction
formations to the perverse tendencies of infancy. They are
brought about at the cost of the infantile sexuality itself. These
sublimations take place in the beginning in this latency period,
and if they do not occur there is an abnormal development and
the result is the latter perversions of life. When we say a man
has no moral sense, we mean not only that he does not know
the difference between right and wrong but that he is not dis-
gusted or shamed at sexual conduct that is held in abhorrence
by most people. Hence those authors who have this indifference to perverse moral conduct in their work, never as chil-

dren in the latency period developed shame or disgust. All this is again evidence of the influence of the sublimations in childhood upon later literary work and view points. Girls as a rule develop this sense of morality earlier than boys, and this no doubt accounts to some extent for the prudishness of some women writers.

It is no exaggeration then to say that the infantile sex life governs the psychology of the future writer and the nature and tendency of his work.

Chapter 11

Sexual Symbolism in Literature

1

THE REPRESSION of the libido includes the damming and clogging up of all the emotional concomitants that go with sexual attraction and make up the feeling called love. Whenever then sex or libido is referred to in psychoanalysis the word has the widest meaning. The man who loves a woman with the greatest affection and passion, without gratifying these, suffers a repression of the libido, as well as the man who satisfies certain proclivities without feeling any tenderness or love for the woman. In the emotion felt towards the other sex called love, in which admiration, respect, self-sacrifice, tenderness and other finer feelings play a great part, there is consciously or unconsciously, however, the physical attraction. If this is totally absent the emotion cannot be called "love." What differentiates our feelings towards one of the opposite sex from those felt for one of the same sex (assuming there are no homosexual leanings) is the presence of this sexual interest. Love then must satisfy a man physically as well as psychically. It is a concentration of the libido upon a person of the opposite sex, accompanied by tender feelings.

Hence when we read the most chaste love poem, we see what the underlying motive in the poet's unconscious is. He may write with utter devotion to the loved one and express a wish to die for her, and though he says nothing about physical attraction, we all know that it is there in his unconscious. It is taken for granted that a man who writes a real love poem to a girl wants to enjoy her love. And when the poet complains because he is rejected or deceived, or of something interfering with the course of his love, we are aware also that his unconscious is grieved because his union is impeded or entirely precluded. The suffering is greater the more he loves, for his finer instincts, as well as his passion, are prevented from being fulfilled.

Let us take at random a few innocent poems and test the theory. There is Ben Jonson's well known toast, "Drink to me only with thine eyes." He tells how he sent Celia a rose wreath, that she breathed on it and sent it back to him. "Since when it grows, and smells, I swear, Not of itself but thee." Odor is an important feature, it is well known, in sexual attraction. In this poem the poet, after having received the returned rose breathed upon by Celia smells her perfume, whoch now submerges the natural fragrance of the rose. In other words the Poet's unconscious says that he wishes to possess Celia physically. He is talking symbolically in the poem.[1]

There is the song in Tennyson's "The Miller's Daughter," beginning "It is the miller's daughter." The poet says naïvely enough that he would like to be the jewel in her ear in order to touch her neck, the girdle about her waist ("I'd clasp it round so close and tight"), and the necklace upon her balmy bosom to fall and rise; "I would lie so light, so light." The unconscious sexual feelings here are only too apparent. The symbols of the earring, girdle, and necklace are unmistakable. The poet is saying in a symbolical manner that he would possess the miller's daughter.

Moreover one may see the sex motive in poems where it does not seem to appear. If certain facts in an author's life are known, we may discern the unconscious love sentiments in poems where no mention seems to be made of them. Let me illustrate with a fine poem by Longfellow, the familiar "The Bridge." Take the lines

> *How often, O how often,*
> *I had wished that the ebbing tide*
> *Would bear me away in its bosom*
> *O'er the ocean wild and wide!*
>
> *For my heart was hot and restless,*
> *And my life was full of care,*
> *And the burden laid upon me*
> *Seemed greater than I could bear.*
>
> *But now it has fallen from me, etc.*

To the student of Longfellow, this poem speaks of the time he found it difficult to win the love of his second wife, Frances Appleton, love for whom he confessed in his novel *Hyperion*, where he drew her and himself. This story was published before she had as yet reciprocated his love. He married her July 13, 1843. He finished the poem October 9, 1845. At the end

[1] This interpretation is not affected by the fact that the poem is based on a Greek original.

of this year he wrote in his diary that now he had love fulfilled
and his soul was enriched with affection. He is therefore thinking of the time when he had no love and longed for it, and now
that he has it, he is thinking of the love troubles of others. In
the olden days he wanted to be carried away by the river
Charles, for his long courtship, seemingly hopeless, made his
heart hot and restless and his life full of care. So we see that
in this poem the poet was thinking of something definite, relating to love (and hence also sex), though there is no mention
of either in the poem.

It is well known that all love complaints are the cries of the
Jack who cannot get his Jill; or who has lost the possibility of
love happiness by desertion, deception, or death.

Read that fine and pathetic Scotch ballad, beginning "O
waly, waly up the bank." The girl (or woman) has been forsaken by her lover and expects to become a mother. She longs
for death. She complains about the cruelty of love grown cold;
she recalls the happy days. Her unconscious sentiment is that
her lover will never give her spiritual happiness or satisfy her
craving. Her life is empty. The poem was based on an actual
occurrence. It contains all the despair of love that was once
given and then withdrawn.

> *O wherefore should I busk my hear,*
> *Or wherefore should I kame hy hair?*
>
> *When we came in by Glasgow town*
> *We were a comely sight to see;*
> *My love was clad in the black velvet*
> *And I myself in cramasie.*

She does not want to dress herself gorgeously now as she has
no lover. Among other great love wails by a woman are the
old Saxon elegy "A Woman's Complaint" and the second Idyl
of Theocritus.

All the pain of frustrated love is due to the repressing of the
tender as well as of the physical emotions, to the damming up
of the libido, which is love in its broadest sense.

Sometimes the poets tell us almost plainly their real loss, or
suggest it in such a manner that we feel the thought has become conscious in the poem. Read in Tennyson's "Locksley
Hall" the fifteen lines beginning, "Is it well to wish thee
happy," and one can see that the victim is suffering because
Amy is in another's embrace rather than in that of the sing-

er's. He thinks with maddening thoughts of the clown she married.

> *He will hold thee, when his passion shall have spent its*
> *novel forces,*
> *Something better than his dog, a little dearer than his*
> *horse.*

He calls sarcastically upon Amy to kiss her husband and take his hand. "He will answer to the purpose." The singer clearly shows his pain because he has been cheated out of physical pleasure.

When we come to the decadent poets, the loss is sung plainly. One of the most beautiful poems of this kind, is Dowson's poem to Cynara. The poem is frankly sexual. The poet, who was rejected by a restaurant keeper's daughter, tries to console himself with another woman for his loss. The words "I have been faithful to thee, Cynara, in my fashion" mean he loves her in others. He tries to satisfy himself partly by thinking he is with her while he is with another. It is a poem showing how a sexual repression seeks an outlet with some one who did not arouse it and how the poet forces himself to imagine that he is with the one who created it. The poem makes this clear, that a love poem is always a complaint that the libido is being dammed.

It is therefore true to say that even in the tenderest and sweetest love lyrics, like those of Burns and Shelley for instance, one sees the play of unconscious sexual forces. This fact does not make the poem any the less moral or the poet any the less pure.

2

Probably the greatest objection to the application of psychoanalytic methods to literature will be made to the transference of the sexual interpretation of symbols from the realm of dreams to that of art. But if the interpretation is correct in one sphere it is also true in the other. Civilization has made it necessary to refer in actual speech to sexual matters in hidden ways, by symbolic representations; our faculty of wit, due to the exercise of the censorship, also uses various devices of symbolization. Dreams and literature both make use of the same symbols.

When Freud attributed sexual significance to certain typical dreams like those of riding, flying, swimming, climbing, and to certain objects, like rooms, boxes, snakes, trees, burglars, etc., he made no artificial interpretations. He merely pointed out the natural and concrete language of the unconscious.

A similar interpretation should follow in literature, much as authors and readers may object. If flying in dreams is symbolic of sex, then an author who is occupied considerably with wishes to be a bird and fly or with descriptions of birds flying —I do not mean an isolated instance—is like the man who is always dreaming he is flying; he is unconsciously expressing a symbolical wish. Many poems written to birds in literature show unconscious sexual manifestations. Shelley's "To A Skylark," Keats's "To A Nightingale" and Poe's "The Raven" are poems where the authors sang of repressed love; there is unconscious sex symbolism in them.

Wordsworth, one of the poets who rarely mentioned sex, has in his "To a Skylark" unconsciously given us a poem of sexual significance. The motive of the poem is the intense longing to fly. But beneath the wish to fly in the poem, as in the imaginary flying in the dream, a sexual meaning is concealed. The poet is sad when he writes the poem "I have walked through wildernesses dreary, and today my heart is weary." He also thinks of the fact that the bird is satisfied in love. "Thou hast a nest for thy love and thy rest."

Very few of the poems addressed to birds harp on the wish to fly to the extent that Wordsworth does in this poem. Nearly half of the poem is taken up with this wish, and for this reason the sexual interpretation is unmistakable.

The first two stanzas are as follows:

> Up with me! up with me into the clouds!
> For thy song, Lark, is strong;
> Up with me, up with me into the clouds!
> Singing, singing,
> With clouds and sky about thee ringing,
> Lift me, guide me till I find
> That spot which seems so to thy mind!
>
> I have walked through wilderness dreary
> And today my heart is weary;
> Had I now the wings of a Fairy,
> Up to thee would I fly.
> There is madness about thee, and joy divine,

In that song of thine;
Lift me, guide me high and high
To thy banqueting place in the sky.

The wish in literature corresponds to the fulfillment in the dream and the psychology of the poet who wishes to fly is like that of the dreamer who does fly.

I quote from memory the chorus of a poem sung in my school days:

Oh, had I wings to fly like you
Then would I seek my love so true,
And never more we'd parted be,
But live and love eternally.

The author here tells us most plainly why he or she wants to fly like a bird—for the satisfaction of love. He is practically saying that merely flying like the bird, he would have the embrace of the loved one. The opening lines of the chorus show that it is no far-fetched idea, to see sex or love symbolism in birds flying or singing.

We recall Burns' famous poem to the bonny bird that sings happily and reminds him of the time when his love was true. "Thou'll break my heart, thou bonny bird," he sings in despair. A false lover stole the rose and left the thorn with him. The entire poem is full of sex symbolism. That he too would like to have love, is what he says when he speaks of the bird singing.

"The more one is occupied with the solution of dreams," says Freud, "the more willingly one must become to acknowledge that the majority of the dreams of adults treat of sexual material and give expression to erotic wishes. . . . No other impulse has had to undergo as much suppression from the time of childhood as the sex impulses in its numerous components; from no other impulse has survived so many and such intense unconscious wishes, which now act in the sleeping state in such a manner as to produce dreams."

This, to my mind, can not be contested, and these wishes appear largely in the form of symbols. In early times sex was given great significance, and we know that in old myths and literature many events and things were sex symbols. When we dream symbolically, we go back to a method of picturing events that in early history had value, but of which the significance has been forgotten. The law of symbol formation is in dreams not an arbitrary one; it is based on forms of speech in the past and on witty conceptions of today. Folklore and wit are full of sexual symbols corresponding to those in dreams. All doubt has been removed of sexual symbolism in dreams by an experiment made by means of hypnotism, where a patient was told to dream some sexual situation. Instead of doing so directly she dreamed a situation in symbolic form corresponding to that in ordinary dream life. Rank and Sachs in their *The Significance of Psychoanalysis for the Mental Sciences* have given us an excellent study of the nature of symbol formation. Freud has furnished us a list of objects and actions that are of sexual significance. W. Stekel has made an exhaustive study of the subject in his *Sprache des Traumes* (1911). Freud recognizes R. A. Scherner as the true discoverer of symbolism in dreams in his book *Das Leben des Traumes* (1896), but he admits that Artemidorus in the second century A.D. also interpreted dreams symbolically.

Freud ventures the opinion that dreams about complicated machinery and landscapes and trees have a definite sexual significance. If this is so, and he gives his reason therefore, it could mean that all those authors who have a partiality for describing landscapes and machinery in their works continually, are unconsciously revealing a personal trait they never intended to convey. Ruskin's work for example, is rich in landscapes. Is there any connection between his propensity for such descriptions and his attachment to his mamma, his youthful love disappointment, and his unsuccessful marriage? Is it not possible that many of the painters who made a specialty of landscape painting were driven to this special choice by an unconscious cause that the world has not fathomed, a sexual one? A colloquial designation for a woman's pubic hair is "the bushes." May Turgenev who has given us so many landscapes, not have been unconsciously thinking of his first love disappointment when he described them? We find landscapes in every literary work that deals with the country, but Freud's theory can have applicability only to the author who has a mania for them. I do not imply that landscapes may not be depicted in and for themselves without any sexual connotations.

Why does Kipling have a keen interest in bringing descriptions of machinery into his works? If dreams of machinery relate to sex, may we not follow the logical conclusion that an *undue* interest in machinery may evince a sexual meaning? We are also aware that a large number of colloquial sexual terms are taken from the machine shop, e.g. screw, plough, instrument, etc.

I do not maintain that objects do not have a literal significance, free from any symbolic intent.

There can be no doubt about the significance of the phallic worship of old times, in which the serpent was symbolic. Dreams where the serpent figures and folk tales telling of dragons are symbolic of the lustful side of man's nature.

Again, if Freud is right in claiming that the dream of a woman throwing herself in the water is a parturition dream, then one would have to conclude that a woman occupied constantly with stories about herself swimming was probably absorbed with thoughts about child-bearing. That this significance for such a dream is not absurd may be seen from the following statement by Freud: "In dreams, as in mythology, the delivery of a child from the uterine waters is commonly presented by distortion as the entry of the child into water; among many others, the births of Adonis, Osiris, Moses, and Bacchus are well known illustrations of this."

3

Freud was not the first one to interpret dreams symbolically. There have been excellent symbolical interpretations in literature. I shall mention one in Chaucer and another in Ovid.

In Chaucer's *Troilus and Criseyde*, one of the greatest love poems ever written and probably a greater work of art than any of the *Canterbury Tales*, there is a true symbolic interpretation of an anxiety dream. Troilus was pining for his love, Criseyde, who had been led back by Diomede to the Greeks in exchange for Antenor. Troilus dreamt that he saw a boar asleep in the sun and that Criseyde was embracing and kissing it. His suspicious of her faithfulness were confirmed by the interpretation given by his sister Cassandra, who told him that Criseyde now loved Diomede; Diomede was descended from Meleager the slayer of the boar, which, according to the myth, once ravaged the Greeks.

Chaucer throughout his works attacks the theory that dreams may be interpreted, but he gives us a true symbolical interpretation in this poem. He also here recorded unconsciously some of his own past griefs in love. Freud taught that anxiety dreams were due to the repression of the libido converted into fear. We also know from anthropology that the boar was a sexual symbol. In the poem Diomede appears to

Troilus as a boar, also, because Troilus had heard the story of Meleager and the boar and of the ancestry of Diomede. Even though he had forgotten the tale, if he did, since he was reminded of it by his sister, it was still present in his unconscious. His anxiety was due to the fear that Diomede had really won Criseyde. The fear that he experienced in daytime, that his sweetheart would be lost to him—the anxiety that his libido would be repressed, become an anxiety dream in which the boar is the symbol of his rival.

In the fifth elegy of the third book of Ovid's *Amores,* the author reports a symbolical dream of the loss of his love. It is correctly interpreted, in a Freudian manner, by an interpreter of dreams. The poet dreamed that he took shelter from the heat in a grove under a tree. He saw a very white cow standing before him, and her mate, a horned bull, near her chewing his cud. A crow pecked at the breast of the cow and took away the white hair. The cow left the spot; black envy was in her breast as she went over to some other bulls. The interpreter told Ovid that the heat which the poet was seeking to avoid was love, that the cow was his white-complexioned mistress and that he was the bull. The crow was a procuress who would tempt his mistress to desert him. The sexual symbolic interpretation shows that Freud's most unpopular idea was known among the Romans. It happened that Ovid's mistress did prove unfaithful to him, and he complained of the fact. His dream arose, however, from his day fears, and he had previously written a poem in the *Amores* against a procuress.

Ovid is one of the greatest love poets in all literature, and his Epistle of Sappho to Phaon in his *Heroides* translated by Pope records some of his own love griefs, though these are recorded in his *Amores* directly.

The symbolism that psychoanalysis deals with is that of the unconscious. Symbols may have the most significance when the dreamer or writer least suspects it. And it is only by the study of folklore, wit, and the neuroses that one gets to see their meaning.

No doubt the critic who examines literary masterpieces to find sexual symbols is not a popular one; but that does not alter the fact that the sexual meaning is there.

It will be seen that many writers who were deemed respectable and pure because they never deal with sexual problems are full of sex symbolism. They unconsciously strove to conceal their sex interest, but their unconscious use of sex symbolism shows that they were not as indifferent to the problems as they would lead us to imagine.

Browning rarely wrote directly of sex. He is admired justly by all lovers of literature; and women are among the most enthusiastic. It is well known that dreams of riding horseback, rocking, or any form of rhythmic motion through which the dreamer goes, are sexually symbolical. In older literature and in colloquial language "to ride" is used in a sexual sense. Browning has given us at least one poem full of sexual symbolism, his "The Last Ride Together." The speaker who is rejected asks his love to give him the pleasure of a last ride with her. Not being able to get love itself from her, he seeks it in another form, a vicarious one. He will now imagine that he receives love; he is prompted to his strange request by unconscious causes. He wants a substitute for the actuality. "We ride and I see her bosom heave," he says. Every stanza says something about riding. "I ride," "We ride," "I and she ride" are repeated throughout the poem. He addresses the poet, the sculptor, and the musician and tells them that he is riding instead of creating art; by this he means that they express their longing for love in art, he does so by riding: "Riding's a joy." He also lies to himself and pretends he is not angry at his mistress and that perhaps it was best he did not win her love; he pretends that he has no regrets for the past. The poem is an excellent example of the unconscious use of symbolism in literature. The meaning is clear.

4

I do not believe that the idea of nature worship in literature has been fully analyzed yet. Critics have refused to see the exact meaning of the expression "love of nature." Some poets, Wordsworth, for example, have told us that they saw in nature lessons for moral improvement and inspiration for humanitarianism. Granting that this is so, the fact still remains that there is much left unsaid by the poets. Some of them recognized the real significance of their love for nature when they told us how they were inspired by her to love, or were reminded of their lack of love.

Wordsworth, who is one of the greatest nature poets the world has ever had, appears singularly free from the expression of passion in his work. Except for the Lucy poems and a few others, he has given us little love poetry. Hazlitt complained that he found no marriages or giving in marriage in

Wordsworth's poetry. But nevertheless the sex element is there, although never directly expressed. There is nothing, it is well known, calculated to make a man long for the love of woman or to miss her more than when he is in the presence of nature. Anthropology teaches us the close connection between love and nature. When Wordsworth sang of the beauties and lessons of nature he was voicing a cry for satisfied love which he did not have up to his thirtieth year, when he married. He was also pining for love of the girl he met in France in his twenty-third year, the mother of his illegitimate daughter. The poet was using symbols, such as trees and daisies, whose glory he sang when he meant he wished he had love. Some things can be enjoyed alone, though not altogether, such as food, plays, pictures, reading, music, lectures, etc. It is the great distinction of nature that she inspires human love.

Most of the old bucolic poets frankly associated their Corydons and Amaryllises with enjoyment of nature. Wordsworth, who had much of the English Puritanism, was reserved. Any reader who takes up the nature poetry of Wordsworth lays it down after a while with the feeling that the poet is not telling the whole truth. It does not follow that Wordsworth was deliberately concealing it, for he may have been unaware of what was in his unconscious. After he married and had love he continued for a while to give us great nature poetry, for the most part a reflection of his early mood. For it must not be assumed that because a man has love he therefore loses his love for nature. Wordsworth's greatest nature poem "Lines Composed A Few Miles Above Tintern Abbey," was written before his marriage; the nature poetry of the last thirty or forty years of his life was rather poor.

The secret of Wordsworth's great nature poetry is this: it was a sublimation of his unsatisfied love cravings and a symbolic means of expressing them. Instead of singing directly of his longing for love, or creating imaginary love scenes for himself, or voicing despair, as other poets did, he expressed his passion for nature and thus vented himself unconsciously of his feelings. True, the impulse of the vernal wood interested him because he believed it taught him much about moral evil and good; it made him also think of love and he sang of his love indirectly by praising that impulse.

This theory which seems so inevitable is one to which we are forced from so many human experiences with nature and yet critics have not dared to advance it. The psychology of nature worship will no doubt be more completely studied by psychoanalysts some day, and we shall understand our nature poets better. The interpretation may offend those who want to persuade themselves that nature has only sermons for us, but let the reader take up some of the sensuous nature descriptions in Keats and Spenser and he will realize more clearly the underlying meaning of nature worship.

It is significant that sexual symbolism is found in two poets who were deemed most reticent on the subject of sex—Wordsworth and Browning.

5

There is no better proof that common objects, when possible, were formerly assigned sexual associations, than the obscene riddles of the Exeter Book. This work is largely attributed to the second great English poet Cynewulf in the eighth century. Certain riddles are propounded which reek with lewd suggestions, and the answer is supposed to be some object innocent in itself; it is apparent, however, from the questions and descriptions given that the interest in this object is because it is sexually symbolic. Thus the answers meant for the 26th, 45th, 46th, 55th, 63rd and 64th riddles of the Exeter Book are leek, key, dough, churn, poker, and beaker, respectively. The reader will note thus how these objects had a sexual symbolic meaning for our ancestors.

Professor Frederic Tupper in his scholarly work *The Riddles of the Exeter Book* says: "By far the most numerous of all riddles of lapsing or varying solutions are those distinctly popular and unrefined problems whose sole excuse for being (or lack of excuse) lies in double meaning and coarse suggestion, and the reason for this uncertainty of answer is at once apparent. The formally stated solution is so overshadowed by the obscene subject implicitly presented in each limited motive of the riddle, that little attention is paid to the aptness of this. It is after all only a pretence, not the chief concern of the jest." He quotes from another scholar, Wossidlo, a number of other objects than those suggested in the Exeter Book, which in other riddle books were invested with sexual symbolism. These are spinning wheel, kettle and pike, yarn and weaver, frying-pan and hare, soot-pole, butcher, bosom, fish on the hook, trunk-key, beer-keg, stocking, mower in grass, butter-cask and bread-scoop.

Freud is apparently correct when he stated that familiar objects of our day like umbrellas and machinery are given a sexual significance by our dreams unconsciously.

That man early expressed his interest in love in symbolical terms is conceded by most anthropologists and philologists. They have traced the origins of many of our customs and institutions, our words and figures of rhetoric, to the veiled eroticism of former times. In our speech are many terms which now have a distinct sexual significance, though they originally had a symbolic one. The word for seed in Hebrew is zera, the Latin word is semen (from sero, to sow). Both words are also used for spermatozoa. Man formerly sought analogies just as he does today; he often feared to violate a taboo, or aimed at a delicacy of expression. He saw the life producing principle at work everywhere, and he found symbols for it in the phenomena of nature, in the sun, moon, water, forest, garden, field, trees, roses; in animals like the serpent, the horse, the bull, the fish, the goat, the dove; in implements like the arrow, the sword, the plough. Common objects assumed for him suggestive meanings. He saw a means of coining new expressions for generative acts and objects; he found associations when he used the fire-drill drilling in the hollow of the wood, or when he threw wood upon the fire. Later he coined new symbolical terms suggested by such acts of his as stuffing a cork in a bottle, or putting bread in the oven, or inserting a key in the lock.

Man speaks in symbolic language especially when it comes to sex matters. This symbolism appears in his dreams and his literature. The language of the unconscious is symbolic, and literature is often expressing the author's unconscious in symbolic terms without his being aware of this.

When poets celebrate the ceremonies about the May pole they may not know that this celebration is related to early phallic worship. When Æschylus wrote his play of Prometheus stealing the fire, or Milton used the Biblical material of Eve tempted by the serpent, they were probably ignorant of the sexual associations of fire and the serpent in ancient times. But their own works thus become symbolical. Shelley, for example, used the metaphor of the snake quite often, and one of the best known passages in his works is the description of the fight of the eagle and the serpent in *The Revolt of Islam*. He often referred to himself also, as the snake. Yet he may not have been aware there was an unconscious connection between his interest in free love and the symbol of the serpent.

The part played by symbolism in love poetry is seen especially in *The Song of Songs*. To moderns and occidentals many of the comparisons and symbolical representations seem very strange, but they had their origin not in the poet's own conceits but in a historic use of the language. These celebrated love poems are filled with sensuous symbolic images. We learn that early man saw lascivious suggestions everywhere in the landscapes, in flowers, rocks, trees, country, city, animals. The speech of our ancestors was sexualized.

The beloved in these poems is like a wall with towers (the breasts); she is a vineyard; she is in the clefts of the rock and the hidden hollow of the cliff. She has eyes like doves, her hair is like a flock of straying goats, her teeth like a flock of washed ewes, her lips like a scarlet thread, her temples like pomegranate, her neck like the tower of David builded with turrets and hung with shields, her breasts like twin fawns feeding among the lilies. She is a closed garden, a shut up spring, a sealed fountain. The roundings of her thighs are like the link of a chain, her navel is like a round empty goblet, her belly like a heap of wheat set among lilies, her eyes like the pools of Hehbon, her nose like the tower of Lebanon.

The lover is like an apple tree among the trees of the wood; he is a young hart. His head is as fine gold, his eyes are like doves, his cheeks are a bed of spices, as a bank of sweet herbs; his lips are lilies dropping myrrh, his hands are as rods of gold set with beryl, his body is polished ivory overlaid with sapphires, his legs are pillars of marble set in sockets of gold; his aspect like Lebanon, "excellent as the cedars."

The embrace of the lovers is described symbolically by means of the tree symbol. It is known that the tree was formerly used to represent both sexes. "The bisexual symbolic character of the tree," says Jung in his *The Psychology of the Unconscious* (P.248), "is intimated by the fact that in Latin trees have a masculine termination and a feminine gender." The lover in the *Song of Songs* calls his beloved a tree and says he will climb up to the palm tree and take hold of the branches; his beloved's breasts will be as clusters of the vine and the smell of her countenance like apples.

Students of anthropology will recognize all the sex symbols in this book of poems and will find analogies in other literatures. It is regarded by many, curiously enough, as a religious allegory. The chapter headings in some English editions of the Bible, represent Christ and the Church as symbols of the lovers. Higher criticism has recognized the fact that the poems are erotic.

6

Psychoanalysis has gone far, indeed, in seeing sex symbolism in many objects and ceremonies and allegories where it was least expected. Freud and Jung, though they differ in their views here, see in many symbols concealed incestuous wishes. They have deal with the subject in *Totem and Taboo* and *The Psychology of the Unconscious*, respectively. I have no intention of going into the differences between their theories.

Artists in the medieval ages, who always drew and painted the Virgin Mary, showed also unconsciously in a symbolic form the infantile incestuous wishes for their own mothers. By this I simply imply that having failed to find love in real life, they took shelter in their love for their mothers. A modern critic has divined the significance of the worship of the Virgin in so fine a poet as Verlaine, who, while he embraced Catholicism, was not a churchman in the strict acceptance of the word. In his *French Literary Studies*, Professor T. B. Rudmose-Brown says of Verlaine: "It is his intense need of a love that will not return upon itself that makes Verlaine turn to Christ's Virgin Mother—the Rosa Mystica in whom he found all the qualities he looked for in vain in his cruelly divine child-wife and his many 'amies' of later life—and crouch like a weary child beneath her wondrous mantle." Verlaine used the Virgin as a symbolic emblem. He unconsciously craved for the love of his mother since in later life he was divorced by his wife.

The symbol then often becomes under our new science the means of recovering the love one felt as a child for one's own mother. The author may not be aware that this use of the symbol is being made by him. He uses the earth today, as man from time immemorial has used it, as a symbol of the mother, when he exclaims he wants to die and go back to mother earth.

The researches of scholars have established, then, the connection between love and symbolic expressions thereof, and it will be the task of future critics to discover the author's unconscious expression of his love life by symbols.[1] Just as the horse shoe, the mandrake and the four-leafed clover, which are signs of good luck among superstitious people, were originally symbols of fruitfulness, so other objects described in books will be seen to have a sexual origin through a study of anthropology.

[1] I did not realize that my prophecy would be as fully realized as it has been.

Chapter 12

Cannibalism: The Atreus Legend[1]

1

IT will be probably a shock to many people to be told that the cannibalistic instinct still is part of our unconscious. It appears in that pathological state known as lycanthropy where the patient often has a craving for human flesh. It is occasionally revived in cases of starvation and shipwreck, when men are driven to eat human flesh. There should be nothing strange about this, for we are descended from people who were cannibals. And we know that men of the old stone age in France were cannibals and cannibalism was practised in Greece in earliest times. It has not yet been exterminated in parts of Africa and Polynesia.

Cannibalism figured considerably in ancient literature. It is not my purpose to go into the question of its origin, or the ceremonials connected with it. There are good articles on the subject in the *Encyclopaedia of Religion and Ethics* by J. A. MacCullouch and in the *Encyclopaedia Britannica* by Northcote W. Thomas. I shall, however, touch on instances where men ate human flesh at sacrifices.

[1] Freud describes the Id as that primitive part of the human mind where our animal desires, our primitive wishes and impulses live. It is a dark jungle, according to Rachel Baker's designation in *Sigmund Freud for Everybody*, made up of primitive and savage desires. Freud held that the primitive emotions are so strong at times that we must not extirpate them too suddenly or drastically. True, when he was thinking of the Id, he was doing so largely in connection with incest. He naturally was not concerned with the cannibalistic instinct which had been completely wiped out among civilized people. Yet we know it took thousands of years to eliminate it, that it was accompanied with human sacrifice and sealed the fate in some localities for prisoners of war. It still flourishes in some islands in the Pacific and perhaps in Africa. In Greek and Roman drama it was depicted as a means of vengeance. We have in this drama a reflection of the horror that cannibalism inspired.

As a means of revenge, enforced cannibalism figures in Shakespeare's *Titus Andronicus* where the general slays Tamora's two sons, has them baked in a pie, and given to her to eat before he kills her.

If Freud's theory expounded in *Totem and Taboo* is true that one day in primitive society, the horde of brothers, expelled by the father, because he did not want them to get possession of his females, finally joined forces, slew and ate him, thus by devouring him acquiring part of his strength, we may then assume that an erotic motive was a source of one species of cannibalism.

130

The subject is worth taking up because of the attention paid to it in literature. We have tales about it today. Conrad has given us in his *Falk* a story of cannibalism. Falk was the survivor on a wrecked ship and was driven by hunger to eat the bodies of sailors, thus saving his life. The memory of the event is of course horrible to him. The young lady he loves marries him despite his experience.

One of Jack London's stories of cannibalism is "The Whale Tooth" in his *South Sea Tales*. It tells how a missionary who went out to convert some Fiji cannibals was betrayed by Ra Vatu, a heathen about to embrace Christianity. The savage desired the missionary's boots to present to a chief. In spite of his acceptance of the religion of Christ he was willing to have his benefactor made a victim of cannibalism. In the same story London refers to a chief who ate eight hundred and seventy-two bodies.

Cannibalism is to us but a curiosity that was once practised. We find no injunction against cannibalism, or eating one's children, among the crimes on the statute books. It is no crime under the Common Law. A man who would commit cannibalism among us would be sent to an insane institution. There are no laws against a thing when no one has the least inclination to do it. Society recognises that the instinct for cannibalism is dead, but it is nevertheless in our unconscious. Our psyche never forgets the episodes in the lives of our ancestors.

The only places where there are laws against cannibalism are in savage countries where there is a disposition to practise it; and these laws are made by colonists.

It is prevalent today in Africa. John H. Weeks in *Among the Congo Cannibals* (1913) tells us he saw savages carrying dismembered parts of human bodies for a feast and that he was offered some cooked human food. He also speaks of a white man who was a dealer in human flesh to a tribe, an example of degradation that finds a parallel in Kurtz's conduct in Conrad's story *The Heart of Darkness*. Mr. Herbert Ward in his *A Voice from Congo* (1910) describes how some human victims were hacked to pieces, alive, for feasts; he witnessed organized traffic in human flesh and saw several cannibal feasts.

2

Let us mark the part played by cannibalism in ancient Greek literature. We shall see that the cannibalistic instinct was part

of the psychic life of the earliest Greeks. There was a reaction
to it as there was to incest of the son with the mother which is
shown in Sophocles' *Œdipus*. Enforced cannibalism, where a
man was made to eat his own children unknowingly, is the
revenge motive of the famous Greek play *Agamemnon*; this
play depicts the reaction to cannibalism.

In the Atreus legend which Æschylus used in *Agamemnon*,
Thyestes eats the flesh of his children, offered up to him by his
brother Atreus, in revenge for having seduced Atreus' wife.
In expiation of Atreus' crime his future descendents suffer.
The unfortunate Thyestes had a son, Ægisthus, as the offspring
of the connection with Atreus' wife—(Pelopia, Thyestes' own
daughter, by the way). Atreus and his son Agamemnon were
later killed by Ægisthus, who had besides seduced Agamemnon's wife Clyemnestra. Agamemnon's son, Orestes, avenges
the murder by killing his mother and her paramour. Orestes
is shown as expiating his matricide in the *Oresteia* trilogy of
which *Agamemnon* is the first play.

In Æschylus' *Agamemnon*, we have the expiation of the
crime of Atreus for enforcing cannibalism on his brother.
There are several passages dealing with the crime. Ægisthus
describes in detail how his father Thyestes ate the flesh of his
own children and how he vomited when he was told what he
had done. When Cassandra, who returns with Agamemnon,
in her insane ravings is telling of the punishment to befall
Clytemnestra she has a vision of the old feast of the children.
The Chorus also tells about the story.

All this shows the horror which was inspired by a deed, the
eating of one's children, and this must mean that far back in
antiquity this act was practised and that the Greeks were now
describing the act as revolting.

There are several other stories of enforced cannibalism in
ancient literature with revenge as the motive. Herodotus tells
us how the King of the Medes punished Harpagus for not killing Cyrus by making Harpagus dine on the flesh of his own
son. This was in the sixth century B. C. Tereus, King of the
Thracians, was served up his son by the latter's own mother,
because Tereus dishonored his sister-in-law, Philomela, and deprived her of her tongue. In one of Grimm's fairy tales, *The
Juniper Tree*, we have the story of a man who is given the flesh
of his own child by his wife, the child's stepmother.

Seneca in the first century A. D. wrote *Thyestes*, drama-
tizing all the repulsive episodes, describing the preparing of
the children for the feast and the feast itself. The most loath-

some theme is made the main idea of the story. Crebillon wrote a cannibalistic play in the 18th century, *Atrée et Thyeste.*

The tale of Saturn, who swallowed his children when they were born so as not to be dethroned in accordance with the prophecy, with the result that he was compelled to disgorge them later by Zeus, has its parallels in folklore among the Bushmen, Eskimos and others. It is a very old story.

Frued saw in the Œdipus legend the horror reaction of the Greeks to two legendary deeds, the killing of a father and the marrying of the mother by the son, deeds which had their basis in reality and which were occasionally repeated in dreams. Similarly we can see in the Atreus legend a reaction to the idea of eating one's children, an act that used to accompany the offering of human sacrifices. But we cannot say that the cannibalistic instinct affects one's future as the Œdipus complex does. It is, however, part of our unconscious. The effectiveness of Swift's famous satirical proposition to help the poor in Ireland by suggesting that they sell the flesh of their own children for food to the rich is due to the fact that children's flesh was actually once eaten. Swift wrote his essay with ironical intent but he was utilizing an ancient historical fact, unknowingly.

We know from the stories of Abraham and Isaac, Jephthah and his daughter, and Iphigenia, as well as from historical records, that children were offered as human sacrifices; the body of the victim was often eaten; hence there is a connection between human sacrifice and cannibalism.

J. A. MacCulloch in his scholarly article on cannibalism in the *Encyclopaedia of Religion and Ethics*, ventures the opinion that human sacrifice rose through an earlier cannibalism, on the principle that as men liked human flesh the God's would also relish it. The worshippers later shared in the human feasts, with the Gods. Westermarck says that the sacrificial form of cannibalism springs from the idea that a victim offered to a God participates in his sanctity and the worshipper by eating the human flesh transfers to himself something of the divine virtue.

There were many cases of orgastic cannibalism in ancient Greece. There is a vase showing a Thracian tearing a child with his teeth in the presence of a god. Pausanias relates that a child was torn and eaten in a sacrifice to the Gods in Boeotia. In Plato's *Republic* we have an account of a survival of an earlier cannibal sacrificial feast.[2] It is related there that a piece of human flesh was placed among the animals sacrificed to Zeus Lycaeus and that in the feasts that followed the eater of the fragments became a were-wolf.

Other people like the Fijis who partook in a human feast first offered part of the slain to the gods.

The custom of human sacrifices and cannibalism died out among the Greeks, and in Æschylus' trilogy we have the horror reaction of the educated Greek against these institutions. The playwright shows the terrible retaliation visited on the man who indulges in cannibalism or makes another do so. Punishment for Atreus' deed is visited upon his son, Agamemnon in many ways, one of which forces him to sacrifice his daughter Iphigenia. Agamemnon is also punished by the infidelity of his wife Ægisthus; he is finally murdered by them.

The tale of Iphigenia thus sheds some light on the subject. She figures considerably in the *Agamemnon*. Æschylus tells us that Clytemnestra felt justified for being untrue to her husband Agamemnon because he sacrificed their daughter Iphigenia. The latter's name is closely associated with human sacrifice in Greek legend.

In the Saturnalia of Rome a human victim was slain as late as the fourth century A. D.

The theory then resolves itself to this: In very ancient times before Greek civilization made its appearance children were sacrificed to ward off evil and the flesh of those children was eaten by the parents. There rose a reaction to this which we see in the Atreus legend.

---

[2] *The Republic*, VIII, p. 566.

Chapter 13

Psychoanalysis and Literary Criticism

1

PSYCHOANALYSIS will put in a new light the old literary controversies between realism and idealism, between classicism and romanticism. Idealistic writers are those who write of imaginary pleasing scenes and characters. Their books are founded on the same principles that are at the basis of dreams; they are the fulfilment of the authors' wishes. We grow weary of a deluge of such literature, because it is too visionary and not related to reality. We prefer to see life as it is, even though it is harsh. Hence our reaction to those ancient types of romances where the heroes are always strong, pursuing false ideals, obeying silly codes of honor, and are always triumphant; we weary still more of the heroines who are always without individuality. The most idealistic books are those dealing with utopias, and though the new visionary societies are as a rule undesirable and impossible, they represent the wishes of the authors fulfilled; such works sometimes, as in the case of Plato's *The Republic* and More's *Utopia*, are full of valuable suggestions. Utopias, however, are generally dreary because they make no allowances for our instincts; the author is insincere to himself and pretends to be what he is not.

Then there is the idealistic literature which builds a dream palace beyond this life. The author wants to live forever and to have things he did not possess here, and he creates imaginary scenes where all that he suffered here is righted. Of this type of literature is the Paradise of Dante, and the Celestial City of Bunyan. Literature of this type pleases many people, as it enables them to get away from reality and to have a ground for believing in the existence of chimeras they cherish.

Idealism in literature is the selection for description of only those features of life that please the fancy of the author. People are described not as they are but as the author would like them to be; events are narrated not as they occur in life but as

135

the writer would wish them to happen. The dream of the author is given instead of an actual picture of reality. When Shakespeare grew weary of London life, he drew a picture of life in the forest of Arden in his *As You Like It* such as he would have liked to have enjoyed. Idealistic literature hence gives us an insight into the nature of the author's unconscious. His constructed air castles show us where reality has been harsh with him. It is true all literature must to some extent be idealistic, as the author must always do some selecting. Idealism will never die out in literature. Man is an idealist by nature; every man who has day dreams is reconstructing life in accordance with his desires.

There is always a large element in the population that hearkens back to its childhood days. Even our most intellectual people like to divert themselves with stories of piracy, battles, sunken treasures, tales of the sea, of adventure and mystery. The people who love romance go back in their reading to their boyhood days; they have in their unconscious, primitive emotions that, unable to find an outlet today very well, refuse to remain altogether repressed; they get satisfaction by seeing pictures of life in which the unconscious thus participates. The perennial interest of *Robinson Crusoe* and *Treasure Island*, of Scott and Dumas, of the sea stories of Cooper and Captain Marryat, of the detective stories of Gaboriau and Doyle, is due to the fact that they make us young again. It is true we often outgrow some of these books and find them dull in later life, but they enchant many of us at all ages because inherited instincts from savage and less cultivated people can only be kept repressed by being given a feigned instead of a real satisfaction.

Old legends like those about Achilles, the Wandering Jew, the Flying Dutchman, Charlemagne, and King Arthur and his knights, never weary us; they continue to furnish artists and writers with artistic material. Psychoanalysis explains the love we feel for these romances. We have never quite grown out of either the barbarous or boyish state. We like the strange, the marvellous, the mysterious, for this was specially characteristic of man in an early stage and of the boy. We also find an affinity for the kind of life our ancestors led. We are interested in tales where men are hunting and fighting. Man's unconscious loves a fight, for he has always fought in the history of the race. He is fascinated by danger and the idea of overcoming obstacles. And he wants such scenes introduced in literature.

Psychoanalysis also explains the affinity that we have for the supernatural in literature. Freud's disciples, Rank and Abraham and Ricklin, have shown in *The Myth of the Birth of the Hero*, in *Dreams and Myths*, and in *Wishfulment and Fairy Tales*, respectively, that fairy tales are to be interpreted like dreams and represent the fulfilled wishes of early humanity. The child who likes fairy tales finds his own wishes satisfied in these tales dealing with the supernatural and improbable. Even when great poets make use of the supernatural in their work, the same principles of wish fulfillment are there. Faust is saved in Goethe's poem, Prometheus is released in Shelley's lyric drama and the Knight of the Cross is victorious over the dragon in Spenser's allegory. The poems give us the fulfilled wishes of the modern poets. True the modern poet introduces advanced ideas of his time and gives different interpretations to the old tales. But we still love the supernatural because we have our limitations in facing reality.

In an essay on Hans Christian Andersen published in 1867 Georg Brandes showed the connection between the unconscious and the nursery tale. Thus he anticipated the discoveries of Abraham, Ricklin, and Rank who noted that folk-lore and fairy tales are, like dreams, realized wishes of the unconscious of early humanity, formulated into endurable form. Brandes objected to the occasional moral tag in Andersen's stories "because the nursery story is the realm of the unconscious. Not only are unconscious beings and objects the leaders of speech in it, but what triumphs and is glorified in the nursery story is this very element of unconsciousness. And the nursery story is right, for the unconscious element is our capital and the source of our strength." Brandes shows how child psychology interests us all because of its unconscious. He distinguished the changes brought in by the nineteenth century where the unconscious is worshipped, while in the critical eighteenth century consciousness alone had been valued.

Nietzsche understood that the romantic life of our ancestors and their ways of thinking were repeated by us in our dreams. He wrote in his *Human All Too Human,*

The perfect distinctions of all dreams—representations, which pre-suppose absolute faith in their reality, recall the conditions that appertain to primitive man, in whom hallucination was extraordinarily frequent, and sometime simultaneously seized entire communities, entire nations. Therefore, in sleep and in dreams we once more carry out the task of early humanity. . . . I hold, that as man now still reasons in dreams, so men reasoned also *when awake* through thousands of years; the first *cause* which occurred to the mind to explain anything that required an explanation, was sufficient and stood for truth . . . This ancient element in human nature still manifests itself in our dreams, for it is the foundation upon which the higher reason has developed and still develops in every individual; the dream carries us back into remote conditions of human culture, and provides a ready means of understanding them better. Dream-thinking is now so easy to us because during immense periods of human development we have been so well drilled in this form of fantastic and cheap explanation, by means of the first agreeable notions. In so far, dreaming is a recreation of the brain, which by day has to satisfy the stern demands of thought, as they are laid down by the higher culture.[1]

Supernatural phenomena, however, in our contemporary literature savor of imitation and the artificial. Writers do not as a rule believe in the supernatural while the creators of the old fairy tales did. From so fine a poet as Yeats, who was said to believe in fairies, we get literature that is both sincere and artistic. We have a beautiful ideal reconstruction of the world in such a play as *The Land of Heart's Desire*. Here the dream principle is still at work.

Among the fairy tales of our day are those centering around psychic phenomena and reporting the conversations of the dead. They are written because they represent the writer's wishes to communicate with the dead and to prove that we do not die. They are needed by some in an era of exact science as old folklore was needed in its time. Needless to say this does not speak well for the intellects of the writers of these spiritualistic works. We make something occur because we want it to transpire. Lodge's *Raymond* is one of the fairy tales of recent times and it has a genuineness because the author, to the amazement of many of us, believed those talks with his son actually took place. The book is really a commentary on his pathetic state of mind after the death of his son and is his dream of hope.

But realistic literature is after all in the ascendant, for it tells us of what we experience in our own life. Don Quixote showed us that love for books dealing with dreams and impossibilities may help to make one mad. Men are interested in

[1] Vol. I, pp. 23, 25-26.

their inner struggles and in the problems of the day. Books treating of these have replaced considerably the old romances as serious literature.

Romantic and idealistic works are like dreams, fragments of the psychic life of the race when it was young.

2

The literary works that we like best are those which tell of the frustration of wishes like our own. We prefer to read about troubles like those we have suffered, to lose ourselves in the dreams and fantasies built up by authors, akin to those we have conjured up in our own imagination.

We prefer a book that apologizes for us, that tells of strivings and repressions such as we have experienced. We get a sort of pleasure then out of painful works, in which our sorrows and wants are put into artistic form, so as to evoke them again in us and hence purge us. It depends often on the character of our repression as to the nature of the books we like. If we have overthrown the authority of our fathers or experienced a painful love repression because we were hampered by social laws, if we have broken with our religious friends or been crushed by some moneyed powers, we may become of a revolutionary trend of mind and hence prefer writers with radical opinions. In our time there have arisen a number of geniuses who voiced such opinions; having experienced repressions on account of the customs of society, they sang and wrote of those repressions and attacked those customs. The great love felt by the young man who does not fit into the social order, for writers like Whitman, Ibsen, Nietzsche, Shaw, and others, is because these writers approve an individualism that he seeks to cultivate. He who is grieved by the tyranny of the philistine and the bourgeois, the hypocrite and the puritan, finds himself consoled by writers who were also victims of such tyranny.

If we are somewhat more neurotic than the average person, or even abnormal, we go to the writers who are neurotic and abnormal. Why did Baudelaire love Poe so much? Because he saw in him another Baudelaire, a dreamer out of accord with reality, a victim of drink and drugs, a sufferer at the hands of women, an artist loving beauty and refusing to be a reformer. Hence he translated Poe's works, swore to read him daily, and imitated him. Baudelaire's unconscious recognized a brother sufferer in Poe; he wanted to have the same ideal conditions Poe imagined in his dreams; he suffered from the same neuroses that Poe suffered. These two writers became the idols of the French decadent writers, and Huysmans, Mallarmé, and others loved them. The French decadents found affinities with ancient authors, especially the Roman poets of the Silver Age, Petronius and Apuleius. Oscar Wilde, Earnest Dowson, and Arthur Symons in our literature belong to the group who found themselves in harmony with the French decadents.

Literary influences are due to definite reasons and follow regular laws. Though sometimes authors appeal to us who are just the opposite of ourselves, we, as a rule, love those writers who write of our own unconscious wishes.

What is the secret of the universal appeal of Hamlet? Is it not because many of us, like him, have been in conflict wherein we could not act because there was an external obstacle? Dr. Ernest Jones found a reason for Hamlet's inability to act in an unconscious feeling of guilty love for his mother. He was jealous of his uncle, the murderer of his father, and also the successful rival to Hamlet in his mother's affections. This psychoanalytic interpretation made by Dr. Ernest Jones adds a new element to the old theory of Hamlet's struggle with fate. Hamlet has given rise to a series of characters in literature characterized by inaction, by thinking and not doing. Russian literature, with its Rudins and Oblomovs, has recognized in this portrayal by Shakespeare a common Russian type. Hamlet, nevertheless, had good reason for not being able to act, and finally did act, though he made a bungle of it all.

Byron and Shelley have had more imitators and lovers than any of the poets of England of their time. We know the influence of each of them on Tennyson and Browning respectively, though the Victorians later departed from the footsteps of their masters and became conservative. But the causes that made Heine, Leopardi, De Musset and Pushkin love Byron were the same as those which drew to Shelley, the republican melodist Swinburne, James Thomson, the atheist author of *The City of Dreadful Night*, Francis Thompson, the Catholic maker of beautiful forms out of his own sufferings, and the unhappy lyricist Beddoes who committed suicide. These later poets found Byron and Shelley singers of unconscious wishes of their own, portrayers of moods and sorrows like those they felt and planners who would rid the world of such griefs by means they largely approved.

The reason for the universal appeal of the Bible lies in the

ariety in this library of books; there is always some chapter
that expresses our unconscious wishes.

The *Old Testament*, especially, satisfies our unconscious.
This is due to the psalms voicing human sorrow, and the
prophecies of Isaiah ringing with a passionate love for justice,
to the pleasant tales that appeal to our youthful fancy like
those of Joseph and his brethren, and Ruth, and the philosoph-
cal drama of Job, to the epicureanism and melancholy of Ec-
clesiasticus, and the heroism of Joshua and David. The Bible
appeals as literature to many who do not believe in the theo-
logic aspects, to many who find parts of it cruel and unjust,
because it is a varied collection of books, and, as a result, the
unconscious wishes and the means of gratification expressed
must meet our own, separated as we are from them by thousands of years.

When we read that Wordsworth soothed De Quincey and
John Stuart Mill, and had a tonic effect on Arnold, so that he
became a leading disciple, that Shaw based his wit and philosophy on Samuel Butler, an almost forgotten contemporary,
that Brandes found an affinity in writers like Shakespeare and
Ibsen, we are aware that the process is the same: the later
author found some earlier one who especially expressed his
unconscious needs.

Consider the literary influences in literature, that of Smollet
on Dickens, that of Dickens on Daudet and Dostoevsky and
Bret Harte, that of Balzac on Flaubert, of Flaubert on
Maupassant and Zola, of Carlyle on Ruskin and Froude, of
Kipling on Jack London. All this means that the author influenced found in his master a kindred sufferer and a kindred
dreamer.

Literature gives each writer or reader the means of choosing
his own father as it were. When a man says he found his whole
life changed by a certain book, it is equivalent to his saying
that the book has merely made him recognize his unconscious;
it did not put anything there that was not there before. The
book had a psychoanalytic effect on him; it taught him to look
at his unconscious objectively; it brought to consciousness
something that was repressed. If the resistance to perceiving
that unconscious had not been overcome the book could have
had no effect. We hate a book often because the censorship
in us is too great. When John A. Symonds describes the effects
of Whitman's *Leaves of Grass*, which he says influenced him
more than any other book except the Bible, he meant Whitman
cured him of neurosis, brought out his repressed feelings and

made him aware of his inner wants and told him how to satisfy them.

The saying, "Tell me what you read and I'll tell you what you are," is true. People differ about the qualities of books because their own unconscious wishes have been met differently in these books.

3

What then is the cause of literary movements and what stamps the peculiarities of a literary age, if all writers draw on their unconscious? Why does a Pope appear in the age of Queen Anne and a Wordsworth at the end of the reign of George III? Why didn't Shakespeare write in the Elizabethan age like Charles Dickens in the Victorian period? How account for the warlike character of the Saxon epic *Beowulf*, for the religious tone of her first poet, Caedmon; for the interest in chivalry and allegory in the *Faerie Queen?* What made Bunyan so absorbed in salvation in *Pilgrim's Progress* at the time the Restoration dramatists were steeped in exhibitionism and immorality? What are the causes of the notes of revolt in Byron and Shelley, of the romanticism of Scott, the realism and moralism of George Eliot? If the unconscious is alike in all people, and genius records the ideas and emotions formed by personal repressions, it would seem the works of all geniuses who have had similar repressions should be alike, irrespective of the ages in which they lived.

Literary historians and philosophers have accounted for the various changes in literary taste fairly satisfactorily, although they have often omitted from their investigations the factor of the personal experiences and idiosyncrasies of the author, and have emphasized too strongly the importance of the predominant ideas of the age. Yet no author starts out to express the spirit of his age. He gives vent to his unconscious which he suppresses more or less, and colors, in accordance with the literary fashion prevailing. His unconscious appears in a background of the literary machinery and ideas of the time. Since in our unconscious are present all the emotions man has had, different events may make any of them burst forth.

On account of the first world war, many dormant emotions were reanimated in us and appeared in our literature. People found that Homer's *Iliad* and other ancient warlike epics appealed to them more than these did in times of peace. Literature in war times becomes more related to primitive literature where the hero is the successful, brave warrior. The military and patriotic spirit had not been extinct, but quiescent.

If Milton had lived in the eighteen nineties he would probably have written problem plays and novels instead of *Paradise Lost.* He was unhappily married, but the fashion of his age was not to create imaginative works based on justifiable causes for seeking a divorce. He did write on the subject of divorce, however, and his views horrified his contemporaries. He stood alone. Had the tendencies of the time been to make works of the imagination out of situations in which he was personally placed, he would have no doubt done so. In his unconscious he felt about women and divorce much as Strindberg did. He retained during the Restoration his early Puritanism and religious interests, and hence published *Paradise Lost.* Even here he found an opportunity for expressing special views about women and describing his own forlorn condition.

Again it is likely that Shakespeare in our generation would not have written much differently from Ibsen or Hauptmann. The marriage problem interested him also, for he was unhappily married and loved another. He expressed his bitterness towards women in his sonnets, in his characterizations of historical characters like Cleopatra and Cressida. But he wrote no special work occupied with the theme of the hard restrictions placed by society upon the lives of unhappily married people. A work of this kind would have been a monstrosity in his age. Shakespeare could not have written exactly as Ibsen did, for though in their unconscious they were alike, each had different traditions and backgrounds to work on. No writer ignores *totally* prevailing literary fashions or tastes.

It is not my purpose to go into the causes of changes in tastes, traditions, ideas, movements. That subject has been dealt with often. Economics is a great factor in developing new literary styles and movements, yet reaction against a preceding age also has much to do with these. The artificiality of the eighteenth century gave way to the love of nature of the nineteenth. The demand for reason, wit, and classicism in literature disappeared gradually, to be replaced by imagination, the utilization of emotion, and romanticism. Wordsworth is a reaction to Pope (even though Wordsworth's nature worship concealed his sex interest). His way was prepared by other poets like Thomson, Collins, Goldsmith, Gray, Cowper, Crabbe, Blake, and Burns. The immorality and exhibitionism of Congreve, Wycherley, Farquhar, Vanbrugh and Dryden in the Resoration period were a reaction to the Puritanism of the age of Cromwell. Bunyan, because of his early training and his physical and mental makeup, however, still clung to his early Puritanism.

Yet Pope and Wordsworth were each men of their ages and wrote in accordance with the rising literary traditions of the time, though they also altered these. For the imitative instinct is powerful and present in the most original writers. Some of Shakespeare's plays are much like those of Marlowe and Fletcher. His "plagiarisms," like those of Milton, were extensive. It is true that often one man sets the standard for a literary age, but he usually has predecessors. His influence is due to the fact that he strikes responsive chords in the unconscious of many people of this time, and the circle of his admirers and imitators increases, so as to make him an authority.

The realistic novels of George Eliot appeared after England wearied of the fanciful fictions of Walter Scott. A generation passed by before the reaction set in with full force. Both writers wrote as they did, largely in obedience to the tendencies of their times, upon which they reacted and were reacted upon. They wrote because of personal repressions. Their methods of expression were different, because of a desire to comply somewhat with literary traditions. Romanticism was fashionable in 1830, while realism was in the air in 1860.

Those readers who think that these views do not give sufficient credit to writers for originality in literary expression should remember that common literary forms are followed by writers who may nevertheless be original in ideas. Only the student of literary history realizes the power of literary imitation.

Take the hundreds of pastorals that flooded European literature from Theocrities to Pope; most of them, except Spenser's *Astrophel*, Milton's *Lycidas*, and a few others were flat and unprofitable. Note the numerous sonnets written since the form was brought over from Italy by Wyatt and Surrey. The extensive use of the sonnet proves poets are imitative.

Recall the allegories with which medieval literature abounded. Even the great short stories of Hawthorne, who was much influenced by Bunyan and Spenser, show traces of medieval forms. Literary tradition is certainly stronger than originality. And the thousands of authors of our day who write novels and short stories, would in medieval times have written allegories.

The ideas and mode of expression change, and hence make much of the old literature obsolete. But many emotions remain eternal. We can still feel with Sappho and the Troubadours, whereas we find our intellect insulted by some of the religious ideas versified by Dante and Milton; although the passages describing secular emotions win our admiration.

When we must look for an author's unconscious buried in the literary trappings of his day we weary of the task and dismiss his work. Why can we not read the hundreds of pastorals and allegories of the medieval writers? Is it not largely because of the feeble intellects, and spirit of imitation present, because of the absence of the personal note? The unconscious is buried too deeply in rigmarole. The works have a psychological and historical but not artistic value. The religious and romantic instincts in many of us are buried too deeply in our unconscious, and hence we do not sympathize with those works.

Those poets live who have been most personal. The Roman poets, Horace, Catullus, Tibullus, Propertius, Ovid, ality of Virgil in the story of Æneas and Dido—it may have been a love affair of his own.

The unconscious is present in all literature, and the literary movement but colors it and gives occasion for the expression or censorship of certain phases of it. Puritan writers are not in their unconscious any different from the "immoral" ones; only the latter relax the censor and give full play to the unconscious, when a liberal age like that of the Restoration or the Renaissance, permits it.

Hence, though all writers draw on their unconscious and base their work on their personal repressions, authors of one age differ in manner and substance from those of another, not because the unconscious is different (which it is not), but because it is fashionable to express only certain features of it in one age; because writers have an instinctive tendency to comply with the literary fashions of their age; because the time spirit colors and censors those elements of the unconscious which appear in the literary product.

4

Freud has shown in his *Psychopathology of Every-Day Life* that we tend to forget the things that are displeasing to us, that unconsciously we avoid what has once caused us pain. The objection has been raised to this theory that as a matter of fact it is the painful things that we never forget, and that these impress themselves most on us. Such critics might have taken it for granted that the scientist who laid down the principles that neuroses date from the earliest painful love experiences which are never forgotten, but merely repressed, would not have overlooked their objections. Certainly we do not forget painful things, but nature has so provided that we have a tendency to repress into our unconscious annoying events and go on our way as if they had never happened; only in symptomatic acts, mistakes, slips of the tongue do we betray ourselves. The man whose wife has lied never forgets it if he has loved her. But if he has, let us say, been slighted by a person who has not been playing a principal part in his life, he will go on living as if that person had never existed for him. He may unconsciously avoid the street where that man lives, and forget about him, until some occasion may arise when he may show his dislike of that person in a manner he never intended; the action is, nevertheless, the voice of his unconscious. Life would be unbearable if we always had before us pictures of our past sufferings. In fact, a neurosis is brought about by the fact that we don't forget. As Freud said, the hysteric suffers from reminiscences or fantasies based on painful events in the past.

The principle of unconscious avoidance of the painful is at the basis of the rejection of the world's great books, both old and new. Literary criticism is influenced by our tendency to ignore what causes us pain.

The world has not always realized the reason for the opposition to a new great thinker, or an advanced idea or book. We have contented ourselves by asserting that the world was not yet advanced enough intellectually to perceive their greatness. We know, however, that often the most intellectual people of an age are the first to reject a new idea. Carlyle and Lord Beaconsfield would have nothing to do with the theory of evolution. Some of Darwin's chief opponents were among the leading biologists of the time.

People born in an earlier generation from the man who propounds the new idea tend to reject it. Another unconscious reason for the repudiation of the new idea is that it would cause us pain if it were true. We would also feel that we had been dupes all our lives. We had been smugly following a pleasant delusion that brought us some happiness and suddenly we see our bubble pricked. We had been following a course of thinking and conduct that is now indicted by the new discovery. If a man has written several books on miracles, original sin, and other dogmas in which he believes, and has spent all his life studying the subjects, he cannot accept a book which rejects his ideas; it would mean that he had wasted his life. His aversion to concur with the conclusions of that new book is nature's means of preventing him from suffering great pain; it is a defence action. If a preacher has advised many couples who were unhappy not to divorce and not to remarry some one with whom they might have been happy, he would be the last man to see the greatness of a work that shows divorce may be a humane and beneficial act in some cases, for it would mean that he would have to admit he has ruined the lives of many people.

The real objection by man to the Copernican theory was that it reflected on his religion and his vanity; it was annoying to hear that the earth was not the center of the universe. The Darwinian theory was a still more painful discovery because it placed man among the descendents of animals and taught that he was a by-product like them. The facts, however, in both cases, were so overwhelming that many managed to accept them and still keep their religious beliefs intact, for these still give consolation. In spite of Copernicus and Darwin, we still live as if the world were the center of the universe and man its most divine creation.

The most human argument in favor of a belief in personal immortality of the soul, of communion with the dead, or a personal God, is that life would be sad if these theories were not true; they must hence be true. Tennyson, in his *In Memoriam*, has the popular attitude. If life didn't continue forever, then "earth is darkness at the core and dust and ashes all that is." But our wishes must recede before logic and facts.

A great idea, then, is not accepted if its conclusions are painful to us when a more pleasant idea has prevailed; every idea is rejected when acceptance as truth would mean that we have been living in error and wasting our lives. New ideas are nearly always made to fit in with the old views.

The theory of evolution became acceptable only when it was demonstrated to the satisfaction of the religionists, at least what at first did not seem apparent to them, that it interfered neither with a belief in a personal God, Christianity, nor the immortality of the soul.

Literary men who are advanced are admired often for qualities that do not constitute their real greatness. The conservatives praise the daring poet for his style, after he has made his way; or they select a few of the minor ideas he champions and ignore the greater ones. They will not accept the Hardy who wrote *Jude the Obscure,* but the Hardy of *Far From the Mad-*

dening Crowd; they will admire the early harmless lyrics of John Davidson instead of the profound testaments and later plays, whose real greatness was shown by the late Dr. Hayim Fineman in his monograph *John Davidson*.[1] They praise Swinburne for his melody, Ibsen for his technique, and Shaw for his wit, but can see no intellectual value either in the *Songs Before Sunrise*, or *Peer Gynt*, or *Man and Superman*. They overlook the value of Byron's *Don Juan* or *Cain*, because these works contain ideas that offend most, and instead they lavish compliments on some innocuous minor poems. They like Shelley's lyrics and see nothing in his ideas.

The "conspiracy of silence" that has often greeted many great men was at times unconscious. People are not prone by nature to investigate something which might bring painful results. They prefer to let it alone altogether. The motive of ignoring a great book is founded on one of displeasure. Hence morbid and pessimistic books, revolutionary ideas, iconoclastic views on religion, morals, or philosophy, new discoveries in science, encounter opposition. We do not want to be disturbed in our complacency. For the disturbance is, after all, made by those who do not fit into the old order; their own discoveries are defence processes. But gradually it is seen that these writers express universal wants.

The opposition met by all investigations to the subject of sex, is an example of man's effort to thrust painful things out of sight. The barrier raised against Freud himself rises largely from three leading ideas of his, those on the sexual significance of symbols in dreams, and the attributing of neurosis to sexual causes, and the theory that the infant has a sexual life of its own. In spite of his broad use of the term sexual and his many demonstrations of the truth of these ideas, man does not want to believe them. Jung and Adler, who lay little stress on the sexual element, have made the theory of psychoanalysis acceptable to many; but Freud objected to the use of the word psychoanalysis by disciples who have taken out of his theory something he considered essential.

---

[1] Published by the University of Pennsylvania.

Chapter 14

Keats' Personal Love Poems

1

STRESS has never been laid on the real unconscious origins of some of Keats' best poems. We know that his sad love affair with Fanny Brawne, who coquetted with him, inspired a few poems directly addressed to her; it is also indisputable that Keats had her in mind when he wrote "La Belle Dame Sans Merci," that he was telling of his own fate in the account of the knight's mishap. But it is rarely recognized that emotions connected with Fanny Brawne inspired his two most famous odes, the one to the nightingale and the other to the Grecian urn; that the tale of *Lamia*, which ranks among his best poems, is a symbolic description of his attitude towards Miss Brawne, and that her presence is felt in other poems and sonnets by Keats. He though of her constantly. When we compare the poems to the letters that he had written to her about the same time, we find that often the same emotions inspired both.

Keats met Miss Brawne in the fall of 1818, when he was twenty-three years old. He quarrelled with her in February, 1819, but, nevertheless, was her declared lover in the spring. His first love letter is dated July 1, 1819, and the last about May, 1820. In the spring and summer of 1819 he wrote same of his best poems, and he showed most emphatically emotions repressed by the coquetries of Fanny. He took a walk among the marbles of the British Museum, in February, 1819, and three months later penned his' 'Ode to a Grecian Urn." In the latter part of April he heard the nightingale in Charles Armitage Brown's garden, and he wrote the famous ode. In the same month he also wrote "La Belle Dame Sans Merci." In August and September of 1819 he worked on *Lamia*. He had his first hemorrhage in February, 1820, left England in September, and died in Italy in February, 1921.

Those who have read the letters to Fanny will remember with what anxiety the poet wrote, how he showed his jealousy and complained and pleaded without pride. In one letter dated June 19, 1819, he said he would resent having his heart made

149

a football, that Charles Armitage Brown, with whom she flirted, was doing him to death by inches, and that the air of a room from which Fanny was absent was unhealthy to him. "I appeal to you by the blood of that Christ you believe in. . . . Do not write to me if you have done anything this month which it would have pained me to have seen." In October he writes, "Love is my religion—I could die for that; I could die for you." The letters are the record of the agony of a man who is being played with and who cries out in helplessness. He cannot bear seeing her smiling with others or dancing with them. Miss Brawne asserted after his death that she did not regard him as a great poet, and thought it advisable for people to let his reputation die. It is also said she referred to him as the foolish poet who loved her.

Let us see how this sad affair influenced his work.

The Keats of the first volume, *Poems*, 1817, is a much different person from the Keats of the *Lamia* volume, in 1820. The three intervening years had brought a maddening love affair, a fatal disease and the famous, though not as once thought fatal review, attacking *Endymion*. His art principles remained much the same. With growing sorrow he worshipped beauty more and sought in it a refuge from grief. His attitude towards women and life was now somewhat different. He paid woman a tribute in the poem in the first volume, beginning with the lines, "Woman! I behold thee," etc. But he had not yet suffered from a Fanny Brawne; here he spoke of woman's being "like a milk-white lamb that bleats for man's protection." And yet before he was twenty he may have had a foreboding that his fate in love might not be a happy one. In the poem, "To Hope," he wrote:

> *Should e'er unhappy love my bosom pain,*
> *From cruel parents or relentless fair;*
> *O let me not think it is quite in vain*
> *To sigh out sonnets to the midnight air.*

Alas for himself such sonnets and other poems were sighed out later!

Before we can, however, quite understand his sad life and the nature of his work and philosophy, something must be said about his relations to his mother. She died from consumption when he was fourteen. Keats, who was her favorite child, sat up nights, mourning her, and was inconsolable; he would hide for days under his master's desk. Once, at the age of five, he guarded her sick room with a sword. His mother remarried a year after her husband's death, when the poet was in his tenth year. She separated from her second husband and went to live with her mother. Keats then had a guardian. The poet was the oldest of five children, and was a seven months' child. All this is significant. The Œdipus Complex was strong in the poet. He was not only deprived of his mother early, but witnessed her marry a second time. This event revived the babyish jealousy he felt of his father and made him unconsciously hate the new husband. He looked for a substitute for the lost mother and thought he found her in Fanny Brawne, and then he learned what grief was. He loved beauty so much because of unrequited love. Some poets, like Wordsworth, seek consolation in nature for lack of love, others like Byron simply voice their woe in a personal note, others like Shelley find it a spur to spread views of reform in connection with the marriage institution. Keats' love of beauty has a strong sexual component. His unfulfilled physical desires were sublimated into poems worshipping beauty. Art was his refuge.

We are now prepared to trace the origins of some of his work. Most critics saw the unconscious allusions in the "La Belle Dame San Merci." It is symbolic of himself in the snares of a coquette. There is an allusion to an old song entitled "La Belle Dame Sans Merci" in Keats' "The Eve of St. Agnes" which Porphyro played to Madeline while she slept; it was a poem composed in Provence; and we all know that most of the love poems of the Provençal Troubadours were complaints about unrequited love. Keats' poem has a simple plot. A knight tells the poet in response to a question as to why he was so woebegone that he met a fairy child and set her on his pacing steed. She pretended to love him, and she lulled him to sleep, and he dreamed that pale kings and princes and warriors told him that he was in the thrall of a lady without mercy. They were evidently also her victims. He wakes and loiters on the cold hillside, realizing that he has been her victim.

The poem was written a few months before the letter to Fanny was penned in which he said he resented having his heart made a football. The poem corresponds to an anxiety dream. Freud tells us that the contents of the anxiety dream is of a sexual nature; the libido has been turned away from its object, and, not having succeeded in being applied, has been transformed into fear. This poem is a proof of one of the least understood theories of Freud. Keats then is the knight and Fanny is the fairy siren.

The nature of his day dreams and his jealousy appears in the "Ode to Fanny," a posthumous poem, probably not meant for publication. It contains some of the substance of his letters to Fanny. He imagines he is watching Fanny at a dance, and jealous thoughts come to him. "Who now with greedy looks eats up my feast?" he asks. His only remedy is to write poetry to ease his pain. He says to Physician Nature, "O, ease my heart of verse and let me rest." He loves her so much he cannot bear that any one profane her with looks. He wants her thoughts and emotions to be wholly his. The poem was probably written about the time of the quarrel, in February, 1819.

Another posthumous poem addressed to Fanny is the one beginning, "What can I do to drive away remembrance from my eyes?" He is now wishing he were free from love, and that he had his old liberty. He wants to devote himself to his muse as freely as he once did. He thinks of wine as he did in the nightingale poem, and asks: "Shall I gulp wine? No, that is vulgarism." He is in hell, he realizes, but he concludes with a wish to satisfy his physical love for Fanny. He wants to rest his soul on her dazzling breast, to place his arm about her waist, and feel her warm breath in his hair. In a posthumously published sonnet he pleads, "I cry to you for mercy"; he wants her entirely, including "that warm, white, lucent, million-pleasured breast." In the sonnet he wrote (not just before his death as usually thought, but as Colvin says, in February, 1819), in a blank page in a volume of Shakespeare facing "A Lover's Complaint," "Bright star, would I were steadfast as thou art," he concludes most sensually. He longs to be:

> *Pillowed upon my fair love's ripening breast,*
> *To feel forever its soft fall and swell,*
> *Still, still to hear her tender-taken breath,*
> *And so live forever—or else swoon to death.*

All this shows in Keats' love reason or moral sense did not play a great part; it was not tender or kindly, but a madness and more than usually physical. There can be no doubt from the evidence given by Keats, that he indulged in reveries of physical satisfaction with Fanny in day dreams.

Keats has himself written that he had sensual night dreams. He wrote in April, 1819, apropos of the sonnet, "A Dream," after reading Dante's episode of Paolo and Francesca: "The dream was one of the most delightful enjoyments I had in my life. I floated about the wheeling atmosphere, as it is described, with a beautiful figure, to whose lips mine were joined, it seemed for an age; and in the midst of all this cold and darkness I was warm." A flying dream always has a sexual significance, even without any female figure to accompany the dreamer. Of course this figure was Fanny Brawne to whom he had just been or was about to be betrothed.

The poet Amy Lowell who was opposed to psychoanalysis said that it did not need knowledge of the theory of dreams and their interpretation as set forth by Freud to grasp the meaning of the poem and passage referred to above. She stated that those who believed in the Freudian hypotheses [and she did not] and find pleasure in examining literature according to psychoanalysis [which she did not] have a perfect study here. But she added that she lets the obvious speak for itself. She had to admit that the experience Keats went through in his dream and his poem was eminently true to the imagination. Nevertheless she could not contradict the psychoanalytical interpretation I set forth in her life of Keats. In fact she there made use of it.

I met and visited Miss Lowell in the spring of 1919, when my book appeared, and the first remark she fired at me was the question "How could you have done it?" referring to *The Erotic Motive* which she had just read, and without waiting for an answer she went on to say that she had numerous manuscripts of poems [undoubtedly referring to those of Keats], that they had corrections and emendations, and that this showed that a poem was a conscious product. I countered that neither Freud nor myself ever held that there was no conscious effort in reducing the final product to an artistic one. We held that the original impulse or emotion or incentive was unconscious and that it remained in the poem even after rewriting.

Miss Lowell did not care for probing into the motives of conduct as her poems show. She hated Dostoesky because he did this, and she told me that much as she loved reading, she would prefer not to read at all rather than to read him.

Shortly after my meeting with Miss Lowell, there was an anonymous review of *The Erotic Motive* in the *New York Times* for May 25, 1919, headed "The Peephole of the Unconscious." It was written by Miss Lowell's friend Helen Bullis Kizer. It was a slating though she had something of a favorable attitude towards psychoanalysis. She approved my interpretation, which had been most objected to, of Achilles' dream about his slain friend Patroclus, the fact that it had originated in a profound affection which Homer himself had for a deceased friend. But she did not think it mattered.

Unfortunately Miss Kizer was killed the following fall by a fall from her horse. Miss Lowell wrote a beautiful tribute to her in the *New York Times* of October 19th. Her article contained the following passage: "She, a well-read Freudian, poking fun at an ill-read one, (myself) [said] 'The Œdipus complex is as inexhaustible as a grab-bag at a church sociable. We have all had parents: we have all loved them, or hated them, or been indifferent to them, and each condition is overflowing with neuroses' ". This was copied by Miss Lowell from Miss Kizer's review of my book in the *New York Times*.

2

We come now to his two greatest odes, the one to the Grecian Urn and the other to the Nightingale. Both were written in the spring of 1819. In both Fanny Brawne is with the poet though there is no direct mention of his love for her or his troubles with her. The lines in the "Ode to a Grecian Urn" that particularly were written with Fanny in mind are those addressed to the lover:

> *Bold Lover, never, never, canst thou kiss,*
> *Though winning near the goal—yet do not grieve;*
> *She cannot fade, though thou hast not thy bliss,*
> *For ever wilt thou love and she be fair.*

Keats saw a resemblance between himself and that youth. He, too, was winning and near the goal, and he no more had her love than did the youth on the urn. He himself knew the passion "That leaves a heart high-sorrowful and cloy'd, A burning forehead and a parching tongue." He had to accept his lot and pretend to see some advantage in it as he did in that of the youth on the urn:

> *More happy love! more happy, happy love!*
> *For ever warm and still to be enjoyed,*
> *For ever panting and for ever young.*

The poem is the song of unsatisfied desires. Keats, frustrated in his love, had one resource, to make poetry and create beauty out of his sorrow. To the future he too would be like that lover created by an ancient artist, panting for love and ever young. The poem has such great appeal because it strikes a note in us all.

In the "Ode to a Nightingale" we also see evidence of his love sadness because of Fanny. He expresses a wish to go away with the bird from scenes.

> *Where youth grows pale, and spectre thin, and dies;*
> *Where beauty cannot keep her lustrous eyes,*
> *Or new love pine at them beyond tomorrow.*

The nightingale has not known like him "The weariness, the fever and the fret. Here where men sit and hear each other groan." Miss Brawne had embittered his life and hence he must fly at least in fancy through poetry with the bird. Again he finds consolation for his unhappy love in poetry.

He has been half in love with death, he has thought of taking to drink; he expressed both these ideas in previous poems. He is reminded that the nightingale's song was heard by Ruth, because love is uppermost in his mind. But he knows his fancied flight with the bird must end shortly. He will soon come back to his real self with the vexing thoughts of Fanny: "Adieu the fancy cannot cheat so well! As she is famed to do, deceiving elf." Then the music ceased, and he is back on earth again.

The unconscious sex symbolism in the wish to fly with the nightingale is a further proof of his unsatisfied love.

The motive of both these great poems was then supplied by his unsatisfactory love affair, but critics have not openly asserted the fact. It wasn't a mere walk in the British Museum or in Brown's garden that gave birth to the poems. These events merely incited him to put on paper the poems which had already for some time past fermented in his unconscious and were really produced by his repressed love for Fanny. Had he been happy in love, it is very likely we would never have had these poems. They are as personal as the poems previously mentioned addressed directly to Fanny, like "La Belle Dame," and the sonnet written in the fly leaf of Shakespeare. The same unhappy longings gave rise to them all, and they were all written within a few months of one another, though I have no evidence as to the date of the sonnet and the lines to Fanny.

But it is in a long poem where Fanny is chiefly present unconsciously, in *Lamia*. We have here the tale of Lamia, a beautiful woman, who is a metamorphosed serpent ensnaring Lycius of Corinth by her beauty. Fanny is Lamia, the serpent woman, Lycius of Corinth is Keats himself. Lycius is about to marry Lamia, as Keats was also thinking of marrying Fanny. It should, by the way, be borne in mind that the period when

Lamia was written corresponds with the date of the first published despairing letters of Keats to Fanny, the summer and
fall of 1819. It would be a rare miracle if during this time he
could have kept thoughts of his sweetheart out of his work.
Unconsciously he felt she acted like a serpent, and hence he
drew her as such.

Lycius did not want his teacher Apollonius, the philosopher,
at the feast. But the preceptor did come, an unbidden guest,
and told Lycius who this beautiful woman really was. Lycius
died of disappointment. Keats did not wish to be told the truth
about Fanny's lack of character, and thus be disillusioned. He
felt that he too would die, hence he fears facts and asks: "Do
not all charms fly at the touch of cold philosophy?" In this
question we see already he suspects Fanny's nature. But he
will not believe his uncertain suspicions nor investigate them.
It is the voice of his own unconscious that he hears in these
words of his preceptor:

> *"Fool! Fool!" repeated he, while his eyes still*
> *Relented not, nor moved; "from every ill*
> *In life have I preserved thee to this day,*
> *And shall I see thee made a serpent's prey?"*

He attacks Fanny in his description of Lamia's pleading,
whose beauty smote while it promised to save. He tells of the
meshes in which he struggled. That he published the poem in
his lifetime is evidence that he himself was not altogether
aware he was analyzing his own love affair and abusing his
fiancée. When he resolved to make a poem of the little tale he
read in Burton's *The Anatomy of Melancholy* it was his unconscious that chose the theme for him, recognizing that he
had many affinities in his life with that of the unfortunate
Corinthian youth. The poem contains more of himself than
any of his long poems.[1]

There are many other poems of Keats where the personal
element enters and where he tells us of his unconscious. The
affair with Fanny colored his entire work after he met her. He
also knew and admired another girl about the time he met
Fanny, whom he calls a Charmian; she was a Miss Cox, but
she did not greatly influence him. It is to the intense affection
Keats had for his mother, of whom he was deprived in boyhood, and the unfortunate affair with Fanny, that we owe some
of his best literary work.

[1] The interpretation I give here of "Lamia" in which I identify Lamia, the beautiful serpent woman, with Fanny Brawne, and Lycius of Corinth with Keats himself, was the first of which I know. It has been followed by Middleton Murry in his *Keats and Shakespeare* (1925). When he was editor of the *Athenaeum* there appears in it a brief but anonymous favorable notice of the *Erotic Motive*. Murry wrote, "Lamia, as Keats wrote it, is imaginative autobiography and of the exact and faithful kind. Keats is Lycius, Fanny Brawne is Lamia, and Appolonius is Charles Browne the realist, trying to break Fanny's spell over Keats by insisting upon her as the female animal. The identification seems transparent. Lamia is a poem of real and living experience. Keats wrote it from his heart."

If the identification seems transparent why was it not made before?

Chapter 15

Shelley's Personal Love Poems

1

SHELLEY'S great love poems were inspired by repressions, and it will be my province to try to trace some of the finest poems in the English language to their sources.

His relations with women have been much criticized and also much misunderstood. The first thing unusual about his life is the slight influence his mother exerted upon him. Shelley, no doubt, loved his mother, but he received very little sympathy from her. As a result he became strongly attached to his sisters; in them he sought unconsciously for the mother he had all but lost. He was alienated from his father in boyhood, and there were definite clashes later. The poet was the oldest of six children.

He loved his cousin, Harriet Grove and was engaged to her. She broke the engagement on account of the views he entertained. Her parents influenced her in this action. It was Shelley's first love affair. The poet was in his nineteenth year when he was jilted; he slept with a loaded pistol and poison near him for some time after this. In January, 1811, in a letter to Thomas J. Hogg, he writes he would have followed Harriet to the end of the earth. He asks his friend never to mention her. He tells of a personal interview with Harriet and laments that she is gone and that he still breathes and lives. On January 11, he wrote: "She is gone! She is lost to me forever!" She married! Married to a clod of earth; she will become as insensible herself; all those fine capabilities will moulder." She had, however, not yet married. It was the recollections of these acute sufferings that he later put into the mouth of the maniac in "Julian and Maddalo"; those poignant ravings were for a half century regarded as impersonal, and were never thought to be directed against a real woman whom he loved.

In the latter part of March, 1811, the poet was expelled from Oxford for his pamphlet on atheism. In the meantime he had met Harriet Westbrook and married her, in a spirit of gallantry, in the latter part of August, 1811; he sympathized with her because of her sufferings at home. He also liked Elizabeth Hitchener at the time, and later asked her to come and live with his wife and himself. She did so about July, 1812. Shelley's wife had no liking for her, so Miss Hitchener was practically bribed by the poet to leave. This she did in November. Shelley was disillusioned in her, and he really had very little in common with her, though she was intellectually superior to Harriet, Shelley's wife.

In July, 1814, Shelley deserted his wife. A few weeks later he left with Mary Godwin, with whom he had been friendly since the spring of the year. In December, 1816, Harriet, who was pregnant, committed suicide by drowning.

Shelley married Mary Godwin legally December 30, 1816. He probably was not madly in love with her. Mention should be made of two cases of unreciprocated affection for him on the part of the poet's two sisters-in-law, Fanny Godwin, who committed suicide, and Jane Clairmont, the daughter of Mary Wollstonecraft Godwin by a previous marriage; the mistress of Byron.

The two women whom Shelley loved after his marriage and who inspired some of his best poetry were Emilia Viviani and Mrs. Jane Williams. Shelley met Miss Viviani about December, 1820. That winter he wrote "Epipsychidion," which was a love poem to her; here he also told us the history of his love affairs. In June, 1822, he refers to his disillusionment with her. About this time his feeling for his friend's wife, Mrs. Williams, overpowered him, and he wrote a number of lyrics to her. He was drowned July 8, 1822, with Mr. Williams.

Shelley never had a satisfactory love affair in his life. He was discarded by his first love, for whom his affection was strong. He did not love his first wife at all, and his second wife did not give him that satisfaction in love for which he craved. Hence he yearned after others. His new affairs brought him no happiness, as he was disillusioned in his Emilia, while Mrs. Williams was married to his friend; social intercourse was for a while stopped between Shelley and the Williamses on account of Shelley's love. Two other women who cared for him did not attract him. This whole state of affairs led to some of his best poems, brought out some of his views on free love, and influenced his lyrics. We shall examine how his poetry arose from the depths of his unconscious.

"Julian and Maddalo" was first sketched in 1814. The maniac's soliloquy, which is one of the most forceful outcries of love disappointment in poetry, inspired by personal experience, and is, with Swinburne's "The Triumph of Time," among the greatest of all such products in literature, is Shelley's own outburst. It is his full fury cast at Harriet Grove, and was not, as surmised by Arabella Shore[1] and H. S. Salt,[2] directed against his first wife. He never loved her as that maniac loved; besides, it was not true of Harriet Westbrook that she ceased to love Shelley. It is said that the poet believed her guilty of adultery while living with him, but even if this were so (and we have no evidence to warrant such a belief), the poet had been casting longing eyes at Mary Godwin for some time before he left his first wife; we have no proof that the poet was heartbroken after he left Harriet Westbrook, though he sympathized with her.

His affair with Harriet Grove was not the ephemeral affair that William Sharp deems it in his biography of the poet. For even when married to Harriet Westbrook, he was still chagrined about the first Harriet. When Miss Grove married a cousin in the fall of 1811, a few months after his own marriage, the poet wrote to her brother, asking how he liked his brother-in-law, and added sarcastically and bitterly, "A new brother as well as a new cousin must be an invaluable acquisition." This was in October 28, 1811. Harriet Grove's conduct had caused him to spend many sleepless nights, and only a few months before his marriage to Miss Westbrook he had suicidal thoughts. He wrote sad love verses and a complaint against love's perfidy. Captain Kennedy describes Shelley, in June, 1813, as playing on the piano a favorite tune which Harriet Grove used to play for him.[3] It was in the next year that he sketched the poem, "Julian and Maddalo," and while it is likely that in the final version, which was written four years later though published after his death, unconscious emotions regarding Harriet Westbrook were fused in the poem with the indignation at Harriet Grove. The reference to the tomb for which the lady addressed in the poem deserted the poet may have been suggested by the dead Harriet Westbrook; but this fact is not sufficient reason for regarding her as the subject of the poem, as Miss Shore and Mr. Salt do. We should look for truth beyond such incidental references. The pain in this poem is the memory of an earlier agony that Shelley experienced because of Harriet Westbrook's alleged infidelity in which he believed; it is rather the grief that Harriet Grove caused him.

[1] *Gentleman's Magazine* [1887], v. 263, p. 329.
[2] *Shelley Society Papers* [1888], p. 325.
[3] Dowden's *Life of Shelley*, p. 390.

The passages in the letters to Hogg prove that the poet's sorrow was too keen for him to forget; he could not help but put them unocnsciously in this poem.

There are references to Harriet Grove in "Epipsychidion" written in the early winter of 1821. Mr. Flea, in an article, "The Story of Shelley's Life in Epipsychidion," contends correctly that Harriet Grove is the "one with the voice which was envenomed melody," from whose cheeks flew a killing air which lay upon the leaves of the poet's heart and made him feel the ruins of age. The bitterness of this passage is equal to that in "Julian and Maddalo," and hence the lines do not refer to some vulgar affair as some critics think.

Shelley had written some of his earliest sad and lugubrious love poems to Harriet Grove, and they appeared in 1810, in the volume *Victor and Cazir*, a copy of which book the poet presented to her. In the November of the same year, when he was losing her, he published *Posthumous fragments of Margaret Nicholson*, and the concluding poem, "Melody to a Scene of Former Times," has all the pain of the Maniac's soliloquy in "Julian and Maddalo," and was written to Harriet Grove. It has similar passages of reproach.

The best-known lines in the latter poem are:

> *Most wretched men*
> *Are cradled into poetry by wrong;*
> *They learn in suffering what they teach in song.*

The reader may think that it is utterly insignificant whether the Julian poem was written about the first Harriet instead of the second, but this is just as important as to know that, let us say, Arthur Hallam, and not some one else, is the person mourned by Tennyson in *In Memoriam*. And we are enabled to learn the influence upon his work and ideas when we understand the nature of the earliest sex repression in the poet's life. This affair in Shelley's nineteenth year was of vast import; it made the Shelley we know, the enemy of society, and the reformer.

He hated intolerance, religion, and monarchy because by his heterodoxy and the offence it gave to Harriet Grove's parents, he lost her; not to mention that he also lost his mother's love because of his radical views. He saw the world steeped in error, and he believed this condition made him lose the love of his betrothed and of his mother. He wrote to Hogg that he would never forgive intolerance. "It is the only point on which

I allow myself to encourage revenge; every moment shall be devoted to my object which I am able to spare." Here in the words of this youth we see the main factor which led to the writing of *Prometheus Unbound* and *The Revolt of Islam*. His plans shaped themselves at the time he was rejected, and he never swerved from them. And in the opening stanzas of the eleventh canto of the Islam poem he again describes the agonies of his lost love, with Harriet Grove in mind, no doubt. This poem was written in the summer of 1817. Shelley then became an uncompromising reformer because he had suffered in love for his radical ideas; hence he would make it his aim to spread the views which he held so that in the future other lovers should not lose their sweethearts because of liberal notions. And in the "Ode to the West Wind" Shelley's prayer is to spread his ideas over the universe.

Though the poet wrote a few good poems to Harriet Westbrook and dedicated "Queen Mab" to her, she had little or no influence on his life except to bring him sorrow because of her suicide. One of the few references to her in his later work is in "Epipsychidion", "And one was true—oh! why not true to me?" which shows that he believed in Harriet Westbrook's infidelity. Stopford Brooke thinks this refers to Harriet Grove, but this is not likely, as Shelley continues, "there shone again deliverance," and he speaks of one who was to him like the Moon. The Moon was, of course, his second wife, Mary Godwin, who immediately succeeded Harriet Westbrook.

2

"Epipsychidion" tells us of the poet's love adventures and gives us his beautiful dream of love. In "Alastor" he had depicted his longing for love; the poem was written in 1815 a year after he left Harriet Westbrook; it shows how lonely he felt and how he longed for love in spite of the fact that he was living with Mary Godwin whom he married the next year. In "Epipsychidion," where he speaks of his lying "within a chaste, cold bed," he says that he had not the full measure of love from his second wife. Hence he took refuge in building a fanciful isle where he satisfies his love with Emilia Viviani. In this great poem Shelley gives us a glimpse into his polygamously inclined unconscious. He states his philosophy of free love in the poem. As physical desire was a strong factor in Keats' one solitary love, the trait most characteristic of Shelley was his polygamous instinct. This is present in the unconscious of the male, and society has tried to eradicate it by the institution of marriage. We all know that there has never been complete success in this direction. The instinct which is suppressed bursts forth especially when the marriage has not been successful, or when the man does not love his wife in full measure, though, as the world is aware, it breaks out even in cases where he does love. Neither of Shelley's two marriages gave him the real love he sought. He wanted other women to live in his houshold. He created fantasies because of his repressions, and gave us the beautiful day dream which closes "Epipsychidion."

Mrs. Williams inspired some of the greatest lyrics in the language. The painful poem to her husband beginning with the words, "The serpent is shut out from paradise," tells how he flies because Mrs. Williams' looks stir griefs that should sleep and hopes that cannot die. The world owes to Shelley's attachment for Mrs. Williams such poems as, "Rarely, Rarely, Comest Thou, Spirit of Delight"; "One Word is too Often Profaned"; "When the Lamp is Shattered"; "Oh, World! Oh Hope! Oh Time;" "Rough Wind, that Moanest Loud"; "With a Guitar, To Jane"; "To Jane—the Invitation"; "To Jane—the Recollection"; "Remembrance"; "Lines Written in the Bay of Lerici"; and "The Magnetic Lady to her Patient." Here are eleven poems that every lover of Shelley knows, yet they are the outpourings of the poet's love for another man's wife, written because he could not attain that love and satisfy his polygamous instincts. Had these instincts been satisfied, these beautiful poems would have been lost to the world.

We now come to two of his greatest odes, "Ode To the West Wind" and "To a Skylark." Here, as in the case of Keats' two great odes, the critics have not seen in the poems a love repression on the part of the poet. In fact, most criticisms of the poems treat them as alien to the subject of love. And yet unconsciously Shelley is here voicing his longing for love and giving vent to his unconscious polygamous instinct. Francis Gribble, in *The Romantic Life of Shelley*, surmises that the poet is really unconsciously expressing dissatisfaction with his married life. When Shelley wrote these poems he was still groping for love; he lived with his second wife, and as far as we know had no love affair. He had not yet fallen in love with either Miss Viviani or Mrs. Williams.

The "Ode to the West Wind" was written in the fall of 1819. The poet at the time was unhappy; a child of his had died, and his wife was suffering great depression. When the poet complained that he was falling on the thorns of life and bleeding, and spoke of the "autumnal tone" in his life, he was referring to the repression of his love life. He lived with Mary whom he did not love passionately. If he concludes his poem with the prayer that the wind drive his dead thoughts over the universe to quicken a new birth, he wants to profit by this in love. He unconsciously meant that if his ideas on free love should prevail, he would be able to take a new love without reproach and without suffering such misfortunes as he did when he deserted his first wife. He had been deprived of his children and was driven to exile from his native land a year and a half previously, March, 1818. It has been one of the ironies of Shelley's fate that the world has admired this West Wind ode greatly, and tabooed his most important idea, that of free love. So if we read between the lines in this great ode pleading for the dissemination of his idea, we find the poet's unconscious stating he is unhappy and is longing for another love than that of his wife. He pleads for a satisfaction of his polygamous instincts. Should the reader think this conclusion untenable, I can reply that the facts we have of the poet's life give it unqualified support. Let us also remember that the fructifying wind was always a sex symbol.

It is the same with "To a Skylark," written nearly a year later. He envies the bird its happiness. "Shadow of annoyance never came near thee," he says to it. "Thou lovest—but ne'er knew love's sad satiety." Here he betrays himself by a few words. He has had his sad satiety of love. He does not love his present wife passionately; he never cared deeply for his first wife; his first sweetheart rejected him; and he had been loved by women whom he did not love. All these facts justify us in selecting the words, "love's sad satiety" and assigning them a definite meaning. Had we known nothing of the poet's biography we could not have spoken with such conviction. He sings, "our sweetest songs are those that tell of saddest thought." His saddest thoughts have been those about the difficulties of finding love's ideal and of loving another when pledged to someone else. Then we have the unconscious sex symbolism in the wish to be happy like the flying, singing bird.

Psychoanalytic methods applied to Shelley reveal him then, in his love poems and in lyrics which were not supposed to deal with love, as a chaste man with polygamous inclinations, married to a woman he did not love passionately. There is a connection between this state of affairs and his interest in scattering liberal ideas. That he also mistook real love for platonic love may be seen by "Epipsychidion" and the poems to Mrs. Williams. Unconscious love elements were at the basis of other poems of his like "Stanzas Written in Dejection Near Naples."

"Alastor," "Julian and Maddalo" and "Epipsychidion" of the longer poems, his dozen lyrics inspired by love for Mrs. Williams, and his two famous odes represent the personal Shelley from the love side, and are among the greatest poems in any language.

A few words should be said about "Adonais," his great elegy on Keats. It is one of his personal poems, and among the best known lines are those describing himself "who in another's fate wept his own." The critics who attacked the work of Keats, though they did not, as Shelley erroneously thought, drive Keats to death, were the very reviewers who attacked Shelley and his ideas. Even in this grand elegy Shelley was also bemoaning unconsciously his failure, and complaining that his ideas on free love, liberal religion, and republicanism were attacked.[1]

---

[1] In a note on page 514 of his revised edition of *Das Inzest-motiv* Dr. Rank takes issue with my chapter on Shelley in the following words:

So noch Albert Mordell, der mit Kenntnis unserer Auffassung des Inzest-Motiv eine Ruckfunrung der Dichtungen Shelleys seine Liebeserlebnisse versucht, onne diese selbst "Symptomatisch" zu beurteilen und auf die infantilen Bindungen Zuruckzufunren.

This passage in the unfinished English translation made by Harold Feldman in the manuscript of the book, is as follows:

"Thus Albert Mordell also, with a knowledge of our conception of the incest motive investigates the return to life experience of Shelley's poems, without either deeming these (experiences) as "symptomatic" or tracing them back to infantile Associations."

This note was a comment on the text which reads, again in Feldman's translation, "The most frequent error that is made in determining the dependence of literary creation on the author's inner life is caused by taking this kind of secondary rationalizations for the original source and final explanation."

Dr. Rank it must be remembered had by this time adopted his view of the birth trauma as being the source of all future anxiety. Yet he seems to have still held to Freud's views that all infantile experiences like castration fear, fear of the dark, etc., must be taken into consideration in determining future anxiety and hence its appearance in a literary work by the author.

I might have dwelt on these infantile matters even though I would have had to take for granted that Shelley did suffer from castration fear, but after all I was also writing, as my title *The Erotic Motive* suggests, of the effect of an author's conscious upon his work. My chapter on Shelley is only partly a psychoanalytic interpretation and was so intended.

Chapter 16

Psychoanalytic Study of Edgar Allan Poe

1

EDGAR ALLAN POE proves an interesting study from the point of view of psychoanalysis. He has been analysed by pathologists and psychologists, but there remains much to be said about the work of this baffling genius. I can take up only a few phases of the pathetic life and great work of Poe.

One question that has interested criticis is, what was the source of those mysterious ladies in his stories, the Ligeias, the Morellas, the Eleonoras? What made him so preoccupied with the subject of the death of beautiful women long before his own wife died? All this brings us to a little emphasized chapter in Poe's life, the history of one of his love affairs before he married Virginia Clemm. Its influence on his work has hardly ever been noted by critics, and yet the effect was of great importance.

Poe lost his parents when he was an infant, and he was adopted by John Allan. He loved the mother of a friend of his, Jane Stith Stanard, and when she died (he was 15 at the time), he was inconsolable. But the history of this boyish love is not fully known to us. As a boy of sixteen he loved Sarah Elmira Royster, whom he again met later in life and to whom he became engaged shortly before his death. At about the age of twenty or thereabouts after he loved his cousin, Miss Elizabeth Herring, and wrote several poems to her.

The real clue to Poe's life and work is furnished in an article, "Poe's Mary," that appeared in *Harper's Magazine* for March, 1889, by Augustus Van Cleef. It reports a conversation with a woman who was Poe's sweetheart and who rejected him. Her name is now known to us as Mary Devereaux. The main facts of the article have not been questioned by his biographers. The substance of the interview is this: Mary Devereaux met Poe through a flirtation. Her memory did not serve her as to the date, which she put in 1835. But since Poe was betrothed to Virginia that year, and had been betrothed to her for some time, the date was probably 1832, as the author of the article surmises, though Killis Campbell believes the year was 1831. Mary returned the poet's love, and he called on her almost every evening for a year. She jilted him, and Poe horse-whipped a relation of hers whom he thought responsible for his loss. He wrote for a Baltimore paper a poem of six or eight verses expressing his indignant sentiments. This passion continued with Poe, buried in his unconscious, even after he married Virginia Clemm. The day before Virginia died, in 1847, Mary was at the Poe household, and Virginia said to her: "Be a friend to Eddie, and don't forsake him; he always loved you —didn't you Eddie?"

There is an account in the article of a scene that occurred in the spring of 1842. Poe tried at the time to see Mary, who was then a married woman, at her home in Jersey City. He reproached her and shouted that she did not love her husband, and he tried to force her to corroborate his words. He had been inquiring for her and made up his mind he would see her even "if he had to go to hell" to do it. When he saw her, he was somewhat soothed, and she sang to him his favorite song, "Come Rest in This Bosom." She had sung this for him in the early days and also on a visit she paid him in Philadelphia not long before his Jersey City call. After this episode at her home the poet was found in the woods wandering about like one demented.

Mary Devereaux scoffed at the idea that the poet's child wife was the great passion of his life. It was always known, in spite of Poe's tenderness for Virginia, that he never found intellectual companionship with her. Poe married Virginia in May, 1836, when he was twenty-seven and she fourteen years old. He was living in 1833 with the Clemms in Baltimore, and had taken out a marriage license on September 22, 1835, but Virginia was then too young for marriage.

The relation of Mary to his work will soon appear. I wish to point out first that the splendid love poem, "To One in Paradise," appearing in the tale "The Assignation," was, with the story, inspired by Mary. "Visionary," the original title of "The Assignation," appeared with the poem in January, 1834, in *Godey's Lady's Book*, and hence was written in 1833, or before. It was among the tales submitted in the prize contest that year in which Poe was successful with one of his stories. When Poe later obtained employment on *The Southern Literary Messenger*, he reprinted here some of his tales; this tale was reprinted in July, 1835. The clue comes now. In the same number of the *Messenger* there is a poem entitled "To Mary," by Poe, beginning, "Mary amid the cares—the woes," which in sentiments and ideas is but another version of "To One in Paradise" in "the Visionary." This poem "To Mary" appears in Poe's poetical works under the title "To F——." He reprinted this poem, which was originally written to his love Mary, in *Graham's Magazine* for March, 1842, and changed the first line and called the poem no longer "To Mary," but "To One Departed," very suggestive of the "To One in Paradise." Poe, who would make a poem written to one lady serve, by a few changes in its text, for another later woman friend, gave this poem its present title, "To F——," when he reprinted it in the 1845 *Broadway Journal* in honor of the poet Frances S. Osgood, whom he met that year.[1]

If we compare "To One in Paradise" with "To F——" there will be no doubt that they were inspired by the same person and written at the same time, 1833, to Mary Devereaux when the affair with her was over. In both poems references are made to his sweetheart being an isle in the sea wreathed with flowers. In each poem mention is made of the desolate condition of the poet who derives happiness from living in dreams connected with her. "To F——" is not as perfect as the other, but the idea underlying each poem is the same. "Sonnet to Zante" also has the same imagery, and was written, at the same time to Mary.

"To One in Paradise" is supposed to be written by the lover in the story "The Assignation," in which it appears. It will be recalled that the lover of Marchesa Aphrodite in that tale had written the poem in a volume of Politian's tragedy, a page of which was blotted with tears. Poe is that lover and Marchesa Aphrodite is Mary. But we know also that Poe is the author of the poem "Scenes from Politian," which was written about the same time he loved Mary. It was published in the *Southern Literary Messenger* in December, 1835, In these scenes Poe identified himself with Politian, who loves Lalage and asks her to fly to America. "Wilt thou fly to that Paradise?" he asks her. The reference to Politian in "The Assignation" is then significant, and the tears on the leaf of the play shed by the lover of

[1] He honored Mrs. Osgood in the same way by republishing another poem from the *Southern Literary Messenger* of September, 1835, written for some Eliza and opening "Eliza, let thy generous heart." This poem in the poetical works of Poe bears the title, "Lines Written in an Album." It originally was written, Woodberry surmises, to his employer's daughter, Eliza White, though Whitty believes it was addressed to his future wife, Virginia Eliza Clemm. Yet it is very likely the poem was written to one of his early sweethearts, Elizabeth Herring.

Marchesa Aphrodite, the dreamer, were Poe's own for his lost Mary. The poet looked upon her as dead to him, and hence in a later version of the poem to her, "To F——," he changes the title to "To One Departed"; when he wrote "To One in Paradise" he looked upon her as dead. Mary was, by the way, a name that haunted him, and in his "Marginalia" he advances his belief in the incorrect theory that Byron's only real love affair was with Mary Chaworth.

I am not so dogmatic as to maintain that in writing "The Assignation" and the three poems I mentioned, and the Politian scenes, his other earlier loves did not unconsciously make themselves felt. Killis Campbell thinks "To One in Paradise" and "Sonnet to Zante" were written to Miss Royster. Poe may also have been thinking of Mrs. Stanard, now dead, in the poem "To One in Paradise. But it is most likely that his love for Mary inspired these poems. They were certainly not written to Virginia, for in 1833 she was only eleven years old.

The poem to Mary Devereaux, supposed to have been written for a Baltimore paper, may, as Woodberry surmises, be the "To F——" poem, although it is not so severe as Mary said the poem he wrote against her was. Either her memory failed her where the alleged severity of the pom is concerned, or the poem has not been discovered. A poem by Poe discovered by Professor J. C. French, of Johns Hopkins University, and printed in the *Dial* for January 31, 1918. It was called "Serenade," and was published in the *Baltimore Visiter*, April 20, 1833. The girl addressed is given a fictitious name, Adeline. Whether she is Mary or not I cannot venture to say with certainty, but most likely she is. It was published when the affair was probably over, and may have been written at the height of his love a year previously. Here are some lines from it.

> *And earth, and stars, and sea, and sky*
> *Are redolent of sleep as I*
> *Am redolent of thee and thine*
> *Enthralling love, my Adeline,*
> *But list, O list,—so soft and low*
> *Thy lover's voice tonight shall flow*
> *That scarce awake thy soul shall deem*
> *My words the music of a dream.*

I think that the tale of "Ligeia," which Poe considered his best story, was unconsciously inspired by Mary, and it hence calls for a new interpretation. It was published in September,

1838, two years after he married Virginia; but the poet's memories still hearken back to Mary. She is the dead Ligeia, and his wife, Virginia, is the Lady Rowena, whom the narrator married after Ligeia died. The story of Ligeia was suggested by a dream. The poem "The Conqueror Worm" did not originally appear in the body of the tale. The narrator's memory, flew back to the dead Ligeia; he called her name in dreams; even after Rowena was dead he had a thousand memories of Ligeia. The emphasis throughout the tale of the love for the departed Ligeia which will not die shows the real love the poet felt for Mary, about whom he was thinking. The narrator imagines that the dead Ligeia put a poison into the cup of his second wife, Lady Rowena, and that hence the latter dies. He then sinks into visions of Ligeia. He imagines that the corpse of his wife becomes alive, and as he looks at it, it is transformed into "my lost love" Ligeia. In other words, the dead love still lives and will not die; it is not forgotten, and haunts the poet, just as love for Mary haunted him. The quotation from Glanvil that man does not yield to death, applies as well to dead love.

In this tale we seen then the unconscious influence which an earlier love held on Poe. It is a tale of dead love as much as of death.

Mary enters into another famous tale where her presence was never suspected, in "Eleonora," a prose poem influenced by Shelley's "The Sensitive Plant"—a favorite poem of Poe. It has been thought that Eleonora was the poet's wife, Virginia, but the tale of the "Valley of Many Colored Grass" refers to the happy days when he courted Mary; the desolation that took place in the Valley, when Eleonora died, points to the poet's grief when Mary jilted him. The story appeared in 1841 in *The Gift* for 1842. It was written before Virginia burst a blood vessel in January 20, 1842. The narrator thinks of a second marriage after the death of Eleonora, and Poe was surely not thinking of a second marriage in 1841. We recall in the tale that the narrator had vowed never to love or marry again after he lost Eleonora, but he does—he marries Ermengrade, who is really Virginia, since Eleonora is Mary, now dead to him. The narrator believes that he hears the voice of Eleonora forgiving him for his marriage. The poet tells us then in this tale that in spite of his great love for Mary he was able after her rejecting him, still to care for and marry some one else.

The strongest passion of his youth in my opinion was Mary and not Miss Royster. When he became engaged later in life to Miss Royster it was due to worldly reasons, and he once broke the engagement. I believe that the fact that Poe and his wife were cousins and that she burst a bloodvessel gave rise to the theory that Eleonora, who is a cousin of the narrator, was Virginia.

Another earlier tale of the period of "The Assignation" and submitted in the prize contest at Baltimore, and hence written by 1833, is "Morella." In "Morella," Mary is still present in the person of the first Morella, whom the narrator marries and who dies; again we have a symbol of Mary's dead love. Morella leaves him a daughter also called Morella, and this may be a description of the paternal feeling Poe entertained at the time for Virginia, who was then eleven years old. In the tale the second Morella also dies.

The sadistic story, "Berenice" of the same period also has memories of Mary.

These stories with fanciful names like Ligeia, Eleonora, Morella, and Berenice were given us by the poet from the depths of his unconscious; love repressions starting from the death of his own mother in infancy, the loss of his foster mother, Mr. Allan's first wife, the grief at the death of his friend's mother, Mrs. Stanard, the quarrel with Mr. Allan's second wife, the love affairs with Miss Royster, and Miss Herring, but especially the rejection by Mary entered into the influences, which made up not only the poems and tales previously mentioned, but much of his later work. He was neurotic because he lost his mother in infancy and had many love disappointments. The only tale where he gives an account of the love emotions is in "The Spectacles," written before or about 1844, and here he drew on his experiences, chiefly from memories of Mary.

Now comes a question that has always puzzled his critics: Why was the poet so occupied with the subject of the deaths of fair ladies or in despicting a man bereaved by the death of his love? Many conclusions have been drawn but not altogether satisfactorily. Some have thought that he was so occupied with the subject because he lost his own wife Virginia. There is evidence to make us believe that "Ulalume" which is now taken to refer to the death of his wife, was commenced before Mrs. Poe's death in January, 1847; ("Annabel Lee" was, however, written after that date and refers to her.) Nearly all of Poe's short stories, too, had been published by that time. He was occupied with the subject of death long before he married; he mourns the death of women in "Lenore," "Tamerlane," and "The Sleeper," all written before he was twenty-two years old. His first tales, "The Assignation," "Ligeia," and "Morella," deal with the subject of women's deaths.

Poe tells us in his "Philosophy of Composition,"—an unconvincing account of the origin of "The Raven,"—that he regards the death of a beautiful maiden the most poetical and melancholy topic.[1] But there were factors that made him think so, and these were the deaths of women he loved and the rejections by girls with whom he was infatuated. He lost his mother when he was three years old. Mrs. Stanard, who is said to have inspired "To Helen," and who was "the first pure ideal love of my soul" died when he was fifteen. (She is also said to have inspired "The Sleeper.") He lost Mrs. Allan, his foster mother, to whom he was greatly attached, when he was twenty. He had also lost three sweethearts by the time he was twenty-three. These he looked upon as departed or gone from him. In "The Bridal Ballad," written probably on the occasion of the marriage of Miss Royster, he refers to himself as a dead lover. All this shows the strong infantile influences on Poe which dammed up his libido. He was, therefore, occupied with the subject of death not because of Virginia's illness or death, but because he lost, before he was twenty-three, six women. His interest in the subject made him hope death could be conquered or stayed, and hence we have "Ligeia" and "The Facts in the Case of Valdemar." There is a philosophic treatment of death in "The Colloquy of Monos and Una."

---

[1] Some have imagined that Poe was led to write of the death of a woman in "The Raven" because his wife's breaking a blood vessel made him think of her possible death, but the idea of "The Raven" came to him before this misfortune happened.

Poe found the idea of his poem "The Raven" in *Barnaby Rudge*, of which Dickens published the first number in January, 1841 completing the book in November, 1841. Poe had eleven chapters of the novel in serial form by May, 1841, and had therefor already noted the introduction of Grip, the raven. Mary E. Phillips, in *Edgar Allan Poe—The Man*, (Volume I, pp. 767-773) gives evidence to show that the poem was in existence in the summer of 1842, at least in part, and was finished by the next year. It was first published in the New York *Evening Mirror*, January 29, 1845. It might be thought that since Poe's wife Virginia burst a blood vessel January 20, 1842, fears and thoughts of her death arose in him and the question whether in that event he might meet her in heaven occurred to him. But since he read *Barnaby Rudge*, the year before and reviewed it in *Graham's Magazine*, in February, 1842, this means that he had written this review before she burst a blood vessel, and that already he had the idea of "The Raven" in his mind. According to *The Home Life of Poe* by Mrs. Susan Archer Weiss "The Raven" was ten years in the writing.

2

Tales of burial alive, such as "The Cask of Amontillado," "The Black Cat," etc., are also characteristic of Poe.

What is the significance of Poe's interest in the subject of burial alive and in people who are guilty of burying others alive? Very few people would probably accept Freud's theory, but that master psychologist as a rule bases his theories on facts, and hence I will quote his views on the subject. In a footnote of his book, *The Interpretation of Dreams*, he says: It is only of late that I have learned to value the significance of fancies and unconscious thoughts about life in the womb. They contain the explanation of the curious fear felt by so many people of being buried alive, as well as the profoundest unconscious reason for the belief in a life after death, which represents nothing but a projection into the future of this mysterious life before birth. *The act of birth, moreover,* is the first *experience* with *fear,* and *in this the source and model* of the emotion of fear."

Would Freud's theory not also account for Poe's great gift for analyzing and depicting fear? [1]

Morbid fear or anxiety is well depicted by Poe, especially in "The Fall of the House of Usher." As we learn from psychoanalysis, morbid fear is inhibited sexual desire; it is a reaction against the libido. The individual's sexual impulses incapable of being repressed strive for forms of wish fulfilment, and these when repugnant are treated like something hostile and provoke fear. Morbid fear differs from normal fear in being continuous and is attributed to a source which is not the real one, the actual source being unconscious. If a woman, for example, is very much in love with a man who turns out to be a vile criminal, her love may become incapable of being fulfilled any longer because of the part played by her moral sense; shrinking from contemplating her love's fulfilment with the man she really still loves, she may develop an anxiety. This is only one of the innumerable cases of misdirected desire that may cause anxiety. Then there are physiological factors responsible also.

[1] I am allowing these passages to stand although Freud kept changing his views on the cause and origin of anxiety till he formulated his new views in 1925 in *Inhibitions, Symptoms and Anxietes.* Otto Rank, however, from whom Freud probably took this idea of anxiety as the result of birth trauma, continued with the exception noted above, maintaining it from 1923 on, when he wrote his

Poe had himself suffered from a damming of the libido. He is Roger Usher, and is describing his own morbid fear. One feels that the narrator of the tale presents a case of psychosis, for he sees impossible things happen. He imagines the house had a pestilent vapor about it. He tells us that Roger's condition infected him, and that the wild influences of Roger's fantastic and impressive superstition crept over him. He must have been deranged, for he imagines that he sees Roger's dead sister, whose coffin had been screwed down, come out of the vault and drag Roger to death. He also thinks he sees the house crumble into fragments and sink into the tarn. Either his whole narrative is a hallucination or only these few parts of it are.

Roger himself, however, is the real type of sufferer from morbid fear. He has inherited a peculiar disposition, and also suffered from repressions, though nothing is said about this. He attributes his disease largely to anxiety about his sick sister, Lady Madeline. But the cause is in his unconscious. Those who are acquainted with the theories of psychoanalysis and the life of Poe will feel that Roger, like Poe, must have lost a mother early, then the mother of a friend, then his foster-mother. He also, like Poe, had been disappointed in love, and probably also drank. His symptoms were such as afflict neurotics. He was in constant terror and felt that he must die soon in some struggle with fear; he dreaded the future. He read strange books and imagined queer things. His sister died, and, with the aid of the narrator of the story, was buried in a vault in the house. He soon entertained fancies that he had buried her alive, and he was in mortal fear that she would wreak vengeance on him. When the teller of the story read to Roger some

book *The Trauma of Birth*. This incited Freud to expound his new theory, to contradict Rank, and to turn a *volte face* himself. He also no longer regarded anxiety as transformed libido, but as a reaction on a particular model to situations of danger. (*The Complete Psychological Works of Sigmund Freud* Vol. 20, pp. 80-81, Editor's Introduction.) As the editor states, Freud even in this book retained elements of his old theory when he said that "What finds discharge in the generating of anxiety is precisely the surplus of unutilized libido." But later in 1933 in his *New Introductory Lectures* he stated that in the anxiety neurosis, too, the appearance of anxiety was a reaction to a traumatic situation; "We shall no longer maintain that it is the libido itself that is turned into anxiety in such cases."

Naturally Freud's disciples followed his original theories as I also did. Freud's later theories are probably right, but there are confusing contradictions and additions in various definitions of them and some unacceptable features.

While Freud admits a certain preparedness for anxiety is present in the infant in arms, he states that this preparedness does not emerge until later, as mental development proceeds and lasts over a certain period of childhood. As a general proposition this presentation of the case sounds plausible—more so than Rank's theory of birth trauma alone.

pages of a romance, Roger interpreted various unrelated actions described there as a rending of her coffin and the grating of iron hinges on her prison. He imagined she stood outside, and then that he was being crushed to death by her. And he died in fear. The vision of his sister was imaginary with him and the narrator as well, for Lady Madeline could not have escaped from the screwed down coffin and the vault, and having lain many days without food, would not have had strength to crush her brother to death. Usher died because of morbid fear.

Poe was a good delineator of the neuroses. Here we have a picture of his own life and know that he must have experienced some sort of anxiety, as the tale is so true to life. He was only thirty when the story was published, and the main character here, as in "Berenice" and "The Assignation" is a neurotic. Behind it all one sees the mourner for the lost Lenore, the orphan, the victim of unrequited love.

Poe had also another trait, and that was a sadistic one. This accounts for his tales of people torturing and begin tortured like "The Pit, and the Pendulum," and the "Cask of Amontillado." He was sadistic as any one can see by his delight in writing critical articles calculated to cause writers intense pain. He punished his enemies by venting his hatred upon them in his essays. He had an unconscious instinct to cause pain for the mere sake of pain. He hints at this in his "Imp of the Perverse," where he lays down a theory which is undoubtedly true, but which moralists try to shun. "I am not more certain that I breathe than that the assurance of the wrong or error of an action is often the one unconquerable *force* which impels us and alone impels us to its prosecution." He was also masochistic, he unconsciously like to cause pain to himself. In his "The Black Cat" he calls perverseness one of the primitive impulses of the human heart, and he speaks of it as "the unfathomable longing of the soul *to vex itself*—to offer violence to its own nature, to do wrong for the wrong's sake only." Poe, as a child, had the sadistic and masochistic instincts. He is fascinated by contemplation of suffering, and in his "Premature Burial" speaks of the pleasurable pain we get from reading of terrible catastrophes.

His sadism and masochism figure considerably in his art. He could not carry out his desires to punish in life, and hence found a refuge in literature. We often carry out in imagination what we cannot actually do; and we wreak punishment and revenge that way; if we are authors we make books with such ideas. A very simple illustration will serve in Poe's case, yet it has never been noted. In Poe's tale "The Cask of Amontillado" the motive is revenge. The narrator vowed vengeance upon Fortunato, who had added insult to injury. He buries him in a vault. In his fancy Poe was punishing a real enemy, and though he had several, he hated none more than the author of "Alice Ben Bolt," Dr. Thomas Dunn English. It is related he once sought the doctor, saying he wanted to kill him. The tale was published in *Godey's Lady's Book* for November, 1846, and was written probably a few months before. In July of that year Poe published the savage and violent letter to English in retaliation for English's reply to a very hostile article about him by Poe in the *Literati of New York*. Poe's hatred for Dr. English is almost murderous. It is plausible to assume that a writer would unconsciously have his most bitter antagonist in mind while writing a bitter tale of revenge at the time of his most intense hatred for him. Poe was not satisfied with his own savage reply, and instituted a suit of damages for defamation of character which he won. In the story Poe wrote: "I must not only punish, but punish with impunity. A wrong is unredressed when retribution overtakes it redresser." He calls Fortunato a quack in painting and gemmary, as he had called Dr. English a charlatan in literature, who did not know the rules of grammar. So this is an illustration of how sadism made him unconsciously write at least one tale of punishing an enemy by burying him alive.

3

After all, Poe is chiefly the dreamer and author of dream literature. The narrator of "Berenice" tells in detail how he was always dreaming. In "The Assignation" the lover says, "To dream has been the business of my life. I have, therefore, framed for myself a bower of dreams." In "Eleaonora" the narrator says those who dream by day obtain glimpses of eternity. Roger Usher was a dreamer. Poe's *Eureka* was dedicated to those who dream instead of those who think. He also wanted to transcend reality. He built an ideal landscape in "The Domain of Arnheim" because he thinks art can surpass nature. He hated the ugliness of today and he tried in "Some Words with a Mummy" to revive a mummy to tell him of ancient Egypt and to give him the secret that enables one to suspend life temporarily and to be revived again centuries hence. He says in an early poem that all his days have been a dream. ("A Dream Within a Dream.")

Poe was true to the psychology of the dreamer; he created things out of his fancies to be as he would like them to be because he did not have them in reality. He was poor and described mansions with wonderful furniture. He was sad because of deaths and lost loves and tried in some tales to conquer death. His "The Raven" is really an anxiety dream. Fear prompted it, the fear that he would never be with his lost Lenore, who probably was Mary. She then inspired this his most famous poem. His characters cannot help being dreamers, for their creator was one. He was so absorbed in his dreams that he never tried to take an interest in reality. Hence we find no moral note in Poe's work; there is one exception, "William Wilson." He took no interest in philanthropy, reforms, transcendentalism, or other movements of the day, and he disliked Emerson. One would never know from his work whether he lived nineteenth or in the eighteenth or twentieth century. One does not know from his work that there was a Mexican war or a slavery problem in his day.

The one moral tale Poe wrote, "William Wilson," also has great value to the psychoanalyst, for it is a study of emotional conflicts and deals with the subject of dual personality, anticipating Stevenson's famous story, *Strange Case of Dr. Jekyll and Mr. Hyde*. It is the history of Poe's own struggle with his unconscious, with evil. He too was a gambler and probably cheated at cards like William Wilson. There are two William Wilsons, one representative of the unprincipled, the criminal, the unconscious primitive instincts in ourselves, and the other William Wilson who is the voice of civilization, the conscious moralist seeking to repress the other.

So we leave Poe. Others may take up the question of his alleged drunkenness and its over estimated effect on his art. But I have merely wished to point a few things in his work made clear with the help of psychoanalysis. Psychoanalysis has given the answer to those who object to Poe because of his lack of moral tone.

It should be added that Poe's great attachment to his mother-in-law, Mrs. Clemm, was due to the loss of his own mother in infancy.

Poe's devotion and love for women in his later life, Mrs. Frances Sargene Osgood, Mrs. Annie Richmond, Mrs. Sarah Anne Lewis, and especially Helen Whitman, did not influence his work considerably in spite of the sufferings they caused him, but produced a few good poems, notably, "To Annie," Mrs. Richmond, and "To Helen," Mrs. Whitman, and the pathetic, masterly letters to these women.

4

Thus far I had written about Poe in the first edition of this work. Poe has especially attracted students of psychoanalysis and literary critics. A number of such studies have appeared, some in book form and some in articles; some followed me in my interpretation and made acknowledgments to this effect, others who either did not know of my chapter or had not read it did not mention it. As early as January 1927 Professor Chauncey Brewster Tinker in an article in the *Yale Review* which he reprinted in *The Good Estate of Poetry*, wrote: "Mr. Albert Mordell, so far as I am aware (although I do not pretend to extensive knowledge of the field) was the first to apply the psychoanalytic method to Poe as it is exhibited in his poems and stories." Professor Tinker stated that he did not like the use of "sadism" which he found a "very ugly and technical name." It happens that the term is one of the most innocuous and least avoidable in the psychoanalytical interpretation of literature.

I shall mention a few of the psychoanalytical interpretations of Poe which have since been published. A very good one was that previously mentioned by Lorine Pruette entitled "A Psycho-Analytical Study of Poe" in the *American Journal of Psychology*, October 1920, giving due acknowledgments to my study. Clement Wood in *Poets of America* (1925) accepted the theory as I propounded it, but thirteen years later in *The Stricken Eagle* made a *volte face*. Edward J. O'Brien in *The Advance of The American Short Story* in 1931 also accepted the theory. Neither O'Brien nor Wood in his first article sought to build up a theory of his own. Joseph Wood Krutch wrote his book on Poe in which he sought to show Poe was impotent, but I believe he ultimately repudiated his thesis.

Unfortunately Krutch was followed in this by Princess Marie Bonaparte in her two volume work on Poe. It is regrettable, almost reprehensible on my part to criticize this noble lady who has done so much for Freud personally and professionally. Issue must be taken with some of the extreme points of view she adopted. Her work appeared in French in two volumes and was translated into English in 1949 by John Rooker. It had a Foreword by Freud which reads as follows: "Many of the characteristics of Poe's work were conditioned by his personality, and we can see how that personality derived from intense emotional fixations and infantile experiences. Investigations such as this do not claim to explain genius, but they do reveal the factors which awaken it and the sort of subject matter it is destined to choose." The theme of my own article is thus summarized here and could not have been better stated. But of the far fetched conclusions, based on false premises and the adaptation of some Freudian theories open to question made curiosities of some of the chapters. Princess Bonaparte never read my article, as she wrote to me, and apparently Freud forgot to remind her I had written a psychoanalytical interpretation of Poe. He collaborated with her and of course endorsed the book.

The chapter dealing with "The Black Cat" was reprinted in *The Partisan Review* of December, 1950. It is (to me) the freakish and absurd interpretation of this story by Poe that I wish to deal with briefly. Princess Bonaparte says a castration fear dominates the tale. She takes it for granted that Poe was impotent. We have no proof of this and certainly his various love affairs would give the lie to this. She assumes that there is no doubt about Freud being right in the later development of his theory about the castration complex and the symbols used by an author unconsciously to set it forth. The story becomes in Princess Bonaparte's interpretation one solely about the penis. The hanged cat represents the penis.

The hanged man in the story "The Loss of Breath" is also supposed to represent this organ, for does it not droop and does not a man who is hanged also droop? Therefore when Poe wrote both stories, he merely presented unknowingly a wish fantasy represented by the hanging, of regaining his penis and thus the sex potency he lacked. But again there is no evidence he lacked such potency and Princess Bonaparte accepted or arrived independently at the theory Krutch abandoned. If a hanged person represented a penis, we have many characters in literature who are hanged to be so designated. Fagin, Tess of the d'Urbervilles, Danny Deever and the subject of "The Ballad of Reading Gaol."

The castration complex figures largely in "The Black Cat," we are told. Of course there is no real castration but in the Freudian theory the putting out of an eye or the loss of a limb is a symbol of castration. The Black Cat has had an eye put out. Miss Bonaparte quotes Freud and says that he has helped her in her interpretation. Therefore when the son—Poe—

reproaches his mother i.e. the cat who is a totem symbol of her, it is really for lacking a penis. He unconsciously gives expression to the reproach by imagining her hanging, thus turning the whole of the human body of the mother into what the body should have but lacks—a penis—the hanging member. Princess Bonaparte admits that Poe would not have accepted her theory—I should think not. "Though a tom and named Pluto," she says "we should not be misled, for the Black Cat as it were is a totem of Poe's mother, conjured up by Catterina's [Poe's own cat] presence round the house and the bed of his consumptive mother—figure, Virginia [i.e. his wife]."

Fatal to Princess Bonaparte's theory about the hanged man in the "Loss of Breath" representing a penis and therefore a wish-fulfillment for a lost penis is the fact that this tale was written before he was married, and published in 1832 while his double marriage to Virginia took place in 1835 and 1836. He could not then be absolutely sure that he was impotent.

I do not wish to go into the matter here of Freud's views on castration which are accepted by his disciples. He did not give full expression to them at the time I wrote the present book, and I did not know of them. They have been applied by many critics since to Ahab because of his lost leg bitten off by Moby Dick, for example. If the loss of an eye or a limb means a castration complex we shall have to reinterpret the loss of a leg by Silas Wegg, the villain in *Our Mutual Friend*, by Long John Silver in *Treasure Island*, yes even by Miss Watson's "nigger" in *Huckleberry Finn*. We shall have to reinterpret similarly the putting out of the eyes of Samson, of Gloucester in *King Lear*, and of the single eye of Polyphemus in the *Odyssey*!

Yet F. L. Lucas in his *Literature and Psychology* (1951) who here also has written a psychoanalytical interpretation of Poe and found castration fantasies says that Princess Bonaparte's book will not appear far fetched to those who think; personally he feels that in general she has made a convincing case with the exception of the treatment of some details.

C. P. Daly in his article "Mother Complex in Literature," *The Year Book of Psychoanalysis* (1948) which was revised and expanded from a paper published in *The American Quarterly* (1935) has a similar interpretation of "The Black Cat" as Princess Bonaparte. He has (to me) also untenable interpretations of other tales like "Eleonora," "The Fall of the House of Usher," and "Ligeia."

In a late interpretation of Poe by David M. Rein in *The Inner Pattern*, he holds several theories such as that Poe never loved his wife, and that her illness drove him to drink, though as a matter of fact he drank before she became ill. This book however does have merits.

The late Professor Arthur H. Quinn, was hostile to psychoanalysis and would not connect any stories of Poe with his unconscious. He does not even see a love affair in Poe's relations with Mary Devereaux.

D. H. Lawrence who did not accept Freud's views on psychoanalysis but had his own, nevertheless realized that "Legeia" and "The Fall of the House of Usher" were love stories.

So much has been made of the role of the mother in psychoanalysis that psychoanalytic critics have seen it everywhere. Some of the Poe interpreters regard Eleonora as a substitute by Poe for his mother who died in his infancy. In interpreting this story they assume that she is the lost love to whom Poe promised to be faithful and not to marry. As I stated above she is most likely Mary Devereaux who was his lost love and whom he regarded as dead. Nor is Eleonora his wife Virginia who had not yet burst a blood vessel when he wrote the tale. Naturally he could not have then been thinking of a second marriage and a promise to Virginia that he would not marry again. He married her after he lost "Eleonora," that is, Mary Devereaux. Virginia figures as Ermengrade whom the narrator marries. Mary was dead to him but he heard her voice forgiving him. As I stated before, the story was influenced by Shelley's "The Sensitive Plant" where also the death of the woman inspires desolation.

Chapter 17

The Ideas of Lafcadio Hearn

1

LAFCADIO HEARN anticipated many of Freud's conclusions. He understood the unity of life, in the past with that in the present, and his most persistent thought is the power and influence of the emotional life of our very distant ancestors upon our own lives.

A word should be said about Hearn's antecedents. He has himself left a tribute to his mother, who exerted a great influence upon him. She was a Greek. Hearn was very much attached to her and lost her when he was only six years old by his father divorcing her. This event colored his entire life. He tells us that there was a miniature painting in oil of the Virgin and the Child, on the wall of the room in which he slept as a child. "I fancied," he says, "that the brown Virgin represented my mother—whom I had almost completely forgotten—and the large-eyed child myself." In this infantile phantasy we see how the repressed love for his mother revived in him and how he identified her with the Virgin.

He wrote to his brother: "My love of right, my hate of wrong;—my admiration for what is beautiful or true;—my capacity for faith in man or woman;—my sensitiveness to artistic things which gives me whatever little success I have;—even that language-power, whose physical sign is in the large eyes of both of us,—came from her. It is the mother who makes us,—makes at least all that makes the nobler man; not his strength or powers of calculation, but his heart and power to love. And I would rather have her portrait than a fortune."

Hearn knew of the existence of the unconscious in the Freudian sense, and also of its influence on authorship. When he was twenty-eight, in 1878, in a letter to Henry S. Krehbiel he said: "Every one has an inner life of his own,—which no other eye can see, and the great secrets of which are never revealed, although occasionally when we create something beautiful, we betray a faint glimpse of it—sudden and brief, as of a door opening and shutting in the night." [1] *"Unconscious* brain-work is the best to develop . . . latent feeling or thought. By quietly writing the thing over and over again, I find that the emotion or idea often *develops* itself in the process,—unconsciously. When the best result comes, it ought to surprise you, for our best work is out of the Unconscious."

Again Hearn realized that fairy tales had their origin in dreams, an idea that has been developed by Rank, Abraham, and Ricklin, disciples of Freud. Hearn saw that there was an intimate connection between literature and dreams. He is one of the first men to have seen the relation between dreams and supernatural literature. The following passages are from the lecture on "The Supernatural in Literature" in the second volume of *Interpretation of Literature.* "Whether you believe in ghosts or not, all the artistic elements of ghostly literature exist in your dreams, and form a veritable treasury of literary material for the man that knows how to use them." "Trust to your own dream life; study it carefully, and draw your inspiration from that. For dreams are the primary source of almost everything that is beautiful in the literature which treats of what lies beyond mere daily experience."

Hearn, with Samuel Butler, is one of the great champions for the theory about the power of unconscious memory over us. This idea is one of the axioms of psychoanalysis, or rather one of its pillars. In his essay, "About Ancestor Worship" in *Kokoro,* Hearn develops his theories of inherited memory at length, and he expatiates on the subject in many of his essays. Here he states one of the leading lessons taught by psychoanalysis. Hearn realized that we should not starve all our primitive tendencies, as this would lead to the destruction of some of the highest emotional faculties with which they are blended. The animal tendencies must be partly extirpated and partly sublimated. This is practically Freud's theory that neurosis is produced by trying to stamp out our sexual impulses (yet Freud does not mean that we should give these full play). The following passage from Hearn's essay is part of the prophylaxis of psychoanalysis. "Theological legislation, irrationally directed against human weaknesses, has only aggravated social disorders; and laws against pleasure have only provoked debaucheries. The history of morals teaches very plainly indeed that our bad Kami require some propiation. The passions still remain more powerful than the reason in man because they are incom-

[1] *See The Life and Letters of Lafcadio Hearn* by Elizabeth Bisland.

parably older, because they were once all essential to self-preservation,—because they made that primal stratum of consciousness out of which the nobler sentiments have slowly grown. Never can they be suffered to rule; but woe to whosoever would deny their immemorial rights."

He has a similar idea in his essay on "Nirvana." "Mental and moral advance has thus far been affected only through constant struggles older than reason or moral feeling,—against the instincts and appetites of primitive brute life. . . . Only through millions of births have we been able to reach this our present imperfect state; and the dark bequests of our darkest past are still strong enough betimes to prevail over reason and ethical feeling."

Hearn regarded man as an entity of millions of cells, a composite of multiples of lives carrying out unconsciously the behests of past ages. Man's instincts are but unconscious memories of the instincts of old. Whitman has this idea in his "Song of Myself," and Buddha taught this idea which Hearn calls "the highest truth ever taught to man, the secret unity of life." Hearn states the view fully in his remarkable essay "Dust." "All our emotions and thoughts and wishes, however, changing and growing through the varying seasons of life, are only compositions and recompositions of the sensations and ideas and desires of other folk, mostly of dead people.—I an individual, —an individual soul! Nay, I am a population—a population unthinkable for multitude, even by groups of a thousand millions! Generations of generations I am, aeons of aeons." Or as he states it in another essay, "Ideas of Pre-existence," in Kokoro: "It is incontrovertible that in every individual brain is locked up the inherited memory of the absolutely inconceivable multitude of experiences received by all the brains of which it is the descendant." There are similar ideas in Jack London's Star Rover.

Hearn laid emphasis on the unity of the past and present, a fundamental principle of psychoanalysis. He saw this idea in Buddhism and hence became attached to the philosophy of this creed, and his reconciliation of it with the theory of evolution is no mere idle dream. Leading Buddhist scholars before Hearn saw the similarity between the theory of heredity as taught by evolution and the doctrine of Karma or transmigration of character. This doctrine of Karma explains also that a man has pernicious unconquered evil instincts because he is allied to ancestors who possessed them strongly. Buddhism taught the theory found in evolution and psychoanalysis, that we contain in ourselves every moral tendency and psychic attribute of millions of people and animals from whom we have descended. We are full of shreds of our ancestors' emotions and characteristics which are buried in our unconscious.

2

Why does Hearn harp on this idea of unconscious memory throughout his work and in his correspondence? Why was he attracted to the question of the eternal persistence of life even before he accepted the philosophy of Buddhism. His pet theory was that nothing could be lost in the universe. In one of his finest essays, "Reverie," in *Kotto*, he gives us the secret of his life. He declares that the mother's smile will survive everything, for life can never disappear finally from the universe. He first states the materialistic position which assumes that eventually all life will die and naught will be left of our labors and struggles, and then he gives the Buddhistic idea, which holds that nothing is lost in the universe. I think in this essay we have the keynote to Hearn's philosophy. He lost faith in Christianity early and with it a belief in the immortality of the individual soul. At the age of six, his mother whom he loved, died and his scepticism on the subject of immortality made him feel that she was gone from him eternally. This was painful to him, and he accepted the philosophy of Buddhism as a solace, for it taught something that was not repugnant to his scientific sense; that life can never die out entirely, for the universe always would exist and even if life died out on our planet, those conditions that made it prevail here would reign either in some other part of the universe or at a later time. Hence we all would contribute to that life as our ancestors contribute to our lives. In fact, Hearn once wrote he would not object to being transformed into an insect. So if life went on forever he would still know that mother's smile he had lost in infancy. The "Reverie" essay is the result of his Œdipus Complex.

In fact, Hearn formulated the idea of the Eternal Recurrence in 1880 before Nietzsche did, who wept when he discovered this by no means new theory in August, 1881, at Silas Maria, 6.500 feet above sea. Hearn's essay on Metempsychosis appeared in the New Orleans *Item* and was concluded in a collection called *Fantastics and Other Fantasies*. But Nietzsche became intensely pessimistic as the result of his discovery, since it meant all life's tragedies would also recur. Hearn, no doubt, abandoned the theory as a literary possibility after he read Spencer, but he retained his belief in some of the main features of it. The theory dates back to Pythagoras.

When we recall that Buckle, who was a free thinker in religious matters, still clung to the idea of immortality of the soul because he could not tolerate the thought of never meeting his dead mother; when we remember that scientists like Wallace and Fiske, who were among the pioneers of the theory of evolution, finally embraced spiritualism as a compensation for their lost faith in religion, it should not appear altogether fantastic to trace Hearn's views on unconscious inherited memory and on the Buddhistic doctrine of Karma to his loss of both his mother and his religion; for in his new belief he could meet his mother and still not sacrifice his intellect to his belief.

Psychoanalysis might be applied to other phases of Hearn's writings,—his concern with the gruesome and exotic. It can explain his interest in other races like the colored people and the Japanese, his passion for physical beauty and his shyness. One thing that impresses the admirer of Hearn is the seeming impersonality of his work. Yet though he says little of himself directly, one can see the sensitive, half-blind sufferer throughout the work. For his ideas when studied and traced to their source reveal of themselves the reasons why he embraced them.

He has described ideal love, such as he must have felt in "Karma" in *Lippincott's Magazine*, May, 1890. Probably he was thinking of Elizabeth Bisland.

His affinity for Poe and his adoption of the name "The Raven" in his letters to Henry Watkin are seen as an identification of himself with that unhappy genius with whom he had so much in common. He, like Poe, suffered from poverty, was engaged in intellectual pursuits, worshipped beauty, and had a love for French literature.

Chapter 18

Conclusion

1

THE question now arises, What effect will a knowledge of the author's unconscious have in making us appreciate his work as literature? Does it matter at all if we know whether a particular affair or a certain woman inspired a poem or not? Many critics protest against the kind of literary criticism that speculates as to whether the heroines celebrated in the sonnets of Shakespeare or Sidney were real or imaginary, whether the emotions felt by the poets were affected or genuine. These critics are not usually inclined to admit any connection between an author's life and his work.

One of the great factors in helping us understand literary works is an acquaintance with some of the episodes of the author's life. Sainte-Beuve revolutionized literary criticism by his dictum that the knowledge of an author's life helps us to follow his work the better. Dr. Johnson once said that he liked the biographical side of literature. Isaac D'Israeli, before Sainte-Beuve, showed in his *Literary Character* that he grasped the nature of the intimate relationship between an author and his work.

It is our contention that a literary work is better appreciated after the facts about an author's life are revealed to us, and this does not usually happen for years after his death. One of the reasons why masterpieces cannot be fully comprehended in an author's lifetime is that we do not know altogether how he came to write the works in question. Shelley and Keats were not fully understood by the critics of their times not only because of their radical views, but because the public did not know the details of the poets' relations with their parents and the women they loved. How could a cold, stern reviewer find anything in "Epipsychidion" or "Lamia" unless he was aware of some facts about Emilia Viviani or Fanny Brawne? How was any fair estimate of either of these poets possible while the information that later times have furnished was not at hand?

187

Many people objected when the letters of Keats to Fanny Brawne were published many years ago, but these have helped us to understand that the cry that pervades them is the same in the "Ode to Fanny," the "Ode to a Nightingale" and in "Lamia."

No true estimate of a man is possible till one reads the plaints of his that were not meant for the public. We should not regret the publication of the love letters of the Brownings and Carlyles. Those wonderful letters are almost as good literature as anything the authors wrote for the public. We are enabled to see the writers in an entirely different light from that in which their printed works put them, and to understand these better.

It was not possible for the age in which Balzac and Goethe lived fully to appreciate them, for it did not have their published correspondence and could not estimate the close connection between unknown episodes in their lives and their works. I do not mean that the contemporaries of these poets could not recognize the fact that these men were geniuses, but they could not get a proper understanding of them.

In former times criticism was busy with the questions of technique, with matters of rhetoric and grammar; a writer's work furnished opportunities for discussing how near to old ideas of authorship the author approached. In spite of T. S. Eliot and the New Critics we study an author in connection with his life. Shakespearean criticism of the last century is worth more than that of the two centuries following his death. Coleridge and Hazlitt devoted their discussions to showing how the great poet discussed problems that touched all of us. A number of studies and books have been published which seek to educe his personality from his work. Walter Bagehot was a pioneer in this kind of work. His essay on "Shakespeare—The Man" appeared as early as 1853. The most successful venture of this kind has been Georg Brandes's great study. Other works of this nature are Frank Harris' "The Man Shakespeare," and "The Women of Shakespeare," both usually regarded as fantastic, but nevertheless deserving credit for their daring, mistaken as they often are. Leslie Stephen's and A. C. Bradley's essays in the *Studies of a Biographer* and *Oxford Lectures on Poetry*, respectively, deserve special mention. Then there are books like David Masson's *Shakespeare Personally*, Robert Waters' *William Shakespeare, Portrayed by Himself*, and Goldwin Smith's *Shakespeare: The Man*. Shakespeare's greatness can be recognized though we knew little about him, yet the keynote of modern Shakespearean criticism is to endeavor to see the connection between the plays and the man.

2

I did not touch on Shakespeare in the first edition from a psychoanalytical point of view. He had been subjected to such interpretation briefly by Freud himself and by Ernest Jones for *Hamlet* and Coriat for *Macbeth*. I wanted to leave the matter for a later full elaboration. Since then there have been good and bad Freudian studies, a good one of *Measure for Measure* by Hanns Sachs in his *The Creative Unconscious: Studies in the Psychoanalysis of Art*; David Daiches has approved of this and has quoted part of it. The interpreter who I think went to unwarrantable lengths was the late Ellen Freeman Sharpe in her article "From *King Lear* to the *Tempest*: A Study in the Cyclic Movement of Shakespeare."

I believe that more can be learned of the life of Shakespeare from his plays than from such documents showing that he sued people for small debts. I hold to the theory that a pattern of similar events, concentrating on a similar emotion occurring in several plays indicates a strong personal motive. I am however opposed to deducing personal conclusions from an isolated episode or often from a casual remark by a character.

Is there such a pattern of events in several plays of Shakespeare? One pattern, as all Shakespearean students know, is that (in three plays) of an innocent wife unjustly accused of being unfaithful by a villain, a portrayal of jealousy. A similar motive appears where a couple is not married and where an innocent girl is charged with fornication by her lover. Shakespeare's attitude in this is well known, from *Much Ado About Nothing* in which he has Beatrice, Leonato's daughter, urge her lover Benedick, the young lord of Padua, to kill Claudio of Florence who had accused Hero of unchastity. Shakespeare found such episodes in his sources, but why did he choose them? They had a special appeal to him. He never forgot that his wife had premarital sexual relations with him before they were married. She was alone year after year except in the summer at Stratford; he was in London, where he carried on a sad affair with a married woman who betrayed him with a friend. The order of the four plays was *Much Ado about Nothing, Othello, Cymbeline,* and *The Winter's Tale*—all belonging to his late period. I came to the startling speculation: whether it was not likely that what motivated the poet in the four plays was his own jealousy, his belief that his wife had been unfaithful and his discovery that his jealousy was unfounded. Had he written only *Othello* I should not have made this deduction. It still may be wrong. Even if the poet never brought the charge of unfaithfulness against his wife, but only entertained it suspiciously with the accompanying feelings of jealousy, I still think the plays would have been the result. The reader may ask what difference does it make in regard to the merit of the plays whether his wife was faithful to him or not? It does give a note of authenticity and accounts for the truthfulness of the depiction of a haunting emotion. Perhaps had Shakespeare never suffered jealousy, (and we may add been credulous) he would never have given us such faithful delineations of that emotion.

This was a theory of mine I had left to be developed with various proofs in a future book. Only recently did I come across Jones's revised edition of his early *Hamlet* essay, *Hamlet and Œdipus*, when I found that he also believed that Shakespeare might have been so familiar with an unjustified jealousy as to be able to depict it to perfection, and that he was affected by his unfortunate belief. Jones did not have this view in the earlier version in 1910 of his Hamlet essay and I was not familiar with it.

All then that I wish to state here is that Shakespeare is more subjective than has been hitherto believed and that a pattern of episodes is more corroborative of this than a pattern of images.

I should like to add a little epilogue. Oscar Wilde had an amusing, fantastic, at times true, view that life often imitates art. This is substantiated in an aftermath of what happened to the poet's daughter Susanna who was married to John Hall in 1607. Six years later she was accused by one John Lane of "the running of the reins" and of having been "naught with Rafe Smith at John Palmer's." The charge was in the air for about five weeks when Mrs. Hall heard about it, and she brought suit against Lane for slander. She had as a witness a man who later became a witness to the poet's will, his personal friend Robert Whatcote. Lane did not appear at the Ecclesiastical Court at Worcester and was later excommunicated. Mrs. Hall was exonerated. Here is a plot from real life that followed the plots, with variations, in his three plays. We assume, naturally, that Mrs. Hall was innocent, and of course it pleased the poet to believe so.

Another deduction I shall make, and which I claim is only a speculation, is with regard to Shakespeare's least noticed poem "A Lover's Complaint" which attracted Keats and led him to write the sonnet "Bright Star, would I were steadfast as thou art" on a blank page in his volume of Shakespeare facing "A Lover's Complaint."

First, let me dilate on the view that the Shakespearean poem may not be by Shakespeare. J. W. Mackail sought to disprove the Shakespearean authorship on the basis of vocabulary, in my view a very ternuous theory. It had always been attributed to the poet. (Even if it were not by him the conclusions that may be arrived at from consideration of the poem would apply to any author of it.) Mackail admits that there were passages in it so good that no one but Shakespeare could have written them. We better accept Thorpe's authority that, like the sonnets, it was by Shakespeare and hence he included it in the volume containing them.

If vocabulary is to prove or disapprove Shakespearean authorship, we may instance the use of a similar phrase in "The Lover's Complaint" and in *Hamlet*. In the poem the girl says that she knew the youth's "vows were brokers to defiling." In Polonius' admonition to Ophelia he says, "Do not believe his vows for they are brokers." The poem is so good that I accept the authorship of Shakespeare.

The poem however lends itself to an interesting interpretation: it is a confession of guilt for a seduction. A girl is telling an old shepherd how she had been seduced by a young man. We have here a tale in which the author out of a guilty conscience relates indirectly that he was the seducer by putting the accusation in the girl's mouth. We read between the lines that the narrator is confessing his guilt but does not want to admit it. He has already admitted it by writing the poem. We have a parallel in the case of Wordsworth. We know that Wordsworth indirectly confessed his seduction of Annette Vallon in some of his poems by having a woman make complaints against a seducer. In Wordsworth's case we now have the facts. In Shakespeare's case all we know is the story of his marriage. The girl's lament is so authentic. Shakespeare represents himself in the person who, concealed on a hill, observes her in despair tearing up letters that her lover had written to her. Shakespeare presents us a portrait of himself in the flattering description of her lover given by the girl to the old shepherd. He, the poet, was the very youth who made that speech, seeking her love, that he has the girl repeat to the old man. He was the one who had an affcted moisture in his eye, a false fire which glowed in his cheek, a forced thunder that flew from his heart, a sad breath bestowed by spongy lungs, and a borrowed emotion that was hypocritical. He is the youth against whom the girl is declaiming. She describes the manner and tricks used in the seduction so vividly that one feels that the poet himself very likely had used them. The author knows human nature so well that he has the girl, while regretting the lapse from virtue, state at the conclusion that she could again yield to her seducer.

A final word on the question of Shakespearean authorship. Rolfe points out in his edition of the poem that there were numerous words and phrases in it that the poet used in his plays. Rolfe depends for his notes largely on Malone. We see that Malone came near penetrating the veil of concealment when he recognized that the poet delineated his own dramatic power in the lines

> *To make the weeper laugh, the laughter weep,*
> *He had the dialect and different skill,*
> *Catching all passions in his craft and will;*
>
> *That he did in the general bosom reign*
> *Of young, of old, and sexes both enchanted,*
> *To dwell with him in thoughts, or to remain*
> *In personal duty, following where he haunted.*

In think Shakespeare was referring to the effect he produced by his two poems "Venus and Adonis" and "Lucrece," his sonnets and his plays. Therefore it seems to me that to represent this poem as an immature early product as some critics like Masefield have done falls short of the mark.

Neither Malone nor Rolfe entertained the view that the poem was not by Shakespeare, nor for that matter did Dowden. I am not convinced otherwise because such Shakespearean scholars as Sidney Lee, Joseph I. Adams, and Hazelton Spencer were converted, or nearly so, by Mackail's views.

3

George Moore and Strindberg did not wait for posterity to make discoveries about their love affairs. They told us about them frankly in their autobiographical works. Other writers, great poets like Yeats and Symons, voiced their loves more or less openly in their lyrics. The emotions these poets expressed in their work had a real basis. The reader who finds the early Kipling cynical about women and who notes that Hardy constantly dwells on tragedies caused by love, may conclude (we now know rightly) that there must have been some reason for this—a personal one. One who reads Wells's *New Machiavelli* or Dreiser's *The Genius* and observes the author's preoccupation with the marriage problem may also draw his own conclusions about how much is inspired by reality. Occasionally an author like Robert Herrick had his domestic affairs dragged into the limelight, on account of the sensational interest of our newspapers, and the reader learns that *One Woman's Life* was somewhat autobiographical. We know now that much in the novels by D. H. Lawrence and James Joyce is taken from their own lives.

There has been a tendency in our day on the part of authors to write autobiographical novels. We need not deprecate this tendency. Fielding, Smollett, Balzac, Stendhal, Flaubert, Zola, Tolstoy, Dostoevsky, Turgenev, Scott, Dickens, Thackeray, and George Eliot resorted to it. I realize that all literary men, novelists as well as poets, are compelled to wear their hearts on their sleeves by virtue of their art. That criticism which reproached Rousseau, Chateaubriand, Senancour, and Musset for having been occupied too much with themselves is unfair. With whom else would the critics have the authors occupied? A man cannot get out of himself. When he undertakes to write a book, he tells us practically beforehand that he is going to talk about himself.

Therefore, such excellent novels of our time as Jack London's *Martin Eden*, Stephen French Whitman's *Predestined*, Maugham's *Of Human Bondage*, and Beresford's *Invisible Event* are to be commended. Should these authors' renown live, posterity will learn that some of the emotional life lived by the characters had been experienced by the authors themselves. It is, however, not a matter of importance whether the mere incidents recorded in these novels actually transpired in the authors' lives.

Many of us are so constituted that we like to sit down with an author like Montaigne or Hazlitt who takes us into his confidence. We dislike reticent and cold people in literature as much as in life. We do not ask writers to tell us about their private affairs, but we want them to talk at least indirectly about things that are close to their heart. And one may be sure they will interest us. Shakespeare unlocked his heart to us in his sonnets and in his plays as well.

It is of the world's great books that it can always be said as Whitman did of his own, "Whoso touches this book, touches a man."

4

Art and literature are realities in themselves. The depicting of an event enshrines it as a thing of beauty; the event itself may be dull. We meet Falstaffs in real life and waste no time on them; put into a play by a master, Falstaff gives us an artistic thrill. How many of the people who enjoy Dickens' novels about humble people would be interested in them in real life? Dickens' magic pen makes us receive a sensation reading about them that they cannot give us themselves. It is the artist's personality and art that count.

Gissing and Flaubert wrote about ordinary people, but they themselves were intellectual aristocrats; they had nothing in common with the people they wrote about (except with those who were disguised portraits of themselves). In fact, they despised them; they personally were recluses and merely sympathized with and were interested in the people they wrote about as subjects for art. If we had met *Madame Bovary* personally and heard her tale from her own mouth, the effect upon us would be small compared to that of the novel.

The domestic troubles of our next door neighbors may be a bore to us. We may not care to meet the people personally, but a great novel or play describing the matrimonial difficulties of fictitious characters gives us a distinct artistic thrill. The sorrows of people who lived centuries ago move us more than those of people we know, because of the magic power of art.

Those who from time immemorial called art magical were right. Many people who disparage art and literature say to the writer and the reader that they should enter the whirlpool of life, and live themselves. No advice could be more foolhardy. To read beautiful books about other people's lives is itself a high form of life, a life that only art can furnish. It also has its advantages when we think of the characters in literature whom we enjoy reading about and yet would never care to meet. Who would really want to meet Becky Sharp or Pecksniff?

That artistic pleasure we get, mingled with actual pain on account of the sorrows of poets, is to us a decided part of our lives. The fact that we are brought into contact with a beautiful series of lines voicing human grief in such a manner that both our human and aesthetic emotions are aroused, is a privileged pleasure that only those who can enjoy poetry may derive.

It does not follow, however, that a man must confine himself solely to the artistic or intellectual life. To know of love only through books and not through experience is not to have lived a full life. To read the views of Aristotle on friendship and never to have had any real friendships is also to lead but an incomplete life.

Literature is real and to read and write it is to live.

Index

196